T0345312

Being a Minor Writer

. . . .

Being a Minor Writer   by Gail Gilliland

. . . .

University of Iowa Press Iowa City

University of Iowa Press,

Iowa City 52242

Copyright © 1994 by the

University of Iowa Press

All rights reserved

Printed in the United States

of America

Design by Richard Hendel

Printed on acid-free paper

Library of Congress Cataloging-in-Publication Data

Gilliland, Gail.

    Being a minor writer / Gail Gilliland.

       p.   cm.

    ISBN 0-87745-473-6, ISBN 0-87745-486-8 (pbk.)

    1. Gilliland, Gail — Authorship.   2. Women and literature — United

States — History — 20th century.   3. Literature — History and criti-

cism — Theory, etc.   4. Authorship — Sex differences.   5. Canon

(Literature).   6. Authorship.   I. Title.

PS3557.I38837Z465   1994

818'.5409 — dc20

    [B]   94-10562

                                                  CIP

01   00   99   98   97   96   95   94   C   5   4   3   2   1

01   00   99   98   97   96   95   94   P   5   4   3   2   1

For my mother and father,

for David and Genevieve,

and for all the unknown artists

who ever were

Contents

. . . .

Preface

. . . .

In a letter to the eldest son of one of his friends, the Roman poet Horace sets up the poetics, or principles of literary criticism, by which he as a practicing poet wishes to be judged. He expresses a particular concern in this letter with his current project, probably a tragic play. As with Aristotle's *Poetics*, Horace's comments in the letter that has come to be called his *Ars Poetica* may be broken down into separate discussions of purpose, subject matter, genre, character, diction, and style.[1]

But the *Ars Poetica* differs from Aristotle's *Poetics* in that, rather than seeking an aesthetics that stems primarily from a reader/critic's standpoint, with examples taken from various literary texts that were well known at the time, Horace sets up a subjective framework in which the practicing poet himself, while he may also comment upon the creative work of others, is primarily concerned with the goals he wishes to accomplish in his own art. The Horatian scholar C. O. Brink says of Aristotle and Horace, "It is hard to conceive of minds more different than those of the two men." While both men discuss the same concepts, Horace concentrates on "the unity of a work of poetry seen by a poet." Horace's is a poetics that links theory with practice, "a poetic restatement" of his own work. While Aristotle attempts the pose of objectivity in discussing the merits of tragedy and epic, Horace finally abandons that pose altogether. He uses the established critical tradition for his own purposes and is not particularly subtle in doing so. In short, he claims "the right to be opinionated" about his art.[2]

This book, *Being a Minor Writer*, is not, however, intended as a scholarly treatise on Horace's *Ars Poetica*. It is itself an *ars poetica*, written from a minor woman writer's point of view. Theoretical arguments abound just now that purport to define *major* and *minor*. Yet so far as I know, little or nothing has been said from the authority of the experience of *being* minor — of being the writer who, according to the definition of author given by the French critic Michel Foucault, does not possess a "name."[3]

I first conceived of this project when, as a writer of short stories and poems that had found their way at regular intervals into little magazines over a period of about ten years, I returned to graduate school and thought that I saw, during my first survey course in literary theory, a decided difference between what I came to think of as the Aristotelian line of theory — that primarily by and for critical theoreticians — and the Horatian line of theory — that by and primarily directed toward practicing writers. Although the two descending lines of theory that I came to see may portray entirely too schematic a picture for some, I nonetheless found myself, as a writer, responding to the pieces in a very different way. In particular, I found that I was searching among the various discussions of purpose in the Horatian line for an answer to the invariably asked question, *Why do I write?* It struck me very forcefully that for the minor writer — at least as that individual was being defined for me by various critical theories deriving from the Aristotelian line — both the question and its answer would have to contain a *still*. That is, in the absence of major recognition, the minor writer must continually ask himself or herself: *Why do I (still) write? Why do I write (anyway)?*

The question, posed in this manner, and especially when viewed within the context of Jean-Paul Sartre's premise in *L'Être et le néant* (translated into English as *Being and Nothingness*) that the ultimate question of all philosophy is suicide (*Why go on living anyway? Why try?*), seemed to me to be as much the basic question of the human condition — of all unrecognized effort, of all unacknowledged human life — as it was the question of purpose for one's art.

Being a Minor Writer, then, is my search for an answer to this question. In addition to using tracts by various writers that have come down through the tradition begun with Horace's *Ars Poetica*, I will also, like Horace, employ existing critical theory (the Aristotelian line) to serve my own purposes. In keeping with the genre, I will claim "the right to be opinionated." But unlike Horace, and unlike most of the authors whose comments about writing I will be quoting, I will claim the right to be opinionated not as a writer who is well known, but from the authority of my experience as a minor writer — as one who does not possess the particular critical validation of Foucault's "name."

Oddly enough, while I will be working within an old tradition, my exploration of the *ars poetica* and its application to the question of being minor seems to me to fit quite neatly into a poststructuralist theoretical scheme of things. In his introduction to *Textual Strategies: Perspectives in Post-Structuralist Criticism*, Josué Harari states that, unlike their predecessors, the structuralists, who in an interdisciplinary framework attempted to turn literary theory into a kind of science in which the model would determine signification, poststructuralist theoreticians express a tendency to question the status of science itself and the possibility of objectivity. There is also, he notes, an eagerness to bring theory back to a specific text, to make it less abstract, and to interrogate the possible points of contact between literature and criticism, the place where conceptual crossings occur that relate the two.[4] Ultimately, I can think of no better place where these conceptual crossings might occur than in the *ars poetica*, where theory and practice have always coalesced.

There is perhaps no end to the authorial references to writing that I might have used here in addition to the clearly self-proclaimed *ars poetica*. These would include all the asides that exist in otherwise fictional or poetic works. In fact, as my interest in this project grew, I began to commit to my marginalia anything at all that seemed to speak to the writer's relationship to art. Mme. de Staël's autobiographical novel *Corinne*, for instance, could probably have provided material on the nature of personal experience and its effect on the writer's work. Keats's *Hyperion* or Wordsworth's *The Prelude* (subtitled, after all, *The Growth of a Poet's Mind*) could both have served in this capacity as well. I could also have referred to a remark made by the main character, a poet, in Thomas Mann's *Death in Venice*, about the relationship between a work's "sympathy" and its considered greatness. Even as I read to my daughter before she went to bed, I found myself gathering comments, such as the link Louisa May Alcott makes between the "moral" and the tale, when she has Jo in *Little Women* beg her mother, "Tell another story, Mother — one with a moral to it, like this. I like to think about them afterwards, if they are real and not too preachy."[5]

There are also short stories whose main themes are art and its aims, such as Isak Dinesen's "Babette's Feast," in which a once-renowned French chef finally exclaims to her austere Danish mentors, after having served them a sumptuous feast that has depleted the small fortune she won in absentia in the French lottery, "A great artist, Mesdames, is never poor."[6] The list of such remarks about art and writing in fiction and poetry could go on and on, but I am going to limit myself to comments on writing that have been made as such.

I know that the language and style of my discussion will at times seem too personal to some. But if Sidney and later Shelley believed it necessary to defend poetry in their contributions to the tradition of the *ars poetica*, I believe that it is much more necessary at this point in literary history, in view of the various linguistic-philosophical systems that bring the subject, and therefore the very existence of the author, into doubt, to defend the authority of my own experience and perhaps thereby to suggest new grounds on which importance might be accorded to written works.

While my coinage of terms to express concepts that may not lend themselves well to existing critical jargon is not without recent precedent, particularly among a number of feminist critics, the personal voice I will at times prefer to use actually has its roots very much in Horace. C. O. Brink points out that while the father of the *ars poetica* at first appears to speak within the traditional garb of rationalistic Graeco-Roman criticism, his *Ars Poetica* contains far more "personal content" than most criticism of his time.[7] Personal content is very natural to me as well. To that end, while I will continue to employ the expected process of quotation to make some points, I will also feel progressively free to employ what may well be termed memoiristic or anecdotal material by some.

For instance, the first chapter, "The Question of Being Minor," is written very much in traditional academic style, in that it explores existing literary theories about minor literature in an attempt to present the importance of the question of being minor in and of itself. The second and third chapters, on purpose and genre, respectively, while I hope they contain new and challenging material, follow in a similar mode. But, like Horace, I found that I had to all but abandon the pose of objectivity by the time I reached chapter 4, which discusses experience — the relationship between the writer's choice of subject matter and the writer's life. I found that I could not treat personal experience — my own or someone else's — with the stiff use of "one." It also seemed logical to me that the treatment of listening as it unfolded in chapter 5, with its various allusions to Walter Benjamin's "The Storyteller," might easily move over into the family narratives I heard when I was a child which left me with a passion for storytelling so deep that I had no choice but to do as my father had pleaded and to *write it down*. Just so, in chapter 6, with its discussion of the writer's need to make a living as it affects what D. H. Lawrence terms his "spirit of place," it seemed natural to talk about some of the menial jobs I have done for a living, if I were really going to be honest about what I believe is the genuine importance to the artist of this kind of work. The last two chapters of the book — the seventh on diction and characterization and the eighth on the subject of motherhood, which has been the most important experience of my life — would have lost their integrity entirely had I felt forced to limit myself to an academic voice.

But I am finally concerned in this book with what I see as the continuing split between the Horatian and Aristotelian lines — between critics and writers. I hope to show that theory and practice cannot be such separate categories after all. The critic needs the writer as subject, and the writer needs the existing critical tradition in order to express, like Horace, the right to be opinionated about his or her art. In an attempt to break down the partition between us, I invite both the critic and the writer into my text.

Acknowledgments

. . . .

Portions of this book were first presented as papers at the following conferences: Boundaries In/Of Literature Conference (Graduate Students of the Canadian Comparative Literature Association), 1987; Dialectic and Narrative Conference (International Association of Philosophy and Literature), 1989; Intellectual Property and the Construction of Authorship Conference (Society for Critical Exchange), 1991; and Conference on Change (International Association of Philosophy and Literature), 1991. An expanded version of the material on Primo Levi and Christa Wolf in chapter 4 appeared as "Self and Other: Primo Levi's *Se questo è un uomo* and Christa Wolf's *Patterns of Childhood* as Dialogic Texts" in *Comparative Literature Studies* 29, no. 2 (1992).

I wish to thank Julie Ellison of the Department of English at the University of Michigan for encouraging me to undertake the writing of this book. I will always be grateful for the depth of her intellect and for her wonderful sense of humor. I am also grateful to the Institute for the Humanities at the University of Michigan, where I completed much of the initial writing. My profound thanks go to Stuart McDougal and the faculty and staff of the Program in Comparative Literature at the University of Michigan. I also wish to thank the research librarians of the Boston Public Library, the Wellesley Public Library, and the Morse Institute of Natick, Massachusetts, for their help during my final revisions.

I am grateful to the editors of the journals and magazines that have supported my fiction and poetry over the years. Specific works referred to here first appeared in the *Christian Science Monitor*, *Dark Horse*, *Primavera*, *Rackham Journal of the Arts and Humanities*, *Sonora Review*, *Villager*, and *Yankee* or in manuscripts which won Hopwood Awards for the novel, short fiction, and poetry at the University of Michigan in 1985. The tale of the Texas Ranger in chapter 5 has been the focus of two published short stories: "The Texas Ranger," in *Swallow's Tale*, and "Permanence," in *Object Lessons*. A poem, "The Texas Ranger," appeared in *Michigan Alumnus Magazine*.

Most of all, I thank my father for his voice.

Being a Minor Writer

. . . .

The Question of Being Minor

. . . .

Over the past few years, scholars have engaged in a lively debate about the previously indisputable literary canon — those works traditionally recognized, primarily by members of college and university literature departments, as being "great," or at least worthy of being taught. That debate has necessarily led to an ongoing theoretical discussion about "minor" literature that ranges on a number of levels — from literally hundreds of in-depth articles in academic research journals to the arguments of some American undergraduates who protest the absurdity of having courses called "Great Books," most of which come out of a Western tradition, in a society that pretends to pride itself upon its diversity.

But it is at least equally important that the participating voices in the increasing controversy over the canon include those who speak from a subjective standpoint, not only *about* the concept of minor literature but from the authority of experience — how it *feels*. The question of being minor — of being unrecognized or little known — needs to be added to the discussion of minor literature, or the discussion will continue to be meaningless in and of itself.

The American novelist Mary Gordon writes, "There are people in the world who derive no small pleasure from the game of 'major' and 'minor'. . . . Exquisite, they will hasten to insist, but minor. These people join up with other bad specters, and I have to work to banish them. Let us pretend these specters are two men, two famous poets, saying,

'Your experience is an embarrassment; your experience is insignificant.'"[1] Indeed, it appears to have been largely the province of "famous poets," or of the literary scholars who study them and write critical articles about them, to have silenced the authority of experience of the minor voice. Yet the so-called minor writer has something very important to say, not only about literature and writing but about the search for purpose, the reason for continuing to be or to do anything, in the midst of a postmodern human condition in which nothing supposedly ever counts. The minor writer must justify an existence and a product that is unrecognized and that will probably continue to go unrecognized throughout his or her life. The minor, or unknown, writer could stop writing tomorrow and no one would notice. This individual's purpose for what he or she does, and is, must contain an *anyway*, as in, *Why do I write anyway, when perhaps only the five hundred people who read this literary journal will hear me out?* For this writer, some sort of poetics of being minor must be borne in mind.

The critical tradition of the *ars poetica* — the writer's own commentary upon his or her art — began with the Roman poet Horace, was later revived in France with Boileau's translation of Horace in 1674, was transferred into the English canon during the following centuries with various "defenses" of poetry such as Sir Philip Sidney's or the subsequent "Defense of Poetry" by Percy Bysshe Shelley, and was then maintained in the Anglo-American canon with works such as Edgar Allan Poe's "Philosophy of Composition" and Walt Whitman's "Preface" to *Leaves of Grass*.[2] The *ars poetica* continues to be a viable, lively genre to this day, with interviews and articles in which well-known writers explore the basic Horatian issues of subject matter, character, diction, genre, and other aspects of their art appearing regularly in periodicals that range from literary magazines or the Associated Writing Program's *Chronicle* to the Sunday book review section of the *New York Times*. But while the *ars poetica* has theoretically allowed space in literary history for the writer to talk critically about (or, in Shelley's case, to defend) his or her art, the tracts that have been saved and available to us in our libraries are almost all by individuals upon whom the reading public has bestowed what the French critic Michel Foucault acknowledges as a "name."[3]

Foucault tells us that the process for determining that the author has a name is based on the same techniques that Saint Jerome, who is widely acknowledged as the individual most responsible for choosing the canon of the modern Christian Bible, employed when he was determining the holiness of script. The process of *name*-ing, Foucault says, essentially involves four steps. First, the author is defined as one who maintains a standard level of quality in the text. Second, the author is one who expresses a certain field of conceptual or theoretical coherence. Third, the author is one who expresses a certain stylistic uniformity. But finally — and most important as it affects the minor, or unknown, writer — the author is a definite historical figure in which a series of events converge.[4] That is, history has recorded this author in its text. The author does not have a name if history, or a history of readers, has somehow managed, for whatever reason, to pass this author by. The argument for determining which authors have something valuable to say to us about writing and literature through their *ars poetica*, then, would be that a Henry James or an E. M. Forster, for example, has somehow earned the right to talk about writing, or why he writes, because of the reputation history has bestowed upon him, while the minor writer — who by definition has no name or established reputation — does not have that right. The minor writer cannot write in the tradition of the *ars poetica* begun by Horace, because that tradition includes "the right to be opinionated," as the Horatian scholar C. O. Brink puts it.[5]

The unnamed voice, in Foucault's sense, is not allowed to speak for itself as a critic. If the unknown, or minor, voice wants to say something important about art — or if it merely wants to "defend" itself — it is expected to use the process of academic quotation. That is, it must glean various sentences and paragraphs from those authors who have been legitimized by history — who have been given names — and then respeak these passages to prove that what it has to say is worthwhile. In this way, history perpetuates its own assumption that the minor voice can have nothing original to say. Yet it is only in that unknown, minor voice, with its particular experience — and not in that voice's dependence on some history of knowledge outside itself — that the question of being minor ultimately resides.

In contemplating the difficulty of modern editors who must defend their criteria for determining major and minor, the French philosopher and critic François Lyotard notes:

Can you give me, says an editor defending his or her profession, the title of a work of major importance which would have been rejected by every editor and which would therefore remain unknown? Most likely, you do not know any masterpiece of this kind because, if it does exist, it remains unknown. And if you think you know one, since it has not been made public, you cannot say that it is of major importance, except in your eyes. You do not know of any, therefore, and the editor is right.[6]

One can only imagine the difficulty a serious scholar would meet in attempting to provide a bibliography of treatises on writing by even a handful of the writers who have been relegated to the status of minor, whether that be taken to mean unimportant or unknown. Lyotard's point, of course, is that it is the editor who has determined that the "masterpiece" will remain unknown. But neither the critic who bestows Foucault's "name" on select authors in history nor Lyotard's editor, who must decide moment by moment whether a work is major or minor, can surmise why it is that the unknown writer goes on writing in spite of them, why he or she still writes.

In his "Polemical Introduction" to the now-classic *Anatomy of Criticism*, Northrop Frye admits that our trust in "public critics" (such as Lamb, Hazlitt, Arnold, or Sainte-Beuve, as he chooses to represent the "historical" critics) to help us "appreciate" literature — to tell us "what we should know about literature" and "something about what it is" — has not of itself provided us with "a systematic criticism as distinct from the history of taste." Frye, with his inherent sense of literary ethics, ultimately argues against the establishment of a "limiting principle in literature," admitting that even the age-old criterion of "marketability," with the public critic as some sort of intermediary, falls back on the history of taste — however short-lived that history might turn out to be.[7] Indeed, if one pushes Frye's observations to the absurd, one comes up with the very real prospect that just about any written text has at least the possibility of becoming part of the canon.

While Frye may have invited us to begin to open up the canon, it was still perhaps the prevailing notion of a prescribed derivation of "great books" within an assumedly closed (and exclusively Western) literature that allowed the American critic Harold Bloom, in his early work, to produce a theory of poetry that had at its base an anxiety on the part of the author of not being original, of not being historically in charge of his or her (now disputably) new text. But the student of literary theory who is familiar with the biblical promise to the Hebrews that there will be a coming Messiah has also had to have noticed the limited Christian nature of Bloom's metaphor in *The Anxiety of Influence*. Just as the assumption for mainstream Christians must be that the highpoint of religious history has already occurred with the advent of Jesus and that therefore the world must necessarily continue to decline until some catastrophic Second Coming brings it all to a halt, so Bloom assumes that the downfall of anglophone literature since Milton's *Paradise Lost* is inevitable.[8]

The ultimate consequence of such a theory, of course, is, as Bloom implies, the total disappearance — or total wishy-washiness, I'd rather say — of future poems. But just as the Christian concept of the messianic promise does not work in the very Hebrew theology that is ultimately responsible for its existence, so Bloom's theory of derivation, or anxiety, does not always work in literatures outside his own anglophone base. Even in French literature — itself a literature within the Western tradition — there is no great lyric poet to coincide with Bloom's precursor poets, Shakespeare and Milton, since the overriding genre of significance in French literature was not the lyric or epic poem, within which Bloom worked out his theory of anxiety, but the *ars poetica* of Horace as it resulted in the prescribed rules set out in the translation by Boileau in the seventeenth century.[9] So although Bloom's primarily Protestant Christian theory of literature may work smoothly in terms of the history of romantic and postromantic poetry in English, with Shakespeare and Milton as literary Christ-figures from whom lesser prophets then emerge, there is no expectation for a catastrophic decline or second fall in French literature. Instead, the great French writer of all time has not already appeared. He or she is yet to come. If Bloom's anxiety is lifted from the author, then each new writer works only under the pressure of the internalized question, *Am I yet great?* The pressure is from within and not from some outside critical vantage point.

But Harold Bloom has always been an original critic, and his more recent work seems to be going beyond his early theory of derivation to allow for the possibility of texts that are less derived. After all, one wants to observe, a theory of poetry that predicts the end of all poetry must also imply the atrophy of the critic's art. In a more recent work, Bloom notes that the issue of unknown, or minor, writers — the issue of inclusion and exclusion — comes up first in the supposedly indisputable texts of the Bible. He observes in *Ruin the Sacred Truth: Poetry and Belief from the Bible to the Present* that *The Book of Jubilees*, a text gathered together by a Pharisee in 100 B.C., which later became the formative text for the modern versions of Genesis and Exodus, methodically excludes the text of the author modern biblical scholars have come to know as J.[10] Was J — nameless as J has turned out to be — the local minor writer of that time?

Bloom suggests in his introduction to *The Book of J* that one reason J's text may have been excluded by the church fathers was that J was a woman in a man's theological world.[11] What he/she/J wrote seems also to have been excluded from the canon in part because readers had a hard time coming to terms with the seeming contradictions in the stories about Yahweh this writer told. In other words, J's stories did not contain the local equivalent of mainstream thought. Bloom ultimately implies that it is the refusal of J's ancient critics (and not of J) to assimilate or to adapt the existing canon that has become the crime. Bloom makes a statement that might justify the view that much that is original (or at least nonmainstream) in literature actually comes from the minor writers of a given time. He writes, "Every crucial trace of the J writer has been totally erased from the *The Book of Jubilees*, whose highly normative author simply refused to assimilate everything about J that is most original and difficult."[12] Bloom's reading of J suggests another criterion for influence — that of the omitted and therefore ultimately subversive text that continues to lie in wait to be discovered over an indefinite period of time (in this case, over centuries). In the wake of this text, everything that has been termed major up to this point must be redefined.

But there is another literary theory about the concept of minor literature that may prove to be an even more positive influence upon the debate. In *Kafka: Pour une littérature mineure*, French critics Gilles Deleuze and Félix Guattari outline, through a careful perusal of marginalia by Franz Kafka, what may be reduced (if admittedly in a simple-minded way) to three criteria by which the minor status of a given work may be approached.[13]

First, a minor literature is not necessarily that written in a minor language (such as Yiddish or Urdu, spoken by a people considered numerically few) but that which a minority produces within a major language. In this context, Kafka, writing in German as a Jew, is producing a minor literature. This view of the term *minor* suggests an exciting realm of possibilities. With this concept, the minor voice, far from being unimportant, is perhaps the only voice that is speaking out. Thus, the African American writer, whether male or female, in predominantly white America is by this definition minor, but by no means can this writer be said at any given moment to be less. The theory approaches an intelligence that refuses to categorize according to mere academic recognition but rather puts into question any outside ability to designate literature as good, better, best.

In *Playing in the Dark: Whiteness and the Literary Imagination*, Toni Morrison suggests through a study of standard works such as *Moby-Dick*, *Huckleberry Finn*, and *Heart of Darkness* that there is no "whiteness" in literature without its accompanying contrast to "blackness" or "darkness." "Explicit or implicit," she states, "the Africanist presence informs in compelling and inescapable ways the texture of American literature. It is a dark and abiding presence, there for the literary imagination as both a visible and an invisible mediating force." [14]

Just as Morrison argues that there is no whiteness without a darkness that the very powers defining it can never know, so there is no major literature without an accompanying contrast with something that has to be defined as minor by those who are least suited to know what it is. Any woman writing within what still remains a predominantly white male tradition must also be minor by the first criterion offered by Deleuze and Guattari.

The second criterion that Deleuze and Guattari list pinpoints the singularity of this minor voice. In the minor literature, they say, all is political. In the *grandes littératures*, they point out, the individual incident, or *l'affaire individuelle*, takes precedence over any collective acts in such a way that familial or marital incidents tend to link all other individual incidents. In the truly minor literature, each individual incident must finally be seen within the context of the whole, because, within each individual incident, an entire oppressed history is struggling to come out.

Working, then, within the context of Deleuze and Guattari's second criterion, the feminist critic might be allowed to account for any disorientation that a white male reader might appear to express upon encountering a work such as Alice Walker's *The Color Purple* for the first time. The director Steven Spielberg, for instance, has rewritten the narrative for the film version of the novel in such a way that the sensuous Shug Avery, who has her own private religion of human love in the almost all-female novel, must have a minister father-figure in the movie to bring her back to life. This kind of readerly disorientation, Deleuze and Guattari might tell us, is innately political. The particular struggle of the traditional white male reader with the text takes place because this reader has no link to the individual experience that is being portrayed.

Until very recently, the black women characters who have been most familiar to us within the confines of the literature that has been prescribed to us as major have almost all been created by white men. Imagination, rather than experience, is their source. And, in so far as these black fictional characters are placed by their white creators in subservient positions, as is William Faulkner's Dilsey in *The Sound and the Fury*, they fit within the confines of the historically prevailing concept of what a white man expects them to be. They are there to serve as the dark contrast to what is white. They cannot have *négritude* — as the Africanist movement pursued by Léopold Senghor and Aimé Césaire attempted to define that essence midway through this century — because the experience that has been defined for them in literature is only the one that has been allowed them by white society in "real" white life.[15]

Much as William Faulkner may have admired the real-life prototype of his Dilsey character — a woman who raised him and was a loyal member of the Faulkner household for many years — in the end we may very well distrust the integrity of Dilsey's voice. In Walker's *The Color Purple*, with its simple epistolary moves back and forth between the separate "common" and "educated" dictions of Celie and her sister, Nettie, we discover this integrity of voice. The Dilsey section of *The Sound and the Fury* is a literary appropriation of a black serving-woman's experience as imagined by a white male writer. And so it is not experience at all.

The third criterion in the strategy of Deleuze and Guattari follows very logically from the second. In the minor literature, they say, everything takes on a collective value. Since there are necessarily fewer "masters" within the microcosm of the particular minority represented in the text, the act which the writer within the minority describes constitutes a communal act. In other words, the minor writer almost unwittingly takes on the responsibility for speaking for the smaller group within the whole. This makes the minor writer's purpose for writing an ethically charged one. The minor writer, by definition, Deleuze and Guattari imply, cannot avoid an ethical involvement with the text. They assert that a minor literature is one that produces an active solidarity, in spite of skepticism. By Deleuze and Guattari's stated standards, then, a minor writer is not necessarily minor because he or she is currently or even historically unknown or financially unsuccessful but because his or her work is counter-skeptical to the prevailing times.

In the postmodern era, when purpose — the reason for

being at all — has become an anomaly, we may even find a few ancient answers to humanity's questions reflected in the persistence of this minor voice. One Hebrew bard, for instance, saw his craft as the means to "sing praises . . . while I have any being." [16] It is a small word, "any," but it says a great deal about the minor voice. It implies that the "being" the poet has left is almost spent but that he is going to sing anyway. It isn't particularly popular — it isn't even particularly literary — at the end of the twentieth century to believe there is a purpose to one's life. So if, as Deleuze and Guattari have pointed out, the minor writer, writing against the current flow, is the one most likely to be counter-skeptical, the minor writer in our era is probably the one most likely to challenge an antibeing or nihilistic view of the question of purpose when he or she writes. "I will sing . . . while I have any being." I will *still* write *anyway*.

The writer's recognition by the reading public is a criterion for greatness at which T. S. Eliot in his "What is Minor Poetry?" finally scoffs. Eliot ends by rejecting any criterion other than what he calls genuineness for judging the poet's craft. [17] The minor writer may just be the one who with this genuineness recognizes the alternative possibilities to the prevailing code and is creatively motivated to include them in a text. In the postmodern era in particular, the minor writer may be more likely to maintain, at times in spite of material evidence, the prophetic or antiskeptical vision that does not disregard the possibility of hope.

In *"A White Heron" and the Question of Minor Literature*, Louis Renza adds yet another criterion for judging a minor work. He suggests that the truly minor piece rejects categorization altogether. Renza systematically shows how each attempt to categorize Sarah Orne Jewett's short story "A White Heron" as "regional" or as "pastoral" fails, and he indicates that this very resistance to categorization is what finally makes the work minor — a judgment that must remain intrinsically nonjudgmental in itself. In his discussion of Jewett's story, Renza implies the use of various "strategies" on the part of this New England writer to *remain* minor, as though she were aware in her writing of making a conscious choice. Renza's suggestion that the conception of minor literature is actually a challenge to the very function of criticism itself is inherently a writer-friendly one.[18]

Yet another critic of minor literature, David Lloyd, in *Nationalism and Minor Literature: James Clarence Mangan and the Emergence of Irish Cultural Nationalism*, also shows how his chosen minor writer avoids categorization by established (or British imperialist, as he terms them) criteria. His reading stresses the political, essentially oppressive, aspects of canonization:

> A major literature is established as such precisely by virtue of its claim to representative status, of its claim to realize the autonomy of the individual subject to such a degree that that individual subject becomes universally valid and archetypal. The subjection of the reader to this canonical form, the alienation of his or her autonomy in the aesthetic work, is as intrinsic an element of the functioning of a major literature as is its perpetuation of the concept of the autonomous subject as the essence of the human.[19]

For Lloyd, then, the individuality or subjectivity of the author, the reader, and the literary character are all at stake in the categorization process.

But Deleuze and Guattari's definition of minor literature is itself most interesting in terms of its possible consequences on the traditional economic value placed upon the writer's ultimate success. In the postmodern era especially, the concept of an ethics of purpose might be extended beyond the traditional treatments in terms of catharsis and/or entertainment to consider the economic consequences of a sense of literary purpose from the minor point of view. Contrary to what has become in the postmodern era the big-business reason for doing anything at all, the minor writer is also most probably the one who writes as an outsider to the worldly or economic concept of success.

This minority economic point of view must necessarily flavor a number of choices that the writer makes. Deleuze and Guattari, Renza, and Lloyd all end by pointing out that the literature traditionally considered major has always had to do with the dominant or wealthy class or race. The *ars poetica*, as conceived by Horace and continued in a predominantly Western white male tradition, has historically treated the writerly questions of subject matter, style, diction, and character as inherently major in the sense of *big*. Horace recommends that literary characters be taken either from "tradition" (in his case the tradition of the Greek male hero Achilles) or that they be "invented," but he leaves us no working model for an invented character whose greatness does not necessarily lie in a fall from aristocratic grace.[20]

Male writers who follow in the historical tradition of the *ars poetica*, while perhaps not always as pointed about their bias for the idea of aristocratic character as the French poet Stéphane Mallarmé, whose adverse idea of the "mob," or general plebeian population, seems to dominate a good deal of his writerly advice, often tend to underscore the aristocratic type.[21] This may be why, when we encounter an alternative comment about choice of characters, we are oddly moved. The playwright Lorraine Hansberry once wrote to her mother in regard to a play she was writing, "Mama, it is a play that tells the truth about people, Negroes and life and I think it will help a lot of people to understand how we are just as complicated as they are — and just as mixed up — but above all, that we have among our miserable and downtrodden ranks — people who are the very essence of human dignity."[22] Here, a bold effort has been made to move the idea of character greatness from the aristocratic to the downtrodden class, with the idea of dignity expressed in humanistic rather than "class-ic" terms.

In a passage that perhaps bears traces of Horace's statement about the sometimes dual, sometimes either/or purpose of literature to entertain or teach, the Italian author Italo Calvino says that he has observed two inclinations contending through the centuries — the one to entertain, the other to make language a "weightless element." He calls this element *legerezza* and says:

> Possiamo dire che due vocazioni opposte si contendono il campo della letteratura attraverso i secoli; l'una tende a fare del linguaggio un elemento senza peso, che alleggia sopra le cose come una nube, o meglio un pulviscolo sottile, o meglio ancora come un campo d'impulsi magnetici; l'altra tende a communicare al linguaggio il peso, lo spessore, la concretezza delle cose, dei corpi, delle sensazioni.[23]

> We could say that two opposing tendencies contend in literature over the centuries; the first tends to make of language a weightless element, that hovers above things like a mist, or rather like a subtle inference, or, even better, like a field of magnetic forces; the other tends to ascribe to language the weight, the substance, the concreteness of things, of bodies, of sensations. (translation mine)

Calvino gives as an example of the concept of *legerezza* the scene in Shakespeare's *Romeo and Juliet* in which Mercutio refutes Romeo's line, "Under love's heavy burden do I sink." At this point, Mercutio is literally dancing at death's door — dancing while he has any being — in a setting that, says Calvino, suggests in microcosm all the illnesses of our own times. Mercutio's dancing contains the lightness that is the profound truth or moral lesson of the play. Calvino regards Mercutio, traditionally held to be a minor character, as the primary vehicle for that moral lesson. Mercutio's role may not be as visible as Romeo's, but it is no less important. It may in fact be more important in terms of purpose.

Purpose must of necessity dominate all other aspects of the minor writer's literary act. In his very astute (and really rather passionate) appeal for what he calls a woman's poetics, the critic Lawrence Lipking implies that the question of monetary success, and the desire for it, must ultimately be at the root of any honest discussion about the purpose of writing. He states, "The silence of most theorists about such issues of publicity and career comes close to being the dirty little secret of current theory: A woman's poetics is likely to take them to heart." It is quite logical that a poetics of being minor would take "the dirty little secret" of publicity and career very much to heart. Indeed, the minor woman writer might claim not only "the right to be opinionated" that follows in the tradition of the Horatian *ars poetica* but also, as Lipking goes on to say, "the right to inquire about the grounds of importance itself."[24]

But if it appears at first that in the postmodern era importance as a criterion for literary judgment has become synonymous with a money-based, *People* magazine kind of publicity or renown, this fundamentally materialistic or economic aspect of postmodern poetics has its roots very much in the tradition from which the genre of the *ars po-etica* is derived. Success and importance are nothing new. In *Ars Poetica*, Horace writes, "To poets to be second-rate is a privilege which neither men nor gods nor bookstalls ever allowed."[25] Horace, with his "second-rate" poets, seems to imply that, for a poet to be first-rate, he or she would nec-essarily have to do well at the "bookstalls," which, one as-sumes, were the Roman Empire's equivalent of our *New York Times* bestseller list or B. Dalton's chains.

The *ars poetica* tradition seems for the most part to have kept this view of major as being connected with sales suc-cess. W. H. Auden remarks at one point that "only a minor talent can be a perfect gentleman; a major talent is always more than a bit of a cad. Hence the importance of minor writers — as teachers of good manners. Now and again, an exquisite minor work can make a master feel thoroughly ashamed of himself."[26] How, one wants to ask Auden in retrospect, is the minor work "exquisite"? And if it is truly exquisite, why was it not determined to be major? Or even great? Once again, one has the feeling that the body of one's artistic work, or corpus, must be big — even pumped up. If the body of one's work is small and/or exquisite — if it is fragile rather than corpulent, if it tends more to-ward the practiced weightlessness of a gymnast rather than toward the sinewy earthboundness of a two-hundred-pound male who makes a practice of lifting weights — then, one may assume, it must by definition be a minor work.

Many literary awards, including the Nobel Prize, are based not on the single exquisite work but on the entire corpus of the artist's work. A number of groups represent-ing the interests of minority and women writers have ar-gued recently that the size of an author's produced work has often been determined by social or economic exigencies and that therefore size should not be seen as one of the criteria for determining the recipient of the Nobel Prize. Reading through the various "answers" proposed to this argument, one soon becomes aware that even the healthy exploration of the ethics of exclusion can have its inequities and biases — its embarrassing moments of racism and sexism in the guise of purist aesthetics.

One defender of the current system for judging the Nobel, for instance, claims that he would "count it a guarantee of literary quality if the next Nobel Prize went to [Seamus] Heaney or [Brian] Friel, [R. P.] Warren or [Peter] Taylor." He goes on to say, however, that if he "were asked . . . not to choose but to bet on the next Nobel Prize recipient in English, I would not put my money on either an Irishman or a male Southerner, but on a woman — say, Margaret Atwood in Canada or Nadine Gordimer in South Africa, or a black writer such as Toni Morrison in the United States, or even, with a little bit of luck, on that thoroughbred of living women writers, Eudora Welty."[27]

Choosing a woman writer for a Nobel, for this particular critic, is more like betting on a horse than reading and comparing texts, and the critical selection process depends less on the genuine importance of the author than it does on luck. For this critic, Eudora Welty is not, like her male peers, a human being, but a thoroughbred mare. According to this reasoning, women still don't make it on their own merit but rather because, as this critic goes on to say, the world suddenly seems to feel guilty and thus feels the pressure to give women and people of color a prize or two. He continues: "To predict that a woman will win the next prize is to admit that the Nobel is often political and social as well as literary, and any honest survey would have to concede that fact."[28] But one wonders here how much "honest" has to do with "fact."

Women writers who have been successful in terms of producing a large body of work may be just as guilty as male critics when it comes to judging another writer's work on the basis of being big. One need only look, for instance, to remarks made by Edith Wharton, who was immensely popular in her own time, and who is enjoying a kind of comeback in ours, about the corpulent size of the writer's work as a kind of proof of genius. Wharton writes, "In all the arts abundance seems to be one of the surest signs of vocation. It exists on the lowest scale, and, in the art of fiction, belongs as much to the producer of 'railway novels' as to Balzac, Thackeray or Tolstoy; yet it almost always marks the creative artist. Whatever a man has it in him to do really well he usually keeps on doing with an indestructible persistence."[29]

Wharton's writer who "keeps on doing with an indestructible persistence" is (still) "a man." For many women writers, the "indestructible persistence" that has meant getting up and writing between four and six in the morning may still not have produced what Wharton calls abundance, even though the resulting few pieces may be very good. Indeed, with constraints of time on women who do not, like Wharton, have ladies' maids, many poorer women writers are perhaps grateful to produce one good poem or story every year.

Women writers who do not have ladies' maids do, of course, have their feminist champions. The critic Carolyn Heilbrun, for instance, says of "privileged" women writers, "Who else has the time and money for such thoughts, for the enactment of such daring?"[30] And who else, if not the minor woman writer, would be motivated to deviate from the traditional male criterion of bigness of body when trying to come up with a working definition of success?

Lorraine Hansberry seems to have been struck at the beginning of our era with the enormous disparity between talent and worldly or economic success. She has one of her characters say in the play *The Sign in Sidney Brusten's Window*, "That is one of the great romantic and cruel ideas of our civilization. A lot of people 'have it' and they just get trampled to death by the mob trying to get up the same mountain."[31] For Hansberry, whose own recognition nevertheless came early and whose audience has become even broader since her death, worth is not determined by the fact that one has made it to the top of the mountain. Literary worth means that one has "it," some writerly quality that is much harder to define. As Hansberry states in a letter to a young writer who had sought out her advice (letters which she is said to have invariably taken the time to answer, and at great length):

> I don't know you but imagine that if your temperament is anything like mine you will find things which make you discouraged and, perhaps, a little angry in the above notes. But as a writer I think you will also discern in them another writer's fraternal sense of the pain of creating *anything* worthwhile. And when all is said and done I imagine that you will also agree with me that life has little else to offer other than the confrontation with a problem to be solved.[32]

Here, "worthwhile" is not necessarily that which sells in Horace's Roman bookstalls but that which confronts a problem to be solved.

Of course, the idea of being minor does not necessarily imply that the minor writer must be indigent, wearing a burlap bag in order to maintain some sort of vague ascetic principle of pure art. Being minor may merely pinpoint where one's artistic priorities more likely lie. The essayist Annie Dillard, though both a popular and critical success, nevertheless tends in writing about her craft to remove the idea of literary worth from the financial realm. Speaking of contemporary fiction, she expands upon an idea she says she took from Buckminster Fuller (characteristically admitting that Fuller probably did not mean it to be taken in quite this way at all) to talk about the relative weight, or value, of what she calls "imaginative acts."

> Imaginative acts actually weigh in the balance of physical processes. Imaginative acts — even purely mental combinations, like the thought that a certain cloud resembles a top hat — carry real weight in the universe. A child who makes a pun, or a shepherd who looks at a batch of stars and thinks, "That part is a throne and that part is a swan," is doing something which counts in the universe's reckoning of order and decay — which counts just as those mighty explosions and strippings of electrons do inside those selfsame stars.[33]

Here, economic definitions of "weight" and "counts" are removed entirely from any universal scheme of artistic accountability. Imaginative acts are "doing something which counts in the universe's reckoning of order and decay." Dillard goes on to apologize for what she calls her "crackpot notion," this "little ghosty story I never tire of telling myself," but she still determinedly notes that, with this "real work," the artist "need not find a publisher, or a gallery, or a producer or a symphony orchestra. Thoughts count. A completed novel in a trunk in the attic is an order added to the sum of the universe's order."[34]

Thoughts count. This is not to say that the artist is duty-bound to leave everything that he or she produces in a drawer, as Emily Dickinson did, at least as she is rendered in the romantic poetic persona we have come to know. In fact, we have no proof that Dickinson *chose* not to place her poems. Her letters imply that she would very much have liked to have found a reader with a listening ear but that she despaired of ever finding one. She wrote in a letter to friends, "Perhaps you laugh at me! Perhaps the whole U.S. are laughing at me too! *I* can't stop for that! *My* business is to love. I found a bird, this morning, down on a little bush at the foot of the garden, and wherefore sing, I said, since nobody *hears?*"[35]

If one believes that one's own literary attempts to make some sort of order out of the prevailing chaos (or perhaps to look beyond the chaos, to take another stand) can make even a minor difference in the status quo, then one also has an artistic obligation to place those stories or poems in places where the receptive reader, the one who hears, can find them. Or at least to try. And trying — doing something that matters *anyway* in the face of threatened oblivion — is what the question of being minor is all about. Like the Hebrew poet, the minor writer continues to sing anyway, to praise with any being that might be left. And so, in terms of both literary history and the overall human condition, there is nothing unimportant about the minor voice.

2

Purpose

. . . .

While no artist can avoid conflict, suffering, and death in dealing with the subject matter of the human condition, the minor writer, as antiskeptic, might well be the one to bring a saving power or presence to the margins of the text. The minor writer, *still* writing, writing *anyway*, despite the threat of historical exclusion, may suggest the possibility of hope.

A number of women writers — by definition minor because they were not writing within what has been until fairly recently the white male whole — have in fact tended to argue for the possibility of hope when they have discussed purpose, or the motivating force that has made them write. The critic Jane Spencer, commenting upon the early-eighteenth-century writer Penelope Aubin, writes, "Morality for her was the proper aim of fiction, and she found the society of her time in particular need of moral advice." Spencer goes on to quote one of the characters in Aubin's *The Strange Adventures of the Count de Veneuil and His Family* as saying, "The few that honour Virtue, and wish well to our Nation, ought to study to reclaim our Giddy Youth; and since Reprehensions fail, try to win them by Virtue, and by Methods where Delight and Instruction may go together." [1]

Aubin does not speak directly about her writing here, as she might in a self-proclaimed *ars poetica*. But by the nineteenth century, women writers can be found on a more regular basis to be making ethical arguments for their writing in a bolder way. They begin to speak, not through the mask of a fictional character, but in separate commentaries that specifically address their creative work.

Horace's *ars poetica* was first of all a letter, we must recall, and so it is perhaps appropriate that as women writers joined the tradition, their comments would take place in letters. Often these were letters to well-read friends who did not themselves write. But in the correspondence between George Sand and Gustave Flaubert, in which the topic frequently reverts to the occupation the two friends had in common, we find a wealth of statements on the affective purpose of writing that Sand espoused. Although she greatly loved and respected Flaubert, Sand felt that the irony — the ambiguous dislike — that her friend felt for many of his characters, including Emma Bovary, was fundamentally detrimental to something that might be termed his artistic health. In her letters to him, she often implied that the vacuum in which he placed his characters denied him an even greater creativity than he had attained. She wrote to him:

> Je ne suis pas dans ton idée qu'il faille supprimer le sein pour tirer l'arc. J'ai une croyance tout à fait contraire pour mon usage et que je crois bonne pour beaucoup d'autres, probablement pour le grand nombre. Je viens de développer mon idée là-dessus dans un roman qui est à la *Revue des Deux Mondes* et qui paraîtra après celui d'Août. Je crois que l'artiste doit vivre dans sa nature le plus possible. A celui qui aime la lutte, la guerre; à celui qui aime les femmes, l'amour; au vieux qui, comme moi, aime la nature, le voyage et les fleurs, les roches, les

grands paysages, les enfants aussi, la famille, tout ce qui émeut, tout ce qui combat l'anémie morale. Je crois que l'art a besoin d'une palette toujours débordante de tons doux ou violents suivant le sujet du tableau; que l'artiste est un instrument dont tout doit jouer avant qu'il joue des autres. Mais tout cela n'est peut-être pas applicable à un esprit de ta sorte qui a beaucoup acquis et qui n'a plus qu'à digérer. Je n'insisterais que sur un point, c'est que l'être moral et que je crains pour toi un jour ou l'autre une déterioration de la santé qui te forcerait à suspendre ton travail et à le laisser refroidir.[2]

I do not agree with you that one must silence the heart in order to hit one's mark. I put a completely opposite view into practice, and it is one I believe is good for many others, probably for the majority. I have just developed my idea in a novel that is at the *Revue des Deux Mondes*, and that will be out after the one due in August. I think that the artist must live according to his nature as much as possible. For him who loves struggle, war; for him who loves women, love; for old folks who, like me, love nature, travel and flowers, rocks, expansive countryside, children too, family: all that moves, all that combats moral anemia. I believe that art has need of a palette that is overflowing with soft or violent tones according to the subject of the painting; that the artist is an instrument upon whom all must have played, before he can play upon others. But all that is perhaps not applicable to a spirit such as yours that has taken in so much and that has only now to digest it all. I would insist only upon one point, and that is that the physical being is necessary to the moral being and that I fear for you a deterioration of your health that will one day force you to suspend your work and let it grow cold. (translation mine)

Apparently, Sand was concerned that the bitter irony of Flaubert's novels — which, she argued, were so unlike his generous human spirit in real life — would eventually cause him to fail both physically and artistically.

At first one may be slightly uncomfortable with this rather motherly warning on Sand's part to her friend Flaubert, especially in our postmodern era when the prevailing sociological code is one of moral constructs, making us hesitant to use such clear-cut terms as "right" and "wrong." One may even begin to hear a voice very much like that of Sylvia Plath's mother in the editorial comments in *Letters Home*, where Aurelia Plath swears that her daughter was always a sunny, happy child, and that she, as the poet's mother, therefore has no idea how her daughter could grow up to write such depressing poems.[3] But only a writer can suffer at any given moment with the frustration of wanting to produce one thing and coming up, instead, with another. Perhaps it is true that to try, like Homer's Achilles, to set the entire community straight, whether it be with one's withdrawal from the group or with one's writing, may be finally an anticommunal act, and an extremely arrogant and self-righteous one at that. Nevertheless, sometimes, after looking at the chaos all around, one may want to help. And so one goes on arguing for moral purpose in literature, even when one knows one may fall short of it oneself.

Few critics seem to have taken note of the fact that, even before she began to write novels, George Eliot was intrigued enough with the moral field to include Spinoza's *Ethics* among her many translations. When it came to speaking to writers about responsibility, she was particularly hard on women writers. In her long essay "Silly Novels by Lady Novelists," she writes:

> It must be plain to every one who looks impartially and extensively into feminine literature that its greatest deficiencies are due hardly more to the want of intellectual power than to the want of those moral qualities that contribute to literary excellence — patient diligence, a sense of the responsibility involved in publication, and an appreciation of the sacredness of the writer's art. . . . The foolish vanity of wishing to appear in print, instead of being counterbalanced by any consciousness of the intellectual or moral derogation implied in futile authorship, seems to be encouraged by the extremely false impression that to write *at all* is a proof of superiority in a woman.[4]

After attacking what she saw as the myth that perhaps those women who wrote "silly novels" needed income and were barred from other income-producing professions, Eliot — almost mimicking the age-old epithet issued by many a misguided but well-meaning mother to a female child, "If you can't say something nice, don't say anything at all" — essentially begs the woman novelist who cannot write anything intelligent not to write anything at all.

But if Eliot seems to single out women for this proscriptive demand, we might reconsider the intent with which the advice is offered. Eliot was fully aware that it was considered unusual for a woman to write at all, and so she probably saw those women writers who did break into print as morally responsible for the standards that they bore, much as the minor writer as defined by critics Deleuze and Guattari feels the particular burden of representation when writing within the whole.[5]

George Eliot doesn't stop with women, however, in her demand for this kind of moral responsibility on the part of the writer. While the fact that she singles women out may imply that she believed women were somehow particularly suited to address what she termed the moral realm, she went on to implore both men and women writers to accept the responsibility that was inherent in their art. In another essay entitled simply "Authorship," she states:

> [The] man or woman who publishes writings inevitably assumes the office of teacher or influencer of the public mind. Let him protest as he will that he only seeks to amuse, and has no pretension to do more than while away an hour of leisure or weariness — "the idle singer of an empty day" — he can no more escape influencing the moral taste, and with it the action of the intelligence, than a setter of fashions in furniture and dress can fill the shops with his designs and leave the garniture of persons and houses unaffected by his industry.[6]

For Eliot, the act of writing is a moral question, a question of for or against and, necessarily, of right and wrong. Her singer here — like the singer in the Psalmist's "I will sing . . . while I have any being" — is not "the idle singer of an empty day." According to Eliot, the singer cannot escape influencing moral taste and the public intelligence. The singer cannot separate the song from its consequences to the community. The office of the writer is inevitably that of teacher and influencer. The writer might protest noisily that he or she is just an idle singer, but that preferred role is not possible. By definition, the writer's office is a moral one. The writer, according to Eliot, has no choice.

Eliot was acutely aware of the danger in her discussion of purpose as moral. If she believed that "it is for art to present images of a lovelier order than the actual, gently winning the affections, and so determining the taste," she seemed, nevertheless, to realize that few writers ever completely accomplish this lofty, somewhat quixotic literary goal.[7] As for her "lady novelists" who wrote "silly novels," she would prefer they not even try. "The most pitiable of all silly novels by lady novelists," she claims, "are what we may call the *oracular* species — novels intended to expound the writer's religious, philosophical, or moral theories."[8]

But Eliot is harshest with those writers who write specifically for monetary gain and material success. Her words are hauntingly attractive to the writer who may in some small way desire to offer, through art, something to the reader that approaches what is perhaps best simply stated as relief. She writes, "An author who would keep a pure and noble conscience, and with that a developing instead of degenerating intellect and taste, must cast out of his aims the aim to be rich."[9] To write for money alone is degenerative. While Sand was concerned with what we might call Flaubert's attitude toward his characters, Eliot seems to be saying here that "the aim to be rich" is just as degenerative to the writer's artistic health. A pecuniary motive, she says, weighs on the writer's conscience and adversely affects the writer's own intellect and taste, as well as those of the community.

Edith Wharton put together a commentary on writing that, despite the fact that she was the first woman to win a Pulitzer Prize for fiction, is still largely ignored because it is said to ape *The Art of the Novel*, those collected prefaces on the genre by her friend and early mentor Henry James. While Wharton's economic and social station tended to make her less aware of the constraints on the time of less wealthy or privileged women writers, her emphasis on the moral in her comments about writing cannot be ignored.

In *The Writing of Fiction*, Wharton states that the process of choosing one's subject matter essentially involves making a moral choice. "A good subject," she notes, "must contain in itself something that sheds a light on our moral experience."[10]

Wharton's choice of the term "moral experience" might in our postmodern era put a good number of deep thinkers on the defensive. What or who is moral? they well might ask. Is there really only one acceptable code of behavior for all of us? Wharton herself never specifically defines the moral, but she does suggest in her commentary a relationship between the writer and reader that is very much like a kind of affection between friends. The writer gives to the reader a work of art that will tend to provide a momentary solace or kindness, even a type of guide, much as Virgil served for Dante-Pilgrim in *The Divine Comedy*. She writes, "In one form or another there must be some sort of rational response to the reader's unconscious but insistent inner question: 'What am I being told this story for? What judgment on life does it contain for me?'"[11] Wharton's "inner question" contains two parts. The writer must first ask, *Why am I telling this story?* And then, *What does it pretend to teach its readers about human life?* If the writer is honestly exploring these inner questions, then the answers to those questions, as they make their way into fiction, may also be a kind of "rational response" the reader can take into real life.

Like Sand, who dared to tell the now-canonized Flaubert that she was concerned that something was missing in his art, Wharton, in a chapter dedicated to the writing of Marcel Proust, whom she admired greatly and whose work she read again and again in the original French, quietly suggests that the great master of things remembered is nonetheless slightly morally flawed. She sees him falling short of a higher peak that, for all his greatness, he could have gone on to attain. Wharton comments, "All through his work there are pages literally trembling with emotion; but wherever the moral sensibility fails, the tremor, the vibration, ceases." She calls moral sensibility "that tuning-fork of the novelist's art," suggesting that dissonance or harmony in fiction is just as much the responsibility of the novelist as dissonant or harmonious strains of music are the responsibility of the composer of music.[12] Part of the art of both the novelist and the musician, she implies, is to serve as a listening ear — as a kind of moral sensor of the times.

Later on in this century, the southern writer Flannery O'Connor, a devout Catholic, goes one step further than Wharton and calls the writer's sense of moral purpose "grace." She says in her book-length comment on writing, *Mystery and Manners*, "I have found . . . from reading my own writing, that my subject in fiction is the action of grace in territory held largely by the devil."[13]

O'Connor's discussion in *Mystery and Manners* of her much-anthologized story "A Good Man Is Hard to Find" is helpful in considering her sense of grace. On first reading, the story may seem particularly vicious. Though we laugh darkly in spite of ourselves, we are aware that this is the laughter of chaos — and that we are ultimately laughing not only at the characters in the story but at ourselves. There is no safety in numbers in this laughter, because no one is on our side. There is no real reason to go on living, no real cause in life.

But O'Connor argues in her afterthought that the point of the story for her is not that chance governs our lives, so that, no matter what we do, The Misfit will end up killing us all in a senseless melee. The point of the story for her, she says, is contained in The Misfit's line about the grandmother: "She would have been a good woman, if it had been somebody there to shoot her every minute of her life." It is only when she meets death face to face that the grandmother, who up until this moment has been completely oblivious to the needs of everybody in the family but herself, moves out of her limitation so thoroughly that she recognizes even The Misfit as deserving of a kind of love. A new kind of seeing or spiritual vision is at hand. "Why you're one of my babies," she cries even as he is about to shoot her in cold blood. "You're one of my own children!"[14] Only a writer who has glimpsed what it means to never stop loving could come up with a line so full of promise. O'Connor sums up her concept of grace and its relevance to a world that appears increasingly graceless in the section about "A Good Man":

> The novelist with Christian concerns will find in modern life distortions which are repugnant to him, and his problem will be to make these appear as distortions to an audience which is used to seeing them as natural; and he may well be forced to take ever more violent means to get his vision across to this hostile audience. When you can assume that your audience holds the same beliefs you do, you can relax a little, and use more normal means of talking to it; when you have to assume that it does not, then you have to make your vision apparent by shock — to the hard of hearing you shout, and for the almost-blind you draw large and startling figures.[15]

Her "startling figures" are very consciously drawn. She goes on in this piece to decry, at least in part, what she sees as the progressive voluntary giving-over of this moral voice on the part of the writer. After tracing the change from omnipresence on the part of the author in eighteenth- and nineteenth-century novels, she notes that a sudden and drastic change takes place with the novels of Henry James. The downward trend, she asserts, continues, so that "by the time we get to James Joyce, the author is nowhere to be found in the book. The reader is on his own, floundering around in the thoughts of various unsavory characters. He finds himself in the middle of a[n amoral] world apparently without comment."[16]

Her observation here, of course, predates what we have come to call the postmodern era, an era in which, in his earliest writings, the philosopher-critic Jean-François Lyotard says that words like "solace" and "consensus" or "sharing" and (certainly) "attainable" are obsolete.[17] But Lyotard himself has come to see that the ultimate danger of the argument for social construct as the final seat of human motivation is the acceptance of the inevitability of total anarchy. At one point he argues that the "positive side" of the doctrine of phenomenology — phenomenology being, in a philosophical nutshell, the belief that everything is merely the outward objectification of subjective thought — "lies in its effort to recover humanity itself." And in *The Différend*, Lyotard ponders — and perhaps even comes to embrace — a more community based or shared ethical approach to criticism.[18]

Other critics besides Lyotard, among them J. Hillis Miller in *The Ethics of Reading* and Tobin Siebers in *The Ethics of Criticism*, have begun to take a closer look at ethics — the collective guidelines for interaction shared by groups of individuals despite their differences — and art.[19] Indeed, at times, the word "ethics" seems to be on every forward-minded tongue. Still, during this period in critical theory, when subjectivity in literature has for the most part been discussed primarily as the taking and retaking of power by the various voices in the text — a kind of war in which supposed author, supposed narrator, and major and minor characters all vie for the primary position in the linguistic system at any given time — it may seem almost whimsical to argue for any responsibility on the part of the author, an individual who, some critics still insist, may not even bodily exist.

The notion that the world is somehow getting worse, and that there is nothing we can do about it, while not always stated in terms as eloquent as Lyotard's, has clearly plagued the practicing writer, man or woman, in earlier eras for which Lyotard would probably tell us we can now only have nostalgia. In an introductory essay to Mark Akenside's long poem *The Pleasures of the Imagination*, the early-nineteenth-century essayist Anna Laetitia Barbauld argues that, in spite of apparent suggestions from her peers that hers is a period in history that is particularly corrupt, there is nevertheless a certain timelessness to morality. Literature, she insists, is not necessarily shaped according to the morals of its times. As Barbauld sums up in her essay, it "would be a very dangerous doctrine" to suppose that "the sense of *moral beauty* itself were dependent on our peculiar formation, and adapted only to our present state of existence."[20]

A good number of classicists are of the opinion that the author Petronius, writing during the corrupt last years of the Roman Empire, placed the deflowering of an eight-year-old girl in his *Satyricon* with the express intention of criticizing the decay of Rome. They point out that Petronius has given us one of the earliest examples of what literary historians have come to call the untrustworthy narrator. That is, we can never be quite sure whether the narrator condones what he is telling us as he watches the deflowering scene, because the author has chosen not to be present — not to appear to comment in the margins or even through another character — in the text. But the female reader/witness of that literary scene may feel very uncomfortable indeed with this interpretation. She is being forced into the position of *voyeuse*, of playing powerless witness to a sexual act against an enslaved female child. The eight-year-old girl is supposedly being raped for literary purposes, so the female reader/witness — particularly if she has been warned of the dangers of deductive reading — knows that she had better not interfere. Her reputation as a rational critic may be at stake. Yet in spite of her training, she may still hear Wharton's "inner question" as it asks: Was there ever a moment in human history when the nonconsensual sexual penetration of an eight-year-old female child, even though she was a slave or servant, was arguable as permissible, since right and wrong are only the social constructs of a given time? In searching for an answer to her inner question, the female reader/witness might ponder the meaning of Wharton's "rational response."

Amidst the obscurities of Lyotard's numbered philosophical *pensées*, Wharton's more simply put inner questions continue to resound. *What ought we to be?* he asks. *What ought we to do in order to be that?* And, finally, more forcefully, *What can we do?* His question of "duty" — responsibility to ourselves and to the they or them — is at the very core of what Wharton terms a rational response by the writer to the reader's questions about the relationship between human literature and human life.[21] It is possible that the author may only be able to prove a "real" existence in this life-threatening, post-Holocaust, postmodern era by taking back responsibility for the text.

This does not mean, of course, that there should be a sudden purging of Petronius' *Satyricon* from all "Great

Books" courses throughout the Western world. Plato might well have liked that sort of mass action, given the strictures he wished placed on literature in his *Republic*. But Plato ends up in bad company in Karl Popper's *The Open Society and Its Enemies*, because his doctrine of censorship is entirely dependent upon the tastes, whims, and limitations of the censor representing those in power.[22] What we might consider, however, is the possibility that the censorship Plato talks about in the *Republic* is a power exercised from the wrong vantage point. In Plato's system, the critic/reader, rather than the writer, ultimately decides what the writer writes. But the kind of inner discretion that emanates from the writer is voluntary and can only be practiced by degrees, as the writer works toward some inner goal. Any author who brings into the *ars poetica* an argument for purpose that is based on affection, rather than on mere titillation, is already setting up self-imposed guidelines that, if taken up with patience, may mean that the writer at some point will approach the utility that under Plato's system is still a too-proscriptive, critic-based ideal.

There can be the very real danger of an internalized loss of artistic freedom in this kind of self-watchfulness. Writers whose special demons, like Socrates' inner voice, will not let them write anything down without first considering its moral consequences may find themselves literally unable to speak. The nineteenth-century writer and activist Margaret Fuller, who wrote the early feminist text *Woman in the Nineteenth Century* and whose life is read by some as being a tempestuous, romantic novel in itself, seems to have fallen for a proscriptive self-censorship to some degree. Her view of what she plainly saw as "women's intuition" may have been extremely anti-artistic. She writes, "The especial genius of Woman I believe to be electrical in movement, intuitive in function, spiritual in tendency. She excels not so easily in classification or recreation, as in an instinctive seizure of causes, and a simple breathing out of what she receives that has the singleness of life, rather than the selecting and energizing of art."[23] At times, this "instinctive seizure of causes," the spirituality that is said to especially motivate "Woman," may result in an all-consuming involvement in human causes that acts to the detriment of the woman's creative output.

The dilemma of the inner censor is by no means one that plagues only the female writer. In his introduction to a volume of the literary magazine *Ploughshares* that chose as its theme the question of "The Virtue of Writing," editor James Carroll discusses the writer's would-be inner censor:

> The fiction writer's greatest enemy is not the would-be censor in society, but the would-be censor in the writer's own head. Morality is a problem for a serious fiction writer first because the writer's own work consists essentially in an unfettered confrontation with his or her own *im*morality. . . .
>
> Fiction writers live in the realm of what is wrong with the world — with their *own* worlds — not of what is right with it. In the age of "no fault," fiction writers are fault-finders. But unlike the moralists and finger-waggers, fiction is never a moral failing of which they accuse others that they have not first — because this is the way the invention of fiction works — accused themselves.[24]

Even so, if the fiction writer — male or female — finds fault with the world and writes about it in order to heal rather than, as Carroll has it here, to accuse, something other than mere moral proscriptiveness might be at work.

For one thing, the writer can avoid the kind of deductive puritanical reasoning that essentially works backward from the text. The American Puritans saw every human tragedy as a sign from God. If a farmer's crops failed, either the farmer was reaping the reward of some hidden sin or a neighbor was praying darkly against the farmer's soul. John Winthrop, governor of the Massachusetts Bay Colony, wrote in his journal in 1638 that "a very proper and fair woman" who was, with her husband, "notoriously infected" with Anne Hutchinson's differing religious thought, was delivered of a "monster" in a stillborn birth. He goes on, ruthlessly, to describe this child:

> It was a woman child, stillborn, about two months before the just time, having life a few hours before; it came hiplings till [the midwife] turned it; it was of ordinary bigness; it had a face, but no head, and the ears stood upon the shoulders and were like an ape's; it had no forehead, but over the eyes four horns, hard and sharp; two of them were above one inch long, the other two shorter; the eyes standing out, and the mouth also; the nose hooked upward; all over the breast and back full of sharp pricks and scales, like a thornback; the navel and all the belly, with the distinction of the sex, were where the back should be, and the back and hips before, where the belly should have been; behind, between the shoulders, it had two mouths, and in each of them a piece of red flesh sticking out; it had arms and legs as other children; but instead of toes, it had on each foot three claws, like a young fowl, with sharp talons.[25]

After this lengthy description, in which the reader cannot help but observe a kind of perverse pleasure being taken on the recorder's part, Governor Winthrop goes on to report that he saw "a providence of God" in the birth defects of this child, a "providence" that is all the more visible to him because the birth happened to coincide with Hutchinson's excommunication from the church.[26]

Thus, birth defects, the death of an infant, are the effects of sin or of Hutchinson's religious interference or, in this case, both. But in the ensuing Puritan tradition as it may adversely influence American writing, the writer notes the tragic situation that is developing for the character as he or she works the story through and then moves backward from there to find some sort of cause for that effect, with the assumption that some essential moral flaw in the character has been at fault. On the other hand, if the writer finds the character innocent with this kind of faulty reasoning, then the awkward insertion of the deus ex machina is the only possible finale that can result. The writer needs as much to be delivered of these kinds of theological superstitions about created characters as he or she would be in regard to human beings who undergo tragedies in real life. In fiction, as in the human condition, it is the individual's action in the face of affliction that finally counts.

A story does not have to end happily to be affective, of course. But just as not all fictional endings have to be happy in order to be ethical, neither does all literature have to be nihilistic to make a point. In the end, the dangers of self-censorship may be fewer than the dangers encountered by writers who go along with the prevailing critical theory that they have no control — neither authority nor responsibility — over what they write.

The critic Carolyn Heilbrun defines literary power as "the ability to take one's place in whatever discourse is essential to action and the right to have one's part matter."[27] In order to be whole, a body of literature needs to reflect this kind of power. It must partake not only of what has

been the historical ideal — the violent and the adventurous — but also of what has been talked about pejoratively as
the feminine — the calm and quotidian, that which takes
place not so much on a battlefield as it does in thought.

In the biblical story of Joseph, the envious brothers of
Jacob's favored son get together and decide to sell him into
slavery, so that they will be rid of him and his coat of many
colors. What may remain in our era to be thought through
is the value, within the whole, healthy body of a society's
literature, of those creative works that essentially allow Joseph the possibility — if not always the actual outcome — of
getting out of his brothers' pit. In the biblical version, Joseph
could have gotten out of the fictional construct of the pit if
some other shift in the narrative had taken place — if, for
instance, the softest of the older brothers, Reuben, had come
back to the scene of the tragedy before the slave-buyers had
bought Joseph and taken him to Egypt. Reuben's change of
heart comes along too late, but its recording in the narrative
allows for possibility in the text.[28]

The topos of Joseph and his brothers can be historically
followed to serve as a useful example of the perpetuation
of inhumanity in the text — of a man as he is brutally dealt
with by other men. Boccaccio's early Renaissance tale in the
Decameron about a horse trader who falls through a trap-
door in a wily prostitute's boudoir into a deep pit obviously
reminiscent of Joseph's — though this time it is a pit of shit —
still adheres to that collection's predominant theme of all's
well that ends well, however unbelievable that theme must
have struck those who had survived the Black Death of
1348. Boccaccio's horse trader picks himself up in the darkness, wipes off the smelly substance that he cannot quite see,
and exits, naked, onto the midnight street, where his own
clever devices finally save him. Boccaccio's horse trader, like

Joseph, gets out alive. Boccaccio's preface to the *Decameron* lets us know that he meant the work as a gift to his readers, not only in gratitude for the solace they may have offered him during the suffering he experienced after a love affair but as a kind of momentary solace for the unavoidable suffering they had endured during the plague.

But a pattern of reversal of the theme of possibility as it is represented in Joseph's exit from the pit and his individual progress despite the way he has been dealt with by his brothers seems to have developed in Western literature in the ensuing years. The downward trend burgeons most noticeably during the modern period, particularly with the American writers Faulkner, Hemingway, and Fitzgerald, and then explodes with violence in the postmodern period, where even the term "a happy ending" must be a joke. By the time Jerzy Kosinski takes up the typology of the pit in *The Painted Bird*, his protagonist — a small child left in Nazi Poland to fend for himself — falls deeper and deeper into a literal pit of shit, with not even the suggestion of some kind of possibility or presence — not even the motley pair of grave-robbing thieves Boccaccio provides for the character in his story of the pit — that could get him out.[29] Kosinski's work mirrors what Mary Gordon says she feels about no less a canonized work than the story of Abraham and Isaac in the Bible. It is "the cruelest story in any language," she says of the story that almost allows a father to sacrifice his son to a silent god. "It could not have been written by a woman."[30]

To assume too broadly, however, that a moral purpose for writing must necessarily spring from a woman who writes, rather than from a man, is immediately to become as unreasonable as Plato. Plenty of evidence exists that women writers can and do write stories with no sense of moral purpose in mind at all — and that they are also perfectly capable of leaving Joseph or his contemporary hero(ine) in the pit. One need only look at the work of Joan Didion, whose completely downward-spiraling novel *Play It As It Lays* leads a woman driver through a Genesis-enough-like desert, at the other end of which is a corrupt Nevada rather than the not-even-hoped-for promised land.[31] There is no affection in that novel. The world is going to blow up at any moment, and no one cares. Perhaps one reason Didion's work is sometimes the sole work by a woman included among the works of male writers in college contemporary literature courses is that, to use the historical compliment, she must somehow have found the key to writing like a man. Didion's avoidance of the moral would make her acceptable in a traditionally male canon that has been shaped and maintained under the oppression of penal force — the prevailing tradition that refuses to recognize as major any work that does not have as its subject matter the contemporary equivalent of epic/heroic war.

The literary trope of Joseph cast into the pit by his brothers seems to have no parallel in the biblical narratives primarily about women. The biblical narratives concerning women characters — as marginalized as those characters inevitably are — usually show women confronting conflict in order to stave it off instead of confronting conflict in order to participate in it. Conflict is not altogether avoided. But the explosive situation is almost always dismantled rather than detonated — the literary result being that the female characters control the bomb.

The biblical character Abigail receives a total of about four columns in the King James translation of the Hebrew Bible, but at the top of the two pages that contain her story in my version, there are these lines: "Abigail by her wisdom / pacifieth David."[32] It is impressive, to say the least, that Abigail could pacify David, since apparently the combative giant Goliath, whose height was "six cubits and a span" and who encountered David when David was still just a teenage shepherd-boy, could not. But in the story of Abigail and David, David is just about to kill her husband, Nabal, and all his men when, because of Abigail, he stops. At the beginning of the story, Nabal has refused the courtesy of providing the vagrant David and his soldiers rest and food. David is so angry about this snub that, as he rides toward the confrontation with Nabal, accompanied by all his soldiers ("Gird ye on every man his sword!"), he promises to wipe out not only Nabal but all the innocent farmhands who work for him as well. "By the morning light," he vows, he's going to kill "any that pisseth against the wall."

Into this all-male scene of violence (men and their possessions caused the explosive situation; men and their possessions will solve it) rides the figure of a lone woman on an ass. She brings David two hundred loaves of bread, two bottles of wine, five sheep ready dressed, five bags of corn, a hundred bunches of dried grapes, and two hundred dried plums. Falling on her face, she presents these gifts to an incensed David, apparently without the slightest fear that this angry and powerful general might choose to lop off her head as well. Abigail knows, in her wisdom, that David has already pledged to kill her husband. Why not her?

But the scribe who has recorded the story seems to have sensed that Abigail doesn't belong in the violence. Not her. The scribe has quoted David as saying that he is going to kill "any that pisseth against the wall," which means that

Abigail has already been written out of the violence because, in fact, she doesn't piss that way. The wisdom of Abigail is to act boldly in an altogether different way than David knows.

Eventually, Abigail convinces David to put his argument with her stupid husband into greater perspective — to remember that, in the end, he is going to be king of Israel, not Nabal, and that therefore he should not even bother to deal with pissants on the level of this man. Abigail does know that her husband is stupid; it's just her lot to be married to this arrogant, greedy man, of whom she says: "Let not my lord . . . regard this man of Belial, even Nabal: for as his name is, so is he; Nabal is his name, and folly is with him."

The miracle, of course, is that David listens to her at all. "Blessed be thy advice," he tells her. In what some might well consider the traditional romantic (if questionably happy) ending, David marries Abigail after her husband dies. But the implication in the story is that David and Abigail are ultimately together because they're friends. It is not to Abigail but to Bathsheba, that forever inadequately explored victim, that David gives his lust.

Abigail represents the possibility in this text. Without her, the story could have — would have — gone the other way. Even if Abigail can be said merely to prefigure the proverbial peacemakers in the New Testament's transcendent (and patriarchally announced) millennial estate, her humanness is somehow much more accessible than the yet-to-come perfection that the still primarily male characters of the New Testament ask us to take on. The various scribes for the text of the Bible do not purport to make the concept of the peacemaker gender-based; they seem unaware of the essentially feminine strain of peacemaking they create. Still, characters such as Abigail perpetuate a minor strain of moral purpose — the implication that there is at least the possibility of getting out alive. At the end of the twentieth century, it may well be the task of the minor writer — singing as counter-skeptic to the times — to take up the wisdom of Abigail and, to some degree, to pacify the anger of the postmodern text.

3

Why I (Still) Write Stories

On Making the Short Story "A Small, Good Thing"

.   .   .   .

In recent years there has been a great deal of talk about the short story in publications such as the *New York Times* and *Publishers Weekly*, in MFA workshops, and at writers' conferences, not in terms of what this little genre is (where it might fit in among its literary neighbors such as the novel or the poem) or, more important, about its philosophical function (what it does in the ideal city Plato mapped out in his *Republic*), but about the ins and outs of publishing — about what sells. This kind of discussion generally involves two different types of speakers — those who speak about what sells with a wistful expression on their faces that lets the whole world know they would be happy enough to adjust their style a little if that would enable them to join the sellers for a while and, conversely, those who speak about what sells through a derisive sneer because they, of course, are artists who are destined to suffer shamelessly at the hands of those dumb popular readers who throughout eternity have been behind the times.

Several years ago, certain short story–market watchers announced that the short story was enjoying a new success. Herbert Mitgang wrote in the *New York Times*, "The conventional wisdom about the fate of short-story collections is that they do not sell — except now and then. But judging by the new book-publishing lists — and the growing number of literary magazines that offer outlets for big names as well as unknowns — the conventional wisdom may no longer hold up." Mitgang presents as proof of the story's new quasi prosperity the fact that, "during the last few years, four authors with short-story collections have turned up on the best-seller charts — Eudora Welty, John Cheever, Ray Bradbury and Garrison Keillor. Collections are being marketed more often than ever as Book-of-the-Month Club selections; Isaac Bashevis Singer and Mr. Cheever have been main choices."[1]

Under closer investigation, however, Mitgang's statistics can hardly be viewed as proving the short story was ready for a new success. Four collections managed to turn up on the best-seller lists over a period of several years. Four collections out of how many hundred best-sellers altogether? one wants to ask. How many out of the total number of best-sellers were novels? Biographies? Self-help books? Furthermore, one has to take into consideration the fact that all four of the collections that Mitgang is celebrating happen to be by writers who were already well known to their audiences. Indeed, one comes to the conclusion that success for the short story, in Mitgang's terms, involves not only a collection's presence on some best-seller list but also, for the short story writer, an aura of personal celebrity as well.

Still, Mitgang seems very sure of the new success of the short story here, even after also letting us know that the "*New Yorker* receives about 14,000 short-story submissions a year and publishes almost 150 — far more than any magazine in the country." But that means that one's possibilities for being published in the *New Yorker* are slightly higher than 1 percent. After providing us with these not-so-encouraging statistics, Mitgang cheerily goes on to report what those few magazines other than the *New Yorker* who do print the short story ultimately think it is worth. He quotes Jennifer Moyers, executive director of the Coordinating Council of Literary Magazines in New York, as saying, "Most of [the publications] pay by giving the short-story writer a free copy of the magazine."[2] The real situation of the short story seems to be that, while more people may be writing stories than ever before (due at least in part, as Mitgang and others suggest, to an increase in college writing programs across the country), there are probably no more — and perhaps there are even fewer — actual outlets for the short story than there have ever been.

Two and a half years after the *New York Times* article celebrating this dubious "new life" for the American short story appeared, the trade magazine *Publishers Weekly* came up with a decidedly different view of the genre's current status. One of the few things all of the short story writers interviewed for the article managed to agree upon, "was that mass market magazines, with a few exceptions, are finding less room for short fiction and are taking a different attitude to publishing it." Short story writer Ann Beattie, for example, though well known and a frequent prize-winner in anthologies such as the Pushcart and O. Henry collections, is quoted as saying, "If I tried to support myself solely by writing short stories, I'd have an annual income of under $10,000 a year, but it's always assumed I'm doing fine."[3]

Even more recently, an update on the short story in the *New York Times*, the second page of which, interestingly enough, ran directly under a review of a new Ann Beattie book, let us know that "the short story is widely perceived to have awakened, shaken off its doldrums and begun to reclaim its place on the American literary landscape. But you wouldn't know it from browsing through mainstream magazines."[4] The article reports that, while more people might be writing short stories and while more people might also be reading them, the only place they may be found is in small literary magazines or, alternatively, in various anthologies grouped around a particular period or theme.

But perhaps the most disturbing trend lately is the proliferation of so-called reading fees. For some time now, small literary or university presses have charged contributing authors an entry fee when they participate in competitions for which the award is publication. These include the annual Associated Writing Program's novel, short story collection, and poetry competitions; the University of Illinois Short Fiction awards; and prestigious competitions held by Purdue University Press, University of Georgia Press, and Milkweed Editions, to name a few. This practice, legitimately begun by these noncommercial publishers who must operate on a shoestring budget that is often itself dependent upon individual benefactors or public grants, has now been adopted by a great crop of new "literary" magazines as well. The serious writer whose usual audience lies in readers of smaller journals must inevitably become suspicious of magazines to whose call for submissions as announced in various writers' publications the writer responds, only to receive by return mail (in the writer's own self-addressed stamped envelope sometimes) an offer to publish the writer's story, poem, or essay for a "membership fee." These fees are often as much as ten dollars per story and three dollars per poem. Editors who engage in these practices sometimes defend themselves by citing economic conditions and the political atmosphere that has made it harder and harder to apply for grants. But one wonders. The term that used to be used for this sort of thing was vanity press.

Given that the short story is among the least economi-

cally feasible ventures for both writers and legitimate publishers (and thus for agents, too), there must be some other
motive that those who write them and those who publish or
read them must have for writing/publishing/reading them,
other than the worldly goals of fame and fortune. The clear
disparity that exists between the world's fame-and-fortune
concept of writerly success and the utter lack of that kind of
success for the short story writer may in some way even be
inseparable from the short story writer's passion for this
peculiarly chosen minor form of art. The Boston-based
short story writer André Dubus, who began seriously writing stories when he was eighteen but who did not publish
his first full collection until he was thirty-nine, draws this
connection between lack of success and the writing of short
stories in a short piece published in *Boston* magazine some
years ago, before critics had begun to recognize him as
a name:

> We short story writers are spared some of the major
> temptations: we don't make money for ourselves or any-
> body else, so the people who make money from writers
> leave us alone. No one gives us large advances on stories
> we haven't written. I have never envied a writer who
> makes a lot of money, because the causal combination of
> money and writing frightens me.[5]

It may be difficult for the minor, or unknown, writer to
claim, as Dubus does here, "I have never envied a writer
who makes a lot of money," if only because one's sense of
human justice doesn't want to admit that, while most jobs
carry some sort of monetary compensation, it is somehow
normal in the literary scheme of things that one not be paid.
What may remain to be explored in a healthy way (once one
has admitted that envy of any sort, and perhaps even espe-

cially artistic envy, cannot be explored in a healthy way), is not the short story's potential for bringing its creators some sort of materialistically based success but rather the story's function — its special adaptability to play a useful role in contemporary literature. The short story is especially well adapted, as a small and flexible literary entity, to provide some balance to the nihilism and textual self-destruction apparent in so many of the the so-called major works that make up the accepted canon of contemporary literature. The short story, because of its very brevity, can play an affective role in literature that can make it great.

Most critics of the short story agree that, as a separate entity (to be differentiated from, say, medieval fables, such as Marie de France's *Lais*, or "framed" tales, such as Boccaccio's *Decameron* and Chaucer's *Canterbury Tales*, or even from congruent tales contained in later narrative poems, such as Wordsworth's *The Prelude*), the short story was essentially born with Edgar Allan Poe's definition of the "brief prose tale" in his "Review of *Twice-Told Tales*." In this genre-coining piece, Poe concludes:

> Were I called upon . . . to designate that class of composition which, next to such a poem as I have suggested [a poem of not more than a hundred lines, as outlined in his "Philosophy of Composition"], should best fulfill the demands and serve the purposes of ambitious genius, should offer it the most advantageous field of exertion, and afford it the fairest opportunity of display, *I should speak at once of the brief prose tale*.[6] (italics mine)

After offering other arguments for the new genre's desirability as a vehicle for genius, Poe goes on to attempt to define the short story's boundaries, the peculiarities that make it what it is. First of all, it will be recognizable by its beginning. He specifically refers to the importance of the "very first sentence." We are to know that we have begun to read a "brief prose tale" as soon as we have read the first sentence, which, given the short time in which the author must accomplish closure, should suggest a sense of place, mood, character, and potentiality.[7]

The opening lines of Poe's own "The Fall of the House of Usher" serve as an example:

> During the whole of a dull, dark, and soundless day in the autumn of the year, when the clouds hung oppressively low in the heavens, I had been passing alone, on horseback, through a singularly dreary tract of country, and at length found myself, as the shades of the evening drew on, within view of the melancholy House of Usher.[8]

Poe's "very first sentence" gives a setting in nature, suggests the solitude of the main character, and looks forward to a denouement. Poe has thus defined, in theory, his "brief prose tale" and then followed through in practice to show in "The Fall of the House of Usher" how it may be done. But while Poe has defined the short story's possible boundaries — suggested its length ("brief"), its language ("prose"), and its fictionality ("tale") — he has left us with no sense of the genre's purpose, its specific role.

Since the time of Poe, none of the other champions of the short story has attempted to suggest a utility for it. Most anthologies of critical essays about the short story contain discussions that only further define its boundaries, essentially centering around the ambiguous question, *What is short?* Many of the discussions necessarily hearken back in some way to Aristotle's pre–short story discussion of length and brevity in the *Poetics*, where he writes, "Beauty is a matter of size and order. . . . Plots must have a length which can easily be remembered."[9]

The impact on memory that is made possible precisely because of the story's brevity may also make the genre a particularly adaptable vehicle for affection. Affection is the utility of a literary work to affect the consciousness of the reader in some positive, humane way, perhaps even to the point of causing the individual to become actively involved in "real" life, thus bringing about some specifically needed effect or social change. The short story, with its special adaptability to affect, might well provide a kind of liberation literature, to be compared to the social/theological concept of liberation theology that has effected progress in human rights in South and Central America in recent years.

The theory that the telling of a short tale or fable might affect the hearer/reader in a positive way is, of course, not new. When Horace observes in the *Ars Poetica* that the poet's main goal is either to teach or to entertain, he notes, "The aim of the poet is either to benefit, or to amuse, or to make his words at once please and give lessons of life. When you wish to instruct, be brief; that men's minds may take in quickly what you say, learn its lesson, and retain it faithfully."[10] Horace implies that the writer's literary goal can go either way, "to benefit" or "to amuse," but he suggests that, when the aim is "to instruct," the hearer's receipt of the lesson may be very much enhanced if the vehicle containing the message is also "brief." In fact, classic sages do often tell short tales to their audiences when they mean to teach — Jesus with his parables, Socrates with his allegories, and Augustine not only with his conversion tales but also with his retellings of the youthful sins he claims, sometimes very seductively, no longer to enjoy. But if a group of ancients may have been precursors for the argument that what Poe came to call the "brief prose tale" can teach, modern and post-modern practitioners and critics of the short story seem to have gone around the discussion of the genre's possible purpose almost entirely and instead have concentrated on the part of Poe's definition that has to do with being brief.[11]

Edith Wharton, in her chapter on the short story in *The Writing of Fiction*, implies that the brevity (or, in Aristotelian terms, the nonmagnitude) and order of the short story are particularly dependent on the author's ability to create a true "beginning" and an "end." She writes, "Of the short story . . . it might be said that the writer's first care should be to know how to make a beginning."[12] Like Poe, she knows the reader's interest in the "brief prose tale" has to be obtained with the "very first sentence"; yet she appears to leave the reason for engaging the reader's interest undiscussed.

Wharton's dry "how-to" on the short story may seem woefully inadequate to the writer facing the high-tech, smart-missile war-world of today. Every night during the first few scenes of the evening news, our attention is invariably engaged, just as Wharton says a well-written short story would engage our attention. Usually, however, the news clips are so violent that television viewers have to finish the sequence in order to deal with the disgust or guilt or pity that they feel, before it will be possible to go to sleep. So, while news producers certainly know how to make a beginning in one sense, it does not necessarily follow that they could write great short stories.

Wharton also tells us that a short story writer should be able to come to an end. Of the dangers of not knowing when to stop she warns, "The failure to end a tale in accordance with its own deepest sense must deprive it of meaning."[13] But what, in fact, is the short story's meaning? News producers also come to an end with their programs, but they probably have no "deepest sense" in mind. One is hard put to make any sense of the news at all. If such scenes from everyday life seem to make no sense, perhaps it can be the job of the short story writer, through the very brevity Poe originally accorded to the tale, to transcend the circumstances of the characters and to provide at least the possibility of making sense.

First, of course, one needs to consider exactly what making sense means. Certainly the human condition as it is presented on the evening news can make no sense. But there is often something in the writer that wants to argue with the assumption that the material evidence is all there is. The possibility of making sense, in short fiction, can challenge the parameters of the cold and apparently indisputable evidence of human beginnings and endings and allow the reader to search for alternatives beyond the text. Tolstoy suggests that it is not one's life experience that should necessarily determine what one writes but rather a working concept of a kind of spiritual intuition or intelligence that might in some small way help suffering humanity to deal with the human condition:

> Truth will be known, not by him who knows only what has been, is, and really happens, but by him who recognizes what should be, according to the will of God.
>
> He does not write the truth who describes only what has happened, and what this or that man has done, but he who shows what people do that is right, that is, in accord with God's will, and what people do wrong, that is, contrary to God's will.[14]

Tolstoy has given the writer the awesome task of determining God's will. While many writers have, even as the poet Carolyn Forché has said, "the usual problems with God" (or at least with talking about God in a text like this), Tolstoy may be making the point that what really happens is not the issue, as long as some kind of recognition of or deliberation over what should be has taken place.[15]

Tolstoy ultimately comes to the astonishing conclusion that, out of all of his works, only two short stories — and none of his novels, including *Anna Karenina* and *War and Peace* — achieve his goal of truth in art. In a sad little footnote, he writes:

> My only purpose in mentioning examples of works of this or that class is to make my meaning clearer, and to show how, with my present views, I understand excellence in art in relation to its subject-matter. I must moreover mention that I consign my own artistic productions to the category of bad art, excepting the story *God Sees the Truth but Waits*, which seeks a place in the first class, and *The Prisoner of the Caucasus*, which belongs to the second.[16]

Perhaps a clue to Tolstoy's privileging of the two stories as the more likely carriers of his *truth* lies in the observation that, while we may have come to expect that a play or a novel — and even a poem, though it is, like the short story, short — will arrive at some sort of closure at the end, we may in fact be much more open, in regard to the brief prose tale, to open ends. In these open ends, infinite possibilities can open up.

Some aestheticians do in fact argue that people make up stories or read them in order to make sense of their world. In *Mimesis as Make Believe: On the Foundations of Representational Art*, the philosopher Kendall Walton suggests that, at least in their artistic endeavors, adults may be more like children than they realize or admit. Children, he implies, "make believe" in order to make sense of the nonsense of the "real" world in which they live.[17] The possibility of making sense may therefore turn out to be the peculiar role of the short story writer's small and gemlike form of art.

More often than not, however, the short story as a genre has been considered more like the fast-food form of literature than its little gem. *Don't have time for a novel? Pick up our finger-lickin' antho, catch a coupla stories while you eat, wait, fly.* The *Publishers Weekly* article cited earlier points out that the writer today whose short story collection is eventually accepted for publication will probably also have to agree to produce a novel as a second book. Literary agent Mary Ann Evans, who handles a number of short fiction writers, including Canadian author Alice Munro, comments that "as an agent representing someone who comes along with a story collection, it still is difficult to sell without a novel in tow. I don't think I've ever sent something out without the editor coming back and asking if the author is writing a novel. It is very hard for an agent to take on someone who *just writes short stories*" (italics mine).[18]

But the "big just has to be better" bias is not limited to the moneylenders of the literary profession by any means. In an essay in the *New York Times*, Annie Dillard asserts, "It makes more sense to write one big book — a novel or nonfiction narrative — than to write many stories or essays. . . . It is no less difficult to write sentences in a recipe than sentences in *Moby-Dick*. So you might as well write *Moby-Dick*."[19] She may be right in pointing out the difficulty of writing well whether one chooses to be lengthy or to be brief, but in doing so she, like most observers of the short story, altogether misses the possibility that there may exist some reason for being brief other than that the writer only has enough time in a busy life to write an occasional short story.

What still seems to be lacking in all of this, even as the short story as a separate literary entity enters its second century, is a discussion of its purpose, its justification for being within the common whole. Brander Matthews, writing on the short story in the early twentieth century, foretold a much-needed relationship between the short story and its possibilities for affection when he suggested that the short story, unlike the novel, did not necessarily have to be about romantic love. Other than that, the short story writer, according to Matthews, could "do as he pleases."[20]

But Matthews's all-encompassing laissez-faire, viewed from the standpoint of the contemporary fiction reader who has been buffeted by the gratuitous chaos, violence, and nihilism of many of the longer works written during the last two decades, may not sound like an edict that has been reserved only for the short story writer. The reader of Jerzy Kosinski's *The Painted Bird* witnesses within the three-hundred-odd pages of that novel Kosinski doing exactly "as he pleases" with any number of characters, almost without intervention from any character in the novel and certainly without the stand the author as omniscient narrator might have made himself. Under the guise of showing us this wicked modern world as it really is, Kosinski risks becoming wicked himself. He is God to the book he writes, to the characters he creates, and he has done "as he pleases" with them, when he has had a choice.

While the entire body of Kosinski's work has now been further complicated by the issues surrounding his death, he has also done "as he pleases" with the rest of us. The reader might very well wonder what purpose is to be served if short story writers, with the necessary brevity of their genre to

hinder them, also do as they please when writers like Kosinski (or Norman Mailer with *The Armies of the Night*) have
already accomplished that in the novel, and at length.

Some critics suggest that, with the short story as well as
with the novel, the severity of the contemporary scene does
not allow for exploration of anything other than the most
depressing of subject matter. One editor of a critical anthology on the short story, commenting on an article by Bonaro
Overstreet, whose task at the *Saturday Review of Literature*
during the 1940s was to distinguish between the "old" and
the "new," between "quality" and "commercial," remarks:

> Noting that the two basic faiths of the nineteenth cen-
> tury — that it was possible to know the difference be-
> tween right and wrong, and that people actually were
> what they seemed to be — have been lost, Overstreet
> claimed that the action or plotted story was no longer
> viable. Since the drama of the century has become the
> drama of what goes on in the mind, the short story has
> more and more become an expert medium for the ex-
> pression of our "deep concern about human moods and
> motives — moods and motives that have shown them-
> selves to be far less transparent than what we once
> thought they were."[21]

While I am not at all sure that Overstreet's claim that the
action or plotted story is no longer viable in fact holds true,
I am equally unsure whether what he says about the purpose of the short story within our worldly situation — that
is, to "become an expert medium for the expression of our
'deep concern about human moods and motives'" — does
not sound a little too much like the language used to support
the all too often gratuitous violence played out on the larger
scale of the novel. As useful or cathartic as some may believe

this created violence may be in its mimetic way, the violence might very well be put into perspective, and its effect enhanced and balanced, by the ethical commentary possible in the short story on its smaller scale. It is indeed important to express our "deep concern about human moods and motives," but many contemporary novels merely enumerate the circumstances which have brought about those deep concerns without condemning the crime itself and (assuming it is not possible to do something about the crime) without even offering the world-weary reader so much as one paragraph of human kindness as a small respite. This respite need not be grandiose, no more than an island must be large to offer refuge to a shipwrecked crew. The short story, that "brief prose tale" explored more for its brevity and plot than for any of its other characteristics, may be the very genre that can offer this retreat.

Italo Calvino perhaps best expresses the connection that might be made between a too often neglected moral valorization of the Horatian concept of purpose and the much discussed but essentially morally specious concept of brevity when, in one section of his *Lezioni Americane: Sei proposte per il prossimo millennio*, he explores the fable and short story in terms of *rapidità*. He defines *rapidità* as having to do with rhythm — knowing when to interrupt one strain with another so that the reader will want to go on to find it again. On first observation, Calvino's *rapidità* would appear to have more to do with the concept of entertainment than with teaching. But Calvino, who with his penchant for the fabulous rather than the mimetic broke away from members of the Italian realist generation such as Cesare Pavese, Elio Vittorini, Carlo Levi, and Ignazio Silone (all of whom wrote almost journalistically about the period between the two world wars), apparently believed that the shorter work was a much better vehicle not only for the production of tension in the reader through the use of rhythm, or *rapidità*, but also for the delivery of a positive ideal. In working through a definition of this concept, he chooses to talk about Scheherazade's serial use of the brief prose tale in *The Thousand and One Nights* to stay alive:

> L'arte che permette a Scheherazade di salvarsi la vita ogni notte sta nel saper incatenare una storica all'altra e nel sapersi interrompere al momento giusto due operazioni sulla continuità e discontinuità del tempo. È un segreto di ritmo, una cattura del tempo che possiamo riconoscere dalle origini: nell'epica per effetto della metrica del verso, nella narrazione in prosa per gli effetti che tengono vivo il desiderio d'ascoltare il seguito.[22]

> The art that allows Scheherazade to save her own life every night lies in her knowing how to build one story upon another and in her ability to interrupt at just the right moment two operations on the continuity and discontinuity of time. It is a secret of rhythm, an element of timing that we can recognize from its origins — in the epic poem through the effect of its metrical verses, and in narrative prose through the sustained effect of keeping alive the desire to hear what happens next. (translation mine)

Perhaps if one were to ask Scheherazade, *Why do you tell stories?* or, alternatively, *Why do you write?* she could very legitimately reply, *Because it keeps me alive.* But storytelling and the writing of short stories might very well include keeping the other person alive as well. Not only does Scheherazade's ability to sustain her listener's interest through the proper brevity and rhythm of her storytelling save her life, it also happens to save the moral life, or soul, of her listener, the sultan. Through some sort of recognition of the value of Scheherazade's serial tales — that is, through the human bond established between the storyteller and her listener — this greedy ruler decides not to make her the latest victim in the serial killings his power legally permits him to commit. It is just possible that in the middle of a postmodern, post-Holocaust world already filled to the brim with bloody serial murders and bloody serial coups d'état and ethnic cleansings, the short story can serve the purpose of standing for, to use the title of a fine short story by Raymond Carver, "A Small, Good Thing."[23]

Carver's story, which won first prize in the O. Henry Prize Stories collection in 1983 and was later included in his collection *Cathedral*, deals with what could very easily turn out to be merely sentimental subject matter — the death of a small boy through a freak accident and the attempts of his parents to come to terms with their sudden grief. One of Poe's major criteria for judging the short story is that we examine the "very first sentence," and this criterion becomes especially interesting in regard to the successfully overcome risk of sentimentality in "A Small, Good Thing." The story's first sentence reads: "Saturday afternoon she drove to the bakery in the shopping center." Far from presenting the foreboding mood so often present in Poe's own gothic tales, and from the very first line at that, the first line of Carver's story suggests only the mundane mood of everyday routine. "She," whoever she is, drove that modern signature of everyday American middle-class family life, the automobile, to a place of business located in that modern signature of speedy American life which incorporates after-work and Saturday shopping at conveniently one-after-another storefronts with a multiplicity of offerings for fast-food breaks, the shopping mall.

No information could seem less foreboding. Many of us drive to the shopping center each week. Yet from its prominent position in the story, Carver's sentence is suggestive of far more than what we merely see. The word "bakery" arrests our attention. Why the bakery? Why didn't she go to Lord and Taylor's or Hudson's or The Limited or The Gap for Kids? The shopping center itself we may frequent often enough. Perhaps she, like a large percentage of American women, works outside the home and needs clothes for work, as well as stone-washed jeans for the kids at school. But a bakery? Why is she going to a bakery? A bakery is a place that many of us postmoderns, working full-time, juggling children's schedules with office or teaching schedules and only occasionally enjoying social gatherings, most probably do not frequent even once a week. It must be a party, an occasion. Carver has suggested with one word, hidden within the deceptively simple "very first sentence," the events that will become important in this tale. This is minimalism, if we have to go along with the latest attempt to categorize short fiction within some kind of school, at its best. This one story shows why Carver's stories, and not necessarily those of his followers, verge on being great.

Because of what will follow in this story, it is important that Carver minimalize the obvious and let us get on with our expectations, which at this point have been set up for some occasion like a party. The second sentence of the story lives up to our expectations: "After looking through a loose-leaf binder with photographs of cakes taped onto the pages, she ordered chocolate, the child's favorite." So we are right. There is going to be a party. And we are correct in surmising that it is going to be a birthday party for a child. Nothing could be more of a relief. In this world of shopping centers and full-time jobs, a child is going to have a birthday party, and she has picked out the child's favorite flavor of cake, in the kind of maternal attention to detail that traverses time.

But this is a story, and we are trained to know that writers do not report on children's birthday parties unless they have something else to tell. So now we're worried. With two sentences that play on our sophistication as short story readers, Carver has established a foreboding mood that in retrospect proves to be just as chilling as the one Poe set up for us in "The Fall of the House of Usher."

It is interesting to note that the child and the parents remain nameless, perhaps because their story is one of those tragedies that is reported in the newspaper every day, which we instinctively read and leave, after tucking away our reluctant gratitude that at least the tragedy hasn't happened this time to us. In his book-length treatment of the short story, *The Lonely Voice*, Frank O'Connor suggests, mainly through examples by Russian writers, that the characters in short stories almost always belong to what he calls a "submerged population." While we may sometimes talk of the "novel without a hero" — and one thinks here of the novels of French surrealists such as Alain Robbe-Grillet and Nathalie Sarraute — in fact, the short story, O'Connor says, "has never had a hero."[24] The short story's characters — even its major characters — are virtually nameless, just as they are here.

O'Connor unfortunately dedicates an entire chapter of *The Lonely Voice* to an unreasoned condemnation of Katherine Mansfield, not as a short story writer (he says he can't quite put his finger on what he doesn't like about her stories, noting only that "she wrote stories that I read and forget, read and forget") but for what he hastily surmises about her life. He abandons his otherwise admirable role as critic when he becomes incensed over what he calls her "legend" as "the creature of flame married to a dull unimaginative man," John Middleton Murry. O'Connor finally concludes about this woman writer, whom he could very well have included more kindly as perhaps another member of his "submerged population," that, "though I know nothing that would suggest she had any homosexual experiences, the assertiveness, malice, and even destructiveness in her life and work make me wonder whether she hadn't."[25] He momentarily abuses his role as poet/critic, in what might well be considered an otherwise superb *ars poetica*, to make a judgment not about another writer's literary output but about her private life. The writer, whether major or minor, loses "the right to be opinionated" traditionally accorded by the *ars poetica* whenever that opinionatedness moves beyond the boundaries of his or her art.

But O'Connor's central idea that the short story accommodates characters who have no other rightful place in literature, because they are too minor to be explored at further length, needs to be taken seriously. The fact that these members of a "submerged population" lead lives that are primarily uneventful, save for one death-defying moment of possibility, is perhaps the very thing that makes short story characters more like us than are the characters in novels. As human beings, most of us are never going to be explored at length by the public. But while our entire lives may rarely be tied up so neatly as in a novel, with a meaningful beginning, middle, and end — even if we let our lives be told by a superb biographer — we might very well make sense of, read infinite possibilities into, a day or two.

Shortly after the matter-of-fact reporting of the mother's

selection of the child's birthday cake, Carver switches scenes, from following the mother in the bakery to following the child himself on his way to school. "On Monday morning," Carver writes, "the birthday boy was walking to school with another boy." Information that we took for granted in the first sentence — that she drove to the shopping center on Saturday (everybody does) — suddenly becomes more important. She ordered the cake two days before the child's birthday, fully expecting the birthday party would be taking place.

Well didn't it?

At this point, Carver presents us with the tragedy we have been expecting all along, in the seemingly disinterested language of a journalist. "Without looking," he tells us simply, the boy "stepped off the curb at an intersection and was immediately knocked down by a car."

This sentence contains, of course, the information of the major event around which the story revolves, the tragedy of the loss of a child. In the hands of a less humane writer, it would probably be the only information we would receive. At the end of Kosinski's *The Painted Bird*, the small child who has been warped by the tragedy of the world dies. There is no moral resolution to his death, which we expected, even took for granted. *Of course he is warped*, we might say. *Look at what he went through. The world, after all, is a wicked place.*

But the endings of too many contemporary novels already ask us to come to exactly this conclusion. The world, after all, is a wicked place. Perhaps it is the very size of the novel that makes it (and us) come to this conclusion. When we view the world as a whole — the world as macrocosm — we might indeed conclude that there is no human kindness in it. Or not enough. But even as the Nazis were systematically killing six million Jews during World War II, even while Kosinski's child character was viewing the evil of the aftermath, even during all that wickedness, small, good things were going on. "Righteous Gentiles" like Raoul Wallenberg were handing out Swedish passports to Jews who were boarding trains to the gas chambers at Auschwitz. A French soldier dying from illness and exposure in Poland during the retreat of his army gave his blanket to a Jewish child he discovered hiding in the woods. The child grew up and had a daughter who lived to tell the tale at an academic conference on post-Holocaust literature. And Primo Levi, a Piemontese Jew who was a prisoner at Treblinka, carefully, almost dispassionately, recorded in his memory the moral choices made each day by the prisoners themselves, so that he might come to an answer later, in his *Se questo è un uomo*, to the Hebrew poet's question, *What is man?*

If we are honest with ourselves as readers, perhaps the small, good things don't interest us in the end. Maybe they're just boring. But I would suggest that they belong in literature, at least in small doses, and sometimes right along with the tragic and chaotic, if only so that they may provide a balance or bear witness to the decency that is occasionally still around to some degree in the human race. Carver, while seeming to capitulate to the postmodern reader's expectation of a tragic ending — in this case, the death of a small child — commits a moral act. He leaves us, in the end, not with a floppy-winged angel who arrives in the nick of time with a promise of life everlasting but with a decent glimmer of goodness in the midst of mortality — with a small, good thing.

As the story unfolds, the father and mother wait in the boy's hospital room for their child to wake up from his unnatural sleep (even as we, as postmodern readers, know he won't), and the event of the mother's having ordered a birthday cake — that act of love — seems to take an ominous turn. The baker, knowing nothing of the child's accident and working long hours to make a living at his trade, begins to phone the couple up at odd hours of the night to remind them that they have forgotten to pick up the cake.

Once again, Carver appears to be delivering that which the postmodern reader naturally expects. We find ourselves thinking, *This is the way people treat other people. They don't care. It doesn't matter to them what happens to other people. They simply hate.* But the baker doesn't even know the tragedy has occurred. He only knows that he is left having baked a cake for which no one seems willing to pay.

As the child's condition deteriorates, the baker's phone calls become more malicious. "Scotty," the voice says into the ear of the dying boy's mother. "It's about Scotty, yes. It has to do with Scotty, that problem. Have you forgotten about Scotty?" As readers, we know that she is far from forgetting about the child. She is hurrying to get back to the hospital, and this phone call is going to delay her. We know that when she gets back to the hospital the child will die. *Of course*, we say to ourselves, *this baker, self-centered like all humans, will deepen her tragedy with his inhumanity. That's what humans do to each other, after all.*

In the end, however, when the child dies, Carver doesn't leave us with the tragedy. He wisely knows that there is no comfort for the loss, but he does imply that is not *all* there is. The dead child's parents, having at last realized the identity of the caller, go to the bakery in the middle of the night. They find the baker working on the next day's baked goods. Once he realizes who they are, the baker is (as we expect) nasty to them. He says, "Just a minute here. . . . You want to pick up your three-day-old cake? That it? I don't want to argue with you, lady. There it sits over there, getting stale. I'll give it to you for half of what I quoted you. No. You want it? You can have it. It's no good to me, no good to anyone now. It cost me time and money to make that cake. If you want it, okay, if you don't, that's okay too. I have to get back to work."

But if Carver has given us our expectations as postmodern readers living in a cruel world, he refuses to leave us howling for some sort of refuge in a desert place. When the baker finds out that the couple's child has died, his reaction is not that of the uncaring, childless midnight caller we thought him to be. Instead, he suffers with the couple. He is sorry, genuinely sorry, for his mistake. He offers them freshly baked cinnamon rolls, even though he knows that the weight of warm dough is infinitesimal when measured against the balance of their grief. "You probably need to eat something," he says to them. "I hope you'll eat some of my hot rolls. You have to eat and keep going. Eating is a small, good thing in a time like this." Then the three sit down together in the familiar anonymity of the shopping center atmosphere that most of us, already suffering from too much tragedy, know only all too well in its uncaring vastness, and they eat and eat.

Were Carver to have left us solely with the event of the child's death, we would only have learned of one more tragedy in the postmodern world. And for a writer merely to manipulate that natural expectation in readers — the expectation of death and sickness, of violence and people's innate inhumanity — is to fail to allow for a certain possibility of multiple meanings or, to employ a term first coined by Northrop Frye, to deny the polysemousness of one's own text.[26]

Much of this possibility has to do with the writer's treatment of the ending. The last chapter of René Girard's *Deceit, Desire, and the Novel*, a work that discusses nineteenth-century novels, celebrates the conclusions of great romantic works. Girard states that "all novelistic conclusions [of the Romantic era] are conversions." Later he notes:

> The great novelistic conclusions are banal but they are not conventional. Their lack of rhetorical ability [and] even their clumsiness constitute their true beauty and clearly distinguish them from the deceptive reconciliations which abound in second-rate literature. Conversion in death should not seem to us the easy solution but rather an almost miraculous descent of novelistic grace.
>
> The truly great novels are born of that supreme moment and return to it the way a church radiates from the chancel and returns to it. All the great works are composed like cathedrals.[27]

If Girard believes the presence of conversion scenes in novelistic conclusions constitutes the single most important quality that makes certain romantic novels great, he might well feel a certain discomfort with the conclusions of many of the novels of modern and postmodern times.

Likewise, E. M. Forster complains in *Aspects of the Novel* that too many novels of the modern period "go off at the end," adding that this is their "inherent defect." He is arguing here not for closure or even for clear-cut resolution, but for what may well be this same kind of possibility of the text. He claims that the writer should strive for "expansion, . . . not completion. Not rounding off, but opening out."[28]

It is conceivable, of course, that the grandiose romantic "miraculous descent of novelistic grace" of which Girard speaks is not possible in the literature of the postmodern age. We may be too cynical, too blasé, too downright experienced to believe in miracles these days. But then again, perhaps it is only a question of size. Maybe grace can be presented in a smaller way. The short story, while it may not work miracles or contain miraculous descents, has a special ability to record small acts of human kindness in the presence of the greater record of human pain.

In *A Room of One's Own*, Virginia Woolf suggests that women writers in particular should be looking on the horizon for the coming of a "new" genre that will be particularly suited to the kinds of stories they have to tell:

> A book is not made of sentences laid end to end, but of sentences built, if an image helps, into arcades or domes. And this shape too has been made by men out of their own needs for their own uses. There is no reason to think that the form of the epic or of the poetic play suits a woman any more than the sentence suits her. But all the older forms of literature were hardened and set by the time she became a writer. The novel alone was young enough to be soft in her hands — another reason, perhaps, why she wrote novels. Yet who shall say that even now "the novel" . . . is rightly shaped for her use? No doubt we shall find her knocking that into shape for herself when she has the free use of her limbs; and providing some new vehicle, not necessarily in verse, for the poetry in her.[29]

The short story, which still had yet to be recognized as a viable genre of its own in Woolf's time, may prove to be that "new vehicle," as she puts it, "for the poetry in her."

While the short story writer — and specifically the woman who is a short story writer — should not avoid the painful issues of our day, the next generation of short stories, many of which will be written by writers who are also mothers, might deal with those issues by balancing them with a sense of human kindness. If enough of them do, the short story could very well become, within the context of the larger whole of contemporary literature, a small, good thing.

4

Experience

. . . .

During my third year of high school French, I became
fascinated with the subtle shades of difference in meaning
between the English verb "to experience" and the French
verb "*expérimenter*." My search for a way to equate experience with experimentation eventually opened up a whole
new question for me about the relationship between real
events and the writer's need, for creative purposes, to experience all there was to life. In my case, as a teenager whose
San Francisco Bay Area real biography happened to coincide with some tumultuous times, including the famous
Flower Power Summer, the word "experiment" implied
that one should be willing to try almost anything and everything at least once — even if that meant the naiveté of

pre-AIDS-era casual sex or what has turned out to be the not-so-innocent-after-all psychedelic drugs.

The notion of writerly experience as it is recorded in literary history does indeed seem to include, at least in part, the expectation that the author consciously seek — even run out and embrace — new experiences or adventures, and preferably dangerous ones, for the almost exclusive purpose of expanding his or her choice of subject matter, like a repertoire. As both Horace and Mme. de Staël put it in the preceding passages, imagination in and of itself has often not been enough; the writer needs to have felt some kind of pain or tempest.

But the idea that the writer must feel every possible form of pain and tempest in order to write convincingly about the human condition may lead beyond reasonable experience to a false kind of experimentation with one's life. What the writer may need in the end, far more than experimentation, is a broader sense of the possibilities that lie within the scope of the text that is the given experience of life.

The question of the source of the story has long plagued readers and writers alike. Perhaps the one question asked most frequently of writers is, Where do you get your ideas? Various writers have attempted to answer this question in terms of specific works. Henry James insists in *The Art of the Novel* that the source for *The Spoils of Poynton* lay in a story he overheard at a dinner party. Edith Wharton is said to have found the basis for *Ethan Frome* in a newspaper article about a sledding accident that occurred in the Berkshire Hills where she was living at the time. And there is always William Faulkner's claim that *The Sound and the Fury* began with the image of "Caddy's drawers" — with the image of a little girl up in a tree, wearing muddied underwear, as she is seen by an on-the-ground bystander who is looking up.[2] Thus, gossip, casual reading, and perhaps even the tendency toward pederasty in a grown man's thought may each in turn have served as the source for some of these particular writers' most respected works.

Yet the feeling one may end with, if one merely surveys a number of writers' anecdotes about where the idea for a story came from, is that, in the words of an old Cole Porter tune, anything goes. And for the writer with a conscience, not just anything can go, and certainly not all the time. Some authors have given more theoretical or ontological answers to the question that French critic Jacques Derrida poses, *Which source?*[3]

The twentieth-century northern Italian novelist and poet Cesare Pavese speaks in *La letteratura americana e altri saggi* of the myth that begins as *un germe*, or seed, appearing suddenly and inexplicably in the writer's thought. According to Pavese, the writer can only receive this germ when he or she is in a kind of childlike state of grace. The human mind most often seems to think of the concept of grace within a religious context, but Pavese does not go on to discuss grace just in terms of God. Grace, for Pavese, is a kind of openness or innocent state of receptivity that to some degree helps to differentiate the poet from other human beings — that makes the poet a prophet, even though he or she be a prophet who may not believe in God.[4]

And indeed, the author's quest for the source of the story must invariably be linked to the quest by philosophers and religionists for a deeper source of being itself. The eighteenth-century Italian philosopher Giambattista Vico in *The New Science* suggests that the labor of great poetry is to do the work of God in the absence of God. Vico states that, in the absence of a belief in God, who "in his purest intelligence, knows things, and by knowing them, creates them," pagan (or as he says "gentile") nations "in their robust ignorance [created things] by virtue of a wholly corporeal imagination." According to Vico, poetry's labor in the absence of God is threefold: (1) to invent sublime fables suited to the popular understanding; (2) to perturb to excess, with a view to the end proposed; and (3) to teach the vulgar to act virtuously, as the poets have taught themselves. But when Vico goes on to describe "an eternal property" that is very much like Pavese's state of grace, he inevitably throws the author back to the question of source. "Of this nature [or source] of human things," he writes, "there came an eternal property, expressed in a noble phrase of Tacitus: that frightened men vainly 'no sooner feign than they believe.'"[5]

The poet may well be the only prophet acceptable to a postmodern age. And so the poet's role as receptor or message-bringer to the human race is an important one, even if, as with the ancient prophets of Israel, those who get the message are very few. As Maurice Blanchot expresses it in *L'Espace littéraire*, the poet is the mediator for whom the poem itself is somehow closer to the origin or source than the mediator/poet alone could possibly be.[6] The poet/prophet is doing more with experience, then, than simply (re)living it for himself or herself through the act that writes. In the role of poet/prophet, the writer, no matter how small the audience, can bear witness to the spiritual evidence that the ordinary material senses have overlooked. The writer can illumine in the narrative the invisible reason there may be for going on with life.

The questions of grace and hope are of particular interest to minor writers, because their very reason for being is fraught with hope. If Jean-Paul Sartre says in *L'Être et le néant* that suicide is the ultimate question of philosophy, I might go further to suggest that suicide, or at least stasis, is also the ultimate question of writing, especially for those writers who have realized that they will probably never be rewarded with tangible fame or success as these are world-defined. It is only logical that Sartre, the same author who poses the question, *pourquoi vivre?* (why go on living?), also asks in another treatise, *pourquoi écrire?* (why go on writing?).[7] The minor writer proclaims *I will go on living anyway* each time he or she still writes. The commitment to life and to its recording are related acts.

Those authors who, like Sartre and Blanchot, ultimately give ontological explanations for the source of their writing do seem to link their writing to some sort of personally lived experience. What may yet be left to be explored in the history of critical contention between imagination and experience is the question of writerly responsibility in regard to the particular poetic or fictional subject matter patterned or imagined after life. The German philosopher Immanuel Kant, in *Critique of Pure Reason*, differentiates between a priori (or universally given) knowledge and a posteriori knowledge, or that which has its roots in human experience. According to Kant, one knows some things without having to go through them; others, for better or for worse, one has to learn.[8]

Among the English and Continental romantics, experience, and more specifically adventure as experience, was something the writer had to participate in bodily himself (and it usually was himself). Theoretically, he could not write of an experience which he had only undergone vicariously. The romantic German writer Goethe asserts rather pompously, "I have never uttered anything which I have not experienced."[9] For Goethe, as for others of his time, one has to go through a specific experience before one knows.

Likewise, Byron seemed to think of his stint in the Greek struggle for nationalism as inseparable from his writing life. He believed he could not have been a poet/prophet without having had the experience in Greece.

And Jean-Jacques Rousseau, the romantic's romantic, perhaps the single most romantic of them all, embraces suffering to such a degree that he claims to transcend it in the production of his art: "Actual misfortunes have little effect on me. . . . My fevered imagination builds them up, works on them, magnifies them and inspects them from every angle. . . . As soon as they happen, they lose all the terrors lent to them by imagination and appear in their true size."[10] Here, Rousseau equates suffering with *l'expériment*, affirming that personal suffering/experience/experimentation provide him with the spiritual food on which his creative imagination grows and thrives.

The American romantics also took their place in an argument for the necessity of actual experience, specifically as adventure. Emerson chastens the poets of his age for their removal from common life when he says, "Even the poets are contented with a civil and conformed manner of living, at a safe distance from their own experience. . . . The highest minds of the world have never ceased to explore the double meaning . . . of every sensuous fact." Poets should be, he says, "children of fire, made of it."[11] Poets are representatives of the sufferings of humanity and must therefore bring a rich experience — preferably rich with suffering — to their art.

Even the levelheaded James Russell Lowell calls for poets who are willing to plunge into the center of their day, making art from their very involvement with the increasingly technological modern world. The poet should "find out what there is imaginative in steam and iron and telegraph wires."[12] Lowell refers here to perhaps a different kind of experience, one that has to do more with work and with technological and political changes. Yet for Lowell, this involvement with machines only adds to the poet's experience in the continuing sorrow of the human condition that is common to all ages — death and loss.

The emphasis on experimentation or adventure as a necessary part of the writer's life, while it may have been first codified by the European romantics, seems to have culminated with American writing in the modern period. During the 1950s, Pavese observed the overall autobiographical nature of American literature with a puzzled curiosity as well as with admiration, implying that contemporary European writing was less centered around the experience of the self.[13] Certainly it is this experience of the self that Stanley Kunitz notes with a kind of pride in his introduction to Carolyn Forché's award-winning first volume of poetry, *Gathering the Tribes*, when he states, "In her search for poetry, in her effort to understand it, [Forché] has bent over the potter's wheel, climbed mountain ranges, ventured into the Mojave Desert."[14]

On first reading, Forché's long narrative poem *The Angel of History*, as it has been unfolding over a period of years, might indeed seem to bear out this kind of all-encompassing, sometimes life-threatening, but always exciting experiment on her part.[15] But the motive for her almost overwhelming participation in what some might prefer to call adventure has never been for the sole purpose of gaining new subject matter, and this must be the pivotal point in any ethical discussion of the relationship between the writer's choice of subject matter and the degree to which one intentionally involves oneself with any adverse or adventurous aspect of real life.

As an active member of Amnesty International, Forché can hardly be accused of using other people's lives for the purpose of her art. On the contrary, she has used her renown as a poet to denounce the apartheid policies of South Africa and other infringements on human rights. In an interview in *American Poetry Review*, she says, "It isn't enough simply to *recount*, in the linear sense of legal discourse, because the work must also be somehow *redemptive*, and the narrative re-structured. I now believe that to write of conditions of extremity is the most difficult." [16] She has gone on not only to research the inequities that become her subject matter but also to bring to the literary world's attention, as with the anthology *Against Forgetting: Twentieth Century Poetry of Witness* which she edited, "conditions of extremity" as they have been recorded in poems by the lesser-known poets who themselves endured the conditions. [17] In her choice of subject matter for her own poems and for her editorial and critical work, Forché is practicing what Sartre may have been talking about with his concept of engagement.

However, if the source is in fact rooted in another's experience, the question of experience must be expanded to include a discussion of the ethics of appropriation — the taking of someone else's lived experience as one's own solely for the purposes of poetry or fiction. The ethical question of the appropriation of another's experience for artistic reasons hinges almost entirely upon the motive for the creative act.

Most critical discussions of appropriation center around Michel Foucault's definition of the term as the reader's appropriation of the writer's text as the reader's own. [18] But Foucault has himself appropriated the original meaning of the word, when it stood for a kind of officially sanctioned if ethically questionable stealing — as in, for instance, the federal government's appropriation of American Indian lands — and has deftly made the word into an ultimately victimless literary term. The reader may have appropriated the writer's text, but, since the writer would in most cases agree that he or she needs the reader, this kind of appropriation is basically acceptable to the writer and so doesn't make the writer a victim on first glance. The term seems to be rarely brought to bear upon the question of the writer's appropriation, for the purposes of fiction or poetry, of a particular human experience that, for whatever reason, he or she cannot have had.

As a Vietnam era teenager, I didn't take the romanticization of war in Ernest Hemingway's novels very seriously for very long. Even though I didn't like Hemingway all that much and didn't want to write anything when I grew up that would resemble in any way his short, dry style, I could not have easily accused him of quite the kind of appropriation I'm talking about here, since his reporter's credentials (taken up primarily because of his need to make a living and still write) seemed to me to allow him an ethical form of participation in the war. It was common knowledge that he had reported on the war for the *Toronto Star*, and I suspected that he had just added a little mundane dialogue between two star-crossed lovers to his facts. Now that those articles have been collected and published, we can make almost phrase-by-phrase parallels with his *A Farewell to Arms*, right down to the images of troops marching in the rain.[19]

However, I was also very aware that, *as a girl*, I could not have written *A Farewell to Arms*. That particular experience or adventure was virtually closed to me, because war correspondents, even peacetime foreign correspondents, were not usually "girls."

Virginia Woolf, of course, writes about this disparity in *A Room of One's Own*, but although she claims there that she likes the unconventionality, the subtlety, and — most important here perhaps — the anonymity of women, she ends that book by advising women to get on with a business of life that is essentially the age-old business of life for men. "You have never made a discovery of any sort of importance," she chastises her female audience. Privileging the historically male choice of subject matter as the kind of adventure that includes war, she writes, "You have never shaken an empire or led an army into battle."[20] In an introduction to a more recent edition of *A Room of One's Own*, the contemporary novelist Mary Gordon sums up one of Woolf's major points as being that "women's writing has . . . been impoverished by the limited access women have had to life."[21]

Perhaps my own early innate desire not to write like Hemingway suggests another point. A number of women writers seem to have had an inner sense of the wrongness of war as subject matter — an inner sense that goes beyond the fact that women haven't had the biographical experience to write about it. Some new feminist critics, such as Sara Ruddick in *Maternal Thinking: Towards a Politics of Peace*, for example, maintain that maternal thinking, as it might be brought to bear not only upon literature but upon world politics and economy as well, would revolutionize and revalorize experience to exclude war.[22]

Maternal thinking would make the business of life, and, in the case of the writer, the lived experience that feeds subject matter, something very much other than shaking empires or leading armies into war. In fact, at least one critically acclaimed novel about war written by a woman — Italian author Elsa Morante's *La storia* — moves away from the traditional heroic struggle of the warrior to treat in detail the effect of war upon women and other civilians as they necessarily go on about their daily lives.[23] Due to the historical literary bias that would perpetuate battleground experience as the only appropriate subject matter to be explored in a novel that takes place during time of war, Morante was the subject of much debate in Italian newspapers over her alleged antifeminism. The charge was that her main character, an almost simpleminded, middle-aged, epileptic, part-Jewish schoolteacher who is raped by a German soldier and who then bears his child, was somehow not strong enough to have come from the pen of an author with truly feminist leanings.[24]

In any case, if women writers haven't appeared to desire to appropriate the predominantly male experience of war as subject matter, there is nevertheless a great deal of literary evidence to show that the appropriation of female experience by male writers abounds. As a younger reader, I always asked myself how D. H. Lawrence, a maturing man, could create me (at least as I saw myself in my early twenties) as the independent Ursula of *Women in Love*. Likewise, I wondered how Henry James came to know me (at least as I saw myself while I was wandering alone around Europe) as the self-destructive American exile Daisy Miller or even (a little later) as Isabel Archer in *The Portrait of a Lady*. I, too (or so I thought), was a runaway hippie heroine who would never get married on purpose, not even to save my life, and, like Isabel, I could envisage nothing more perfect than "a swift carriage, of a dark night, rattling with four horses over roads one can't see."[25] That was the unmarried Isabel Archer's idea of happiness, and it was mine. In short, I wondered how these writers, who were middle-aged men rather than young single women, could get *me* so right. Meanwhile, I couldn't seem to get through what I saw then as Jane Austen's tame little comedies of manners. *I* was going to escape marriage completely. *I* was going to go on living by the skin of my teeth in Europe all my life. *I* didn't care, as a reader, whether Jane Austen's boring and obedient and passive Miss Bennett married that complacent wimp of a Mr. Darcy. Furthermore, I would have been far happier with Charlotte Brontë's *Jane Eyre* if it had ended, *Reader, I didn't marry him after all.* What could Jane Eyre possibly do that would be of interest to me if Brontë went on writing out Jane's experience after that? I thought to myself, *Ah ha! Wishful thinking, Charlotte. You may want to get married, but I don't. I'm the Gingerbread Woman. And he can't catch me, he can't, he can't.* And yet, supposedly, these were the books that one might assume, since they were written by women and since I was also a woman, I should have identified with and loved.

In a *New York Times* article several years ago the novelist Edna O'Brien explores this very question, asking why the few "true heroines we have in our serious literature" were created not by women but by men.[26] While O'Brien seems to want to imply that women writers have been somehow reluctant to create "true heroines," it is much more likely that my own earlier preference for the stormy heroines and the more adventurous "female" subject matter in James's and Lawrence's books was due more to a centuries-old manipulative valorization of adventure (preferably dangerous) as subject matter than it was to women writers' artistic failures or to any connection I might have been making in my reading with my own real life. In other words, to some degree I had allowed male writers to tell me about my life and how they expected me to live it if I was going to be interesting enough in fiction for the likes of them.

This is experiential reading at its worst. Through the appropriation of female experience, the major male writers have convinced women readers, and the women writers who have allowed themselves to derive from that reading, of the specific way in which they must re-create their lives. Jonathan Culler's kindly "Reading as a Woman" bears re-reading in this context.[27] And one critic argues that the Italian novelist Alberto Moravia (coincidentally, the husband of Elsa Morante) is a kind of pseudofriend to women who exploits them as objects in his writing — through a male romanticization of what one might say should be their self-destructive lives or through what this critic himself calls an "appropriation of female experience."[28]

More recently, Carolyn Heilbrun makes some interesting observations in *Writing a Woman's Life* about the parallel assumption, both in fiction about women and in biographies about real women's lives, that the only lifeline options open to female heroines (whether real or fictional) are "the conventional marriage or erotic plot."[29] The romantic heroine of Mme. de Staël's novel *Corinne* tries to evade involvement with a man but ultimately fails, to her own artistic detriment, even while the real-life Mme. de Staël, although married, lived separately from her husband for almost their entire married lives and frequently made verbal references to the fact that her own artistic self-destruction was linked to her stormy affair with Benjamin Constant.

J. Christopher Herold's now very outdated biography of de Staël, in keeping with its title, *Mistress to an Age: A Life of Mme. de Staël*, sticks to the idea of Heilbrun's biographical "erotic plot," while it completely ignores or underplays other major areas of her life that may have been even more critical to her creativity. He barely mentions childbearing or child-rearing, though she was apparently passionately involved in both. Eager to explore the literary side of sexual passion, he neglects the possible influence of *maternal* love upon her writing. The birth throes she underwent are treated merely as logical effects to follow this romantic heroine's assignations with famous men.[30] I cannot think of Herold's title without inadvertently picturing the otherwise respectable Mme. de Staël, after having gone to bed with an entire age of literati, now come to bed in Wellesley-Newton Hospital's birthing room, or some nineteenth-century equivalent thereof, as this mistress to an age squats and pushes to bring forth the entire nineteenth century. *O bear down, bear down!*

But the treks I took as a single woman to Europe and the adventures I had there (*Here I am, adventure, open up!*) — while some of them did in fact show up in my stories — eventually left me lonely, homeless, unhealthy, and hungry for something I wasn't getting — something else. After a while, none of that transiency looked so romantic as when I'd started out. Now that I'm more mature, not only as a married woman with a growing child but as a reader and as a writer, my reading tastes have tended away from James and Lawrence to Austen and Eliot and, to name a few more recent writers, to Alice Walker, Gloria Naylor, and Gail Godwin. And I'm beginning to find that the kind of adventure I really want to read about — and write about — these days just may lie in what others would call the minor moments of the day. They are events that take place not on the battleground, as in Homer's epic *Iliad*, or in the bedroom, as in the *Odyssey*, but in the smooth or troubled channels of human thought as it attempts to navigate through just one more day.

The traditional denigration by both men and women of the more mundane female experience — that of home and family and motherhood (mom and apple pie) — as subject matter is an issue that the minor writer, and the minor woman writer in particular, might very well explore. As a female reader/writer might well have guessed, Raymond Carver's "A Small, Good Thing," the story I dealt with in the previous chapter in terms of purpose, strikes me all the more, with its mainly domestic setting and its quiet sense of balance between the tragic and humane, because of the questions of writerly experience it brings up. Carver has dealt with the tragedy of child loss in the story, and he has dealt with it from the mother's point of view perhaps even more heavily than from the father's. So far as I know, he did not himself experience as a parent the loss of a child. I know for a fact that he did not experience that loss as a mother. Yet his understanding and compassion for the feelings of both parents in that particular event still come across. Ann Beattie, as a married but childless woman, has tackled this same subject matter in her story "In the White Night" — a story that was included in the O. Henry awards collection in 1985 — and yet, to my mind, she is far less successful in bringing it off. For one thing, she risks bathos in the hospital scene where the couple's daughter dies:

> She remembered him in the hospital, pretending to misunderstand Sharon when she asked for her barrette, on her bedside table, and picking it up and clipping the little yellow duck into the hair above his own ear. He kept trying to tickle a smile out of her, touching some stuffed animal's button nose to the tip of her nose and then tapping it on her earlobe. At the moment when Sharon died, Vernon had been sitting on her bed (Carol was backed up against the door, for some reason), surrounded by a battlefield of pastel animals.[31]

Carver has somehow managed to stay within the ill-defined appropriate boundaries, or boundaries of appropriation, in taking over someone else's — in this case a woman's, a mother's — experience and thought. And yet if one accepts in one's mode as a fiction writer the part of the Mosaic Decalogue that goes "thou shalt not steal," or some sort of literary counterpart thereof, then in order to have an ethics of authority one must ask, *When is it all right to write about someone else's* (in this case, tragic) *lived experience, and when is it not?*

The critic Craig Owens touches upon this question in his essay "The Discourse of Others: Feminists and Postmodernism" when he notes, "Despite his or her benevolence in representing those who have been denied access to the means of representation, the photographer inevitably functions as an agent of the system of power that silenced these people in the first place. Thus, they are twice victimized: first by society, and then by the photographer who presumes the right to speak on their behalf." [32] Appropriation — even appropriation that is done in order to speak for those who cannot speak for themselves — is to some degree, according to Owens, victimization.

But then again, women in general — and women writers in particular — have become so accustomed to minimizing their traditional experiences and, most recently, to viewing their experience as socially constructed impositions upon their lives that perhaps the Carver story is one that could only have been written by a man. Perhaps no real mother would have thought it was interesting or universal enough to write about. Or perhaps if she had, no one would have been willing to read it. Although she is the one who has the authority of experience to write the mother down, the preferred subject matter in courses on literature exclusively by women — the so-called Women Writers courses — is more likely to include some variation on the Jamesian and Lawrencian theme of breaking free, as in Kate Chopin's rediscovered *The Awakening*, first published in 1899.

I am certainly not alone among those currently challenging this entrenched male sense of adventure. One need only pick up a current issue of a feminist journal such as *Signs* to read the arguments from an informed theoretical basis. There are also forward- and freethinking male writers who are calling for a redefinition of adventure in the text. In his address at the 1990 Hopwood Awards in Creative Writing ceremony at the University of Michigan, Pulitzer Prize–winning novelist William Kennedy remarked, "The writer who believes he has a ready-made work of fiction spread out before him in his notes, needful only of a bit of sprucing and spicing, is deluded. He is a victim of the cult of experience, the impulse that sends writers, who can find no value in the quotidian, off to wars and revolutions to find something to write about. More than experience is called for."[33]

More than experience is called for. What is called for may in fact be a sense of ontological involvement in the human condition that is beyond anyone's present concepts of plot and narrative structure and/or style. In keeping with what I believe is Kennedy's intent here — the adage to write what you know, even if what you know has been historically considered too quotidian to be worthwhile — I suggest that it is high time that those of us who have experienced motherhood and are in the creative arts should put this experience into our art as a kind of leaven, rather than leave this subject matter either entirely (safely) untreated or treated only through the appropriation of however talented, however well-meaning writers who have not experienced this relationship themselves. Those of us who are capable of writing about that particular subject through lived experience would do well to undertake the expression, in artistic terms, of what I still believe, in spite of all the attempts by both men and women to minimize its importance (the quotidian), is the single relationship that contains, more than all others, at least the potential, the possibility, for being the most powerful saving force on earth.

After I had experienced the pain of childbirth and of trying to raise a child in a fundamentally hostile-to-children postmodern world, I encountered on the streets of a city in Germany one day a young, frazzled-looking American blond who was coming out of McDonald's pushing a child of mixed race in a stroller. Mother and child were awkwardly caught in the doorway as great numbers of Germans walked by, eyeing them with that tight-lipped, disapproving silence I myself had come to know on occasion. At the time, I was teaching writing and American literature at Johannes-Gutenberg Universität in Mainz, and as this was before the tearing down of the Berlin Wall, United States service personnel (most of whom, in the all-volunteer army, were African Americans) along with their dependents probably accounted for about 20 percent of the pedestrians I was seeing on German streets. I was sure this woman and her baby were just such dependents.

I began to imagine her as a character in a story. I saw her as a simple person, somewhat like the character in Flaubert's "Un Coeur Simple," but one who could not possibly believe, the way Flaubert's character believed, in any structured religion — certainly not while living as a much-despised American in a NATO-occupied foreign country in the nuclear-destructive, postmodern age. *So what could she possibly believe in?* I wondered. And then, remembering my own almost transcendent experience in childbirth, I thought, *Why, of course. Her child.*

To say that I knew more about that woman than my one explosive picture of her in front of McDonald's on the Bahnhofstrasse would be, in a very fundamental way, to lie — to be guilty of the falsehood Plato charges the poets with in the *Republic*, because they pretend, he says, through the voices of their characters, not to be speaking for themselves.[34] Yet I cannot help thinking of the line from one of John Donne's meditations that Hemingway made commonplace, "No Man is an Iland, intire of it Selfe. . . . And therefore never send to know for whom the *bell* tolls; It tolls for *thee*."[35]

Any suffering the artist encounters as a human being, however small, must open a window onto all human suffering. That is what it means to be human, even with all critical jargon about ethics and literature and politics and government aside. It is what the artist chooses to do with that vision of human suffering that finally counts. And so, even though I had not directly experienced this woman's specific pain and tempest, I had experienced the same feelings of isolation and bewilderment, living as a dark-haired, olive-skinned person in a country that, no matter how hard I tried intellectually to combat the collective memory, had still managed not so very long ago to murder six million Jews. *Was für Leute sind sie, Mutti?* I had once heard a little girl on a train ask her mother about my husband and daughter and me. *What kind of people are they, Mommy?* Or, *What for?* Her mother answered, *Ich glaube, sie sind hebräisch, mein Liebchen.* I think they may be Jewish, honey. (But still, Mutti, Mutti, won't you tell me, Mutti, *what are they for?*) My eight-year-old daughter had been placed upside down in a trash can to the taunts of *Ausländerin, Ausländerin! You foreigner, foreigner!* by the other children during recess in her German school. A woman on a bus had once screamed at me that I had no right to be sitting where I was sitting and continued to insist this, very convincingly, until I moved, after which she turned to another passenger and said, *This is the way that we must deal with these new Jews!*

That is why, when I saw the American woman with her mixed-blood offspring looking lost and scared in front of a fast-food restaurant on a German street, I immediately felt drawn to her and thought, *I will write your story, because I know.* I could not possibly have found that story on the sidewalk in Germany had I not also had the given experience of being a mother with a child in a hostile place.

Tillie Olsen, in *Silences*, notes that "almost no mothers — as almost no part-time, part-self persons — have created enduring literature . . . so far." Even so, she is careful not to suggest that a woman who wants to write should have children. But if, as Olsen so wisely observes, a woman wants to treat in her literature "ways in which innate human drives and capacities (intellect; art; organization; invention; sense of justice; love of beauty, life; courage; resilience; resistance; need for community) denied development and scope, nevertheless struggle to express themselves in fiction; what goes on in jobs; penalties for aging; the profound experience of children — and the agonizing having to raise them in a world not yet fit for human life," then perhaps she should be willing to entertain the possibility of this particular experience in her real life.[36]

The brilliant French critical theorist Julia Kristeva (herself a mother) has pointed out:

> As far as I am concerned, childbearing as such never seemed inconsistent with cultural activity. . . . Mallarmé asked, "What is there to say concerning childbirth?" I

find that question much more pungent than Freud's well-known, "What does a woman want?" Indeed, what does it mean to give birth to a child? Psychoanalysts do not talk much about it. . . . The arrival of a child is, I believe, the first and often the only opportunity a woman has to experience the Other in its radical separation from herself, that is, as an object of love.[37]

The mother's unique experiencing of "the Other in its radical separation from herself," the Other "as an object of love" makes her peculiarly fitted, when she happens also to be a writer, to be the carrier of this unconditional love into her art. We already have enough Hemingways, Mailers, and Kosinskis telling us in graphic detail about all the horrors of human life. Women writers in today's contemporary literary scene — Joan Didion, for instance, with her frail female automatons that seem to be blown about as freely by the threat of the atom bomb and violence done to them by male characters as they are by California's Santa Ana winds — may risk becoming mimetic repetitions of characters already created by male writers, through what may appear to be a new freedom of experience but which may really be only forms of imitation or appropriation of the kind of subject matter reader and writer have come to expect from the violent text. It may be also that the woman writer who repeatedly follows these existing patterns knows that, if she goes outside them, she will be excluded from the established criteria for success.

Of course, to theorize is one thing; to put into practice one's theories is something else. Shortly before giving birth to her second child, Mary Gordon published a piece in the *New York Times* on the relationship between her mothering and her creative work. Like many women, she found that the experience of birthing caused her for a period not to be able to write. A child needs more attention, deserves more attention, than the book. She writes of the waiting manuscript, "I have not even looked at it, partly because any action is physically difficult for me; I could excuse myself this way. But the truth is, it is impossible for me to believe that anything I write could have a fraction of the importance of the child growing inside me, or of the child who lies now, her head on my belly, with the sweet yet offhand stoicism of a sick child." [38]

Yet it is very likely that that very experience — the fact that she has lived it and the knowledge gained that it is impossible to believe that anything she writes could have "a fraction of the importance of the child" — can save her from writing the merely sentimental or the morose naive. In the article, Gordon reflects, shortly after her son is born, upon the fact that in twenty years he may well be drafted for some war. Immediately, she catches herself. "This is sentimental," she says. And she is right. It *is* sentimental; the depth of the birthing experience itself has told her that. But then she comes up with the bare bald truth, which is not in the least sentimental. "The loss of him," she says simply, "would be the end of my life." [39]

The creative move to make with this kind of all-absorbing love may finally be to take the love one step beyond one's own child and to put it in the book. Gordon comes very close to doing just this in her novel *Of Men and Angels*. But she is less successful in accomplishing this kind of statement in her shorter works. Her collection of stories, *Temporary Shelter*, is disappointing in that many of the stories border on the very sentimentality which it is crucial — if she is to carry out her theory — to avoid. In her piece on authoring and motherhood, Gordon maintains that the ancient biblical story of Abraham and Isaac (in which a father is asked by God to be willing to sacrifice his only son and is stopped just in the nick of time by an angel) is "the cruelest story in any language" and that it "could not have been written by a woman" since it tests parental love. Yet she herself is guilty of killing off a number of her own characters for what appear to be rather trivial reasons in relation to the story as a whole. There is something unreal, something unlived, about a number of her characters, something that does what is expected of her as a modern writer rather than challenging contemporary fiction from a brand new front. In "Delia," for instance, she kills off a female character she clearly likes by making her die in childbirth. *What else do women do in books and stories and in* Bonanza-*style television westerns?*, one wants to ask. This has been the romantic way of dealing with women characters who threaten to be of any substance all along. Just so, in the first line of "Agnes" (many of the stories have women's names) she tells us, "The truth was that Ag was right to hang herself, except she should have done it earlier. The truth was women like that were better off not being born, and if you saw you had a girl child growing up like that you'd be best drowning it straight off, holding its head under the water till the breath went out of the doomed creature, so you'd save it all the pain and trouble later on."[40] As the mother of her characters, like the Abraham figure in the Genesis story she deplores, Gordon kills off her main character Agnes because she cannot love her as much as she does the literary angel looking on. It is as if there is a joy in Mary Gordon that she is afraid to show.

Tillie Olsen, on the other hand, has proven to be a practitioner of her own ideals. Her much-anthologized short story "I Stand Here Ironing," from the almost legendary collection *Tell Me A Riddle*, is the imagined answer of a twice-married, working-class mother to the schoolteacher of her gifted oldest child. The teacher has written in a note, "I wish you would manage the time to come in and talk with me about your daughter. I'm sure you can help me understand her. She's a youngster who needs help and whom I'm deeply interested in helping." There, in the very language — in the "manage the time" and the "youngster," in the "whom I'm deeply interested in helping" is where we find it: the gap between educated and uneducated, between working and middle class, between the mother who cares simply because she has had the child and the woman who perhaps cares professionally because she has not. Olsen's mother, with two other children by another marriage, will probably not have the time to go to the school, and so in her pain she reflects on her relationship with this child, whom she had to send away at one crucial point to be cared for by others because she had to work. Like the fictional parents in Kosinski's *The Painted Bird*, the mother in Olsen's short story did the best she could at the time, sending the child to a place where she felt her daughter would be safe. But, unlike the message with which we are left at the end of Kosinski's tale of a child left to grow up on his own, the message at the end of Olsen's story asks us to ask for more. "Let her be," the mother says in her imagined conversation with the schoolteacher. "So all that is in her will not bloom — but in how many does it? There is still enough left to live by."[41]

There is still enough left to live by. It could be the one antiskeptical message that is meek enough, conditional enough, to be accepted in our postmodern world. Olsen's stories — even though there have been too few of them, due specifically to the ironic fact that the source of much of her subject matter was her own experience as a lower middle-class mother who had to work — give us, perhaps even more than the story by Raymond Carver, a small, good thing.

Of course, a discussion of the ethics of appropriation need not be limited to the topic of male appropriation of female experience, or vice versa. The same quandary is posed, in an even more dramatic way, in the question of the white writer's appropriation of the black experience. I think here not only of William Faulkner's "Dilsey" section in *The Sound and the Fury* but also of William Styron's *The Confessions of Nat Turner*, a book which, for me, embodies the traditional white fear and expectation that all black males are potential killers and rapists, even though Styron may have felt he could justify that expectation of violence, writing within the context of the civil rights struggles of his times.

But the ethics of appropriation perhaps become the most fragile in incidents involving the literary recording of torture or gratuitous suffering by a nonparticipant, by a so-called innocent bystander or noninvolved witness. The entire issue of this kind of appropriation may be best explored in the continuing debate over the ethics of Holocaust literature, whether that literature is produced by a true witness or a nonwitness.

While some so-called revisionist historians argue that in legal terms the Holocaust never happened because there are no witnesses, some Jews who lived through the Holocaust respond that the experience was too horrible to deserve perpetuity in words. Yet one of the recognized criteria for judging the relative greatness of written art has always been the individual work's capacity to break through the boundary of the unspeakability topos — to transcend the limits of human speech and, in spite of everything, to write it down.

In the first canto of the *Inferno*, Dante establishes inexpressibility as one of the prerequisites of the experience of hell. He has Dante-pilgrim sigh:

> Ahi quanto a dir qual era è cosa dura
> esta selva selvaggia e aspra e forte
> che nel pensier rinova la paura!
>
> Ah, it is hard to speak of what it was,
> that savage forest, dense and difficult,
> which even in recall renews my fear:
> so bitter — death is hardly more severe.[42]

The memory of hell renews Dante's fear of the experience, and it is at least "hard to speak" of it, but Dante-narrator nevertheless pursues the task of describing the indescribable to readers who have not experienced it for themselves. To some degree, then, Dante's *Inferno* is defined as poetry because of its very ability to express the inexpressible.

Simultaneously, the *Inferno* might further be defined as poetry because, in giving knowledge of the otherwise inexpressible, it also brings about an alterative effect. Julia Kristeva says of poetic language:

> While poetic language can indeed be studied through its meaning and signification, . . . such a study would . . . amount to reducing it to the phenomenological perspective and, hence, failing to see what in the poetic function departs from the signified and the transcendental ego and makes of what is known as "literature" something other than knowledge: the very place where social code is de-

stroyed and renewed, thus providing, as [Antonin] Artaud writes, "A release for the anguish of its time" by "animating, attracting, lowering onto its shoulders the wandering anger of a particular time for the discharge of its psychological evil-being."[43]

The alterative effect of this "place where social code is destroyed and renewed" is the ethical system at work in the writing of Primo Levi, the Piemontese Jew who survived Auschwitz. One pauses in awe to imagine the struggle Levi must have undergone, with the writing of *Se questo è un uomo*, in trying to translate into any human language — even into his native tongue of Italian — an experience which was not human by any standard the world had known and which was thus beyond human expression — an experience that was not, in literary terms, merely a metaphor for hell, but hell itself. *Se questo è un uomo* goes beyond giving us the knowledge of the concentration camps to explore "the very place where social code is destroyed and renewed." In expressing the inexpressible, it affects or alters the social code which makes the concentration camp possible.

Fiora Vincenti writes in her early book-length study of Levi's work that his differs from the majority of works which are grouped together under the appellation "Holocaust literature" because it shows a "validità letteraria in quanto il messaggio in esse contenuto trascendeva la pura testimonianza."[44] ("The message it contains transcends mere testimony.") It goes beyond. Or as one reviewer of the Spanish translation describes the book, "Definitivamente, se trata de un libro poético, porque sólo la poesia expresa con realismo lo imposible."[45] ("Finally, it is a poetic book, because only poetry expresses the impossible with realism"; translation mine.)

Levi comments early in his description of the Lager that it was precisely at the point at which the German community found it possible to put into "expressibility" what had hitherto been "inexpressed dogma," and thus to make that inexpressed dogma a major premise of a syllogism, that the concentration camp became a possibility. He writes:

A molti, individui e popoli, può accadere di ritenere, più o meno consapevolmente, che "ogni straniero è nemico." Per lo più questa convinzione giace in fondo agli animi come una infezione latente; si manifesta solo in atti saltuari e incoordinati, e non sta all'origine di un sistema di pensiero. Ma quando questo avviene, quando il dogma inespresso diventa premessa maggiore di un sillogismo, allora, al termine della catena, sta il Lager.[46]

It is quite possible that many individuals, even whole populaces, hold more or less consciously that "every foreigner is an enemy." For most, this conviction lies at the depth of the soul like a latent infection; it is manifested only in unpremeditated and uncoordinated acts, and is not at the source of a system of thinking. But when this occurs, when inexpressed dogma becomes the major premise of a syllogism, at the end of the chain is the Lager. (translation mine)

When inexpressed dogma becomes the major premise of a syllogism, at the end of the chain is the Lager. As the Self (here, the German Self) allows its inexpressed dogma to become a major premise of its spoken and written language, the Other is eventually removed "infinitely far away," as Jacques Derrida puts it in his discussion of Nietzsche, to be found "at the end of the chain" of human language, in the Lager.[47] Levi can only retain his integrity as a human being by continuing, within the written text, to insist that the Lager is unspeakable, beyond description. At the point at which the experience becomes expressible, he, too, will be cooperating in this perpetration upon humanity. Therefore, he cannot allow this expressibility to take place in his text.

His first realization of this rule comes shortly after he has descended from the train at Auschwitz and has been stripped nude with all the other arrivals. He comments, "Allora per la prima volta ci siamo accorti che la nostra lingua manca di parole per esprimere questa offesa, la demolizione di un uomo."[48] ("Now for the first time we realize that our language lacks the words to express this offense, the demolition of a man"; translation mine.) He speaks in the first person plural, as he often will throughout the book, because "we" are the collective Other to the German Self. If "we" find for the first time that "our language" (the language of human beings, for "we" speak in several linguistic systems, not only in Italian) has no words to describe the destruction of a man, that is because "we" are "men," and "we" cannot conceive of the possibility. That is what differentiates "us" from "them," the Germans who run the camp, who cannot be "men," for "they" have found the words to demolish a man.

For a number of years, Levi refused to enter into the lengthier dialogue between himself and the postwar Germans that a German translation of *Se questo è un uomo* might provide. The book was first published in Italy in 1947, but the German translation, as *Ist das ein Mensch?* (*Is That a Man?*), did not appear until 1960. The Italian literally means *If this is a man*. It follows the idea of the syllogism "*if . . . then*," suggesting that there are prerequisites by which one proves *if one is a man*. Yet of all the translations into major languages, the German title is the only one to incorporate a question mark — to throw into question the *man*-ness of the inmates of the camp. The question mark in the German title offers a puzzle which may in the end have to be at the very center of the dialogue which the German translation should have opened up.

Vincenti suggests that the title in Italian constitutes an "interrogation of conscience," which by its very nature renders the question mark superfluous. There can be no morality in asking the question, she says, because to ask is to imply doubt on the speaker's part. To pose the question about the Other (and not to question the position of the Self in regard to the Other) is ultimately to fail in the interrogation of conscience of the Self.[49]

Levi's language of inexpressibility is at once Dante-esque and biblical in the way that it transcends the possibility of language to describe the hell that has been created by the question mark. Like biblical allegory, his language suggests that some sort of moral premise — whether or not it is recognized by the characters in the allegory — is still at work. It does not merely "bear witness"; it transcends.

But the issue of appropriate subject matter, even when the writer is a "true witness," is not an easy one. I found myself feeling slightly uncomfortable, for instance, when reading an interview with Levi, conducted by the American writer Philip Roth, to find Levi *almost* imply that what he had witnessed was somehow necessary to his art:

> Family, home, factory are good things in themselves, but they deprived me of something that I still miss: adventure. Destiny decided that I should find adventure in the awful mess of a Europe swept by war. . . . When I found myself as uprooted as a man could be, certainly I suffered, but this was far more than compensated after-

wards by the fascination of adventure, by human encounters, by the sweetness of "convalescence" from the plague of Auschwitz. In its historical reality, my Russian "truce" [the time he spent in the USSR after liberation, the story of repatriation told in *La tregua*] turned to a "gift" only many years later, when I purified it by rethinking it and by writing about it.[50]

The ethical question for the writer here once again revolves around the key word "adventure." There are two ways in which one may read this passage. Either Levi is saying, *I could not have been a writer without this adventure* (in which case I find myself responding, *But this is an adventure all of us could have done without*), or he is saying, *Even in the midst of suffering, some sort of "compensation" can be found* (in Levi's case, artistic compensation). I believe Levi meant the latter, if only because I have read the "I sommersi e i salvati" section of *Se questo è un uomo* and the longer work by the same name, and in both, individuals are either drowned or saved, no matter what their situation, according to some sort of working answer Levi has provided for the biblical question, *What is man?*

As the witnesses who did not themselves die in the Holocaust slowly disappear, some writers have felt impelled to appropriate such experiences and to write them down. Cynthia Ozick's award-winning story "The Shawl," first published in the *New Yorker* and subsequently included in *Prize Stories: The O. Henry Awards, 1981*, is a case in point. This very brief story tells, in straight reportage fashion, of a Jewish mother and her two daughters, one twelve, the other an infant, who, during the Nazi occupation of Poland, are captured and incarcerated in a prison camp after three days of walking and trying to hide. The mother tries for a long while to keep the infant hidden in her shawl, but eventually the growing child learns to walk and can no longer be hidden. What should be a joyous occasion for the mother — the eventual independence of her offspring, as symbolized by the baby's first faltering steps — turns out to culminate in the baby's death.

The cruelty of the ending — the picture of a Nazi soldier flinging the starving toddler against an electric fence — is almost impossible to bear. One feels, *there is nothing in the world that I can do.* There can be no stir to action — the impetus one felt, for instance, during the civil rights marches of the sixties — because there is no outside presence in the text to offer hope. The reader experiences only the curious feeling of being finally and irreversibly overwhelmed. Ozick's particular form of appropriation depends on an absence of affection in the text.

The editor of the O. Henry collection, William Abrahams, in his introductory remarks, prefigured the controversy that still surrounds the publication of the tale. "Conventional wisdom," he wrote, "would have us believe that the subject is 'too great,' 'too important,' 'too difficult' for fiction. The magnitude of the historical event is beyond art — I am summarizing the argument against the imaginative writer taking up the subject at all — and it is better left to scholars and journalists. The facts in all their terribleness speak for themselves: what can the artist add?"[51]

The facts in all their terribleness indeed. What *can* the artist add? Abrahams goes on to attempt to answer this question by implying that Ozick adds nothing and that in fact adding something is not the artist's job. Instead, he says, she evokes the emotions we were unable to feel during the real-life Holocaust. He asks, "Who reading 'The Shawl' will not feel an anguish of the heart?"[52]

While some may believe that the "argument against the imaginative writer taking up the subject at all" is "better left to scholars and journalists," I disagree. It must continue to be an ongoing internal argument for the individual artist that in the end has little or nothing at all to do with scholars and journalists. While the outside debate may be interesting and healthy, the question of the ethics of appropriation is left to the writer.

The East German writer Christa Wolf is also deeply troubled by the notion of the innocent bystander or non-participating witness who, for the supposed purpose of telling the world about it, takes it upon himself or herself to record the facts without having had the historical engagement. In *Patterns of Childhood*, she tells of a photographer who takes a picture of a murder in order to get the facts straight, when if he had not taken the time to take the picture, it is possible that he might have saved the murder victim's life.[53] In this case, the only moral witness is the victim; the only moral photograph of the murder is the picture that the murder victim somehow might have managed to take himself.

A writer such as Primo Levi, since he was himself a victim, is also a moral witness; he is in the ethical position to write the murder down. In a review of *The Drowned and the Saved*, which came out after Levi's death, the critic Irving Howe writes, "Shortly before his suicide . . . Primo Levi remarked that in writing about 'the tragic world' of the camps he hoped to avoid the frayed rhetoric of pathos or revenge; he chose instead to 'assume the calm, sober language of the witness.'"[54] Ultimately, however, Howe's review lacks the generosity and strength of Levi's voice. When Howe states that "Mussolini, the brutal clown who ruled Italy, began to copy the anti-Semitic obscenities of his friend Hitler," he is repeating the commonplace names, the weary epithets, the very "frayed rhetoric of pathos or revenge" he had agreed would accomplish nothing in the end. What is needed is a language that arrests attention, that affects — the language of poetry, Levi's language, a language, in short, that can transcend.

In 1988 at the University of Michigan, I heard a public dialogue between Helen Waterford, an Auschwitz survivor, and Alfons Heck, the highest ranking member of Hitler's youth groups to survive the war. At one point during the question-and-answer session that followed their exchange, a young woman got up to condemn modern Germany on the basis of a report she had heard from a lecture on anti-Semitism in Germany today. Waterford asked the young woman if the woman giving the lecture had herself been a survivor. When the student said that she had not, Waterford ended the conversation with a wave of her hand as if to say, *So that doesn't count. Sit down.* I glimpsed in Waterford's testimony what it meant to have an unconditional humanity, a non-*event*-ual kind of love. Hers was not a question of simpleminded forgiving. There is no possible forgiveness for the evils perpetrated on humanity by the Third Reich. Rather, it is as if some of these survivors are saying that only those who have experienced this hell beyond all suffering can have seen what it means to survive it — to literally live on top of it — to drop the "frayed rhetoric of pathos or revenge" and to still go on. To borrow from Tillie Olsen, it seems that, for Waterford and others, "there is still enough left to live by." Even after that.

Finally, then, unless a work that has the Holocaust as subject matter can influence the reader to guard against all the minor holocausts one may encounter in one's life —

to guard against the hatred and verbal violence against others that one ultimately confronts every day in one's own thought — then this story has in some way failed the reader, however much it may have succeeded in horrifying and however imaginatively written it may have been. The work should make the reader more aware of the *ends* of words — not only of the Lager at the end of the chain but of the chain itself. During the time I lived in Germany a few years ago, when antiforeigner, particularly anti-Turk, sentiment was on the rise, a certain thought-provoking bumper sticker kept cropping up that showed that a number of modern Germans were very aware of the power of words. Playing on the German word *Witz*, or joke, it read: *Judenwitz* . . . *Türkenwitz* . . . *Auschwitz*. (Jewish joke, Turkish joke, Auschwitz.) At the end of the chain is the Lager.

In any case, whether or not lived experience on the part of the writer is involved, the subject matter is only ethical when and if the literature also bears witness to some other possibility, as Primo Levi's does. The narrative itself might not take the direction of the other possibility. Holocaust literature, as it is based on history, cannot. But by examining the links in the chain that leads to the Lager, the work can show the places where another direction, another story, might just as possibly have been told.

Eventually, in any thoughtful working through of the interrelated questions of experience and appropriation, the writer, while not wanting to take literary advantage of history's victims, might be left with what may seem like a paltry few subjects to choose from if he or she be limited solely to the sources in his or her own life. In *Il testamento letterario*, the Italian author Count Giacomo Leopardi insists that any imitation of *una persona ignota* — that is, the persona the writer has never been or whom the writer through some sort of lived experience has never come to know — will necessarily be unfamiliar to the reader and will cause the reader the discomfort of disbelief.[55] For Leopardi, the boundaries of one's own subject matter are mapped out by one's own experiences as a human being rather than by questionable experimentation.

But it may be just as dubious for the writer to exploit a real event in his or her own life for the purposes of self-aggrandizement in fiction. The one-time sixties student activist now turned social/literary critic Bettina Aptheker expands upon the ethical aspects of subjective appropriation when she implies in *Tapestries of Life* that there is a kind of unethical self-appropriation that can take place. When one identifies one's experience as being somehow wholly representative — perhaps even exclusively representative — of a particular kind of experience or suffering, much as Rousseau did in *Reveries of the Solitary Walker*, one may already have overstepped boundaries. Aptheker tells of a college-educated daughter who returns to her southern black roots and demands certain objects — a quilt, a butter churner — from her less-educated mother, with the intention of putting them on display as a kind of proof of her solidarity with the working-class blacks she has left behind. "To appropriate a heritage by displaying it to garner status," Aptheker points out, "makes it into just another 'thing,' inert and useless."[56] It is the displaying of the object (or of experience) merely in order to "garner status" that makes the appropriation ethically questionable, and this, Aptheker implies, is true even if the experience or heritage one is exploiting is biologically or culturally one's own. Thus, writing what you know may have more to do with a capacity for human feeling than it has to do with rigid biographical experience or fact. One cannot write in order to become famous; one cannot write to "garner status." One can only write because one loves.

I am acutely aware of the theoretical can of worms I could open up by trying to argue for motive as intentionality in the text. W. K. Wimsatt, Monroe C. Beardsley, and other New Critics of the forties and fifties in America argued voraciously for an "objective" criticism that would view the work as itself alone, despite the author's biography and/or intention, and, for the most part, they won.[57] Jean-François Lyotard, in *The Postmodern Condition*, takes intention away from the author as well, to place it, not necessarily with any one reader (*the* reader), but rather in multiple readings of the text, the success or accuracy of which depends largely on the competency of the participant.[58] But in order to go on writing, the practicing author must believe in at least the possibility that writing is the individual author's subjective act. In the end, the old adage to write what you know may have a great deal more to do with the motivation behind the writer's choice of subject matter — the *why I write* — than has been explored so far.

Throughout the history of written literature, a number of writers have concerned themselves with the concept of selection of subject matter. Horace, as the first, starts the process off with a simple admonition to "choose a subject . . . equal to your strength." He says, "If a man's subject be chosen effectively, neither ready speech will fail him nor clearness of order."[59] The writer's ultimate responsibility for the choice of subject matter is no less implied in this statement merely because the translator has chosen to render the condition Horace offers — "if a man's subject be chosen effectively" — in the passive voice. Horace also implies a sense of authorial responsibility, apparently in response to his correspondent's argument that poets should be allowed a certain "license." He further writes:

> "Poets and painters," you say, "have always had an equal license in daring invention."
>
> We know it: This liberty we claim for ourselves and give again to others; but it does not go to the extent that savage should mate with tame, that serpents should couple with birds, or lambs with tigers. [60]

Horace's warning about taking too much license with one's given material seems good advice. Sometimes the writer should have the wisdom — or humility — to turn down story ideas. The turning down of a poetic or fictional assignment need not be any more mystical than the turning down of an inappropriate assignment that has been mandated by an inhuman boss.

During the time that I worked as a features writer for a small, family-run weekly in the Berkshires in western Massachusetts, I thought my boss was the crudest individual I had ever known. No subject matter was off-limits, so long as it increased our advertising or our sales. To give an example of his ethics, he once suggested with a nasty chuckle, when another reporter was doing a series on abortion, that he should include an X ray of me in the story, since I happened to be pregnant at the time. I quickly learned that I was not going to accept every story this editor assigned me or else I would find myself writing stories (that's what newspaper people call features articles) about local characters (in this case, real people who lived in the Berkshires) whose plots (my boss leaned heavily toward the imaginative schemes these people claimed could make just about anybody get rich quick*)* I couldn't like, from a slant (that's the journalistic word for point of view) so awkward that my readers might not be able to determine whether the slant was my editor's, the local character's, or mine. Ostensibly, my boss was the authority in that office, but I was responsible for both my byline (that's name for a journalist) and my writing time.

My point in bringing up this not-so-pleasant story these good eighteen years later is not to remember this failed old tyrant so unkindly but to suggest that if the writer of fiction cannot be as ruthless with the stories given (to again do away with the responsibility inherent in the active voice) as I finally had to be with some of the stories that my editor gave me, then the writer is accepting a rather limited definition of himself or herself as a blown-up persona who is somehow electrically zapped by a story as it comes flying by.

The Greek word for character is in fact persona, which just means mask. The temptation to think of a writer as somehow this (specifically, *this*) body through which some great source out there might deign to speak is to discount personal accountability and to point, with an apologetic shrug of one's authorial shoulders, at an empty mask. The great source out there giving me story ideas while I worked for this tabloid was this man; yet I did have something to do with the story that came out, and I was accountable for it. The writer has no military directives, no *I was under orders*, no higher-ups.

Selectivity in subject matter need not imply that certain precensored subjects are beyond the bounds. In dealing with this concept of selection, writers stressing the role of subject matter have seemed almost always to concur that, in the end, the message is more important than the chosen plot. Sir Philip Sidney picks up on the dual role of literature to teach and to delight when he writes in the sixteenth century, "Whatsoever action, or faction, whatsoever counsel, policy, or war stratagem the historian is bound to recite, that may the poet, if he list, with his imitation make his own, beautifying it both for further teaching, and more delighting . . . having all, from Dante's heaven to his hell, under the authority of his pen."[61] But while one may have, as Sidney says here, all from heaven to hell as the breadth of one's choice of subject matter under the authority of one's pen, one should take this possibly dangerous authority seriously and not just with the proverbial grain of salt.

John Dryden, taking up this question again in the seventeenth century states, "The poet is not obliged to expose to view all particular actions which conduce to the principal: he ought to select such of them to be seen, which will appear with the greatest beauty."[62] Dryden is, of course, taking the entire English stage to task here with the Continental Model as it was shaped by Pierre Corneille, but he is certainly also trying to work through the problem of selection for himself. What sometimes seems like the pretentiousness of his argument should not make us overlook the fact that he, like Sidney, calls for "beauty" as one of the criteria for that selection. Perhaps the beauty they are both alluding to is that of the resiliency and persistence of the human spirit in the very midst of physical and moral drought. It may well be unreasonable to try to allude to immortality and divinity today the way the ancient Greeks did. Very few postmodern readers would be convinced. But resiliency and persistence are spiritual qualities we encounter every day, in spite of the overwhelming negative evidence of the material senses, and as such, they are the closest figures for immortality we have.

Tolstoy connects a need for compassion in literature with

the author's choice of subject matter when he writes, "Only two kinds of feeling do unite all men: first, feelings flowing from the perception of our sonship to God and of the brotherhood of man; and next, the simple feelings of common life accessible to everyone without exception — such as feelings of merriment, of pity, of cheerfulness, of tranquility, and so forth. Only these two kinds of feelings can now supply material for art good in its subject matter."[63] Tolstoy goes on to give examples of writers whose life experience did not coincide with their choice of subject matter but who nevertheless, through an expanded sense of this "brotherhood," were able to imagine or to legitimately appropriate subject matter that was not their own. Tolstoy apparently offers the term "brotherhood" in a generic rather than gendered sense, in that he shows this brotherhood of authors to have been exemplified by women as well as by men. He cites Victor Hugo's *Les Misérables*, most of Charles Dickens's work, Harriet Beecher Stowe's *Uncle Tom's Cabin*, most of Dostoyevsky's writings, and George Eliot's *Adam Bede*. Ultimately, he seems to hold that an ethical approach to the *appropriate*-ness of subject matter need not necessarily preclude the appropriation of another's experience; the depth of the writer's humanity decides the point.

While I was working for the weekly paper, I found a good number of stories occurring to me that grew out of real events. One story was based on a thought that I kept having each day as I walked home from the bus, past the shoe repair shop that had been set up in what had once been, in the eighteenth century, someone's tiny clapboard house. I knew the kind of people who might have lived in that kind of house. Their families had settled in the Berkshires as small tradespeople almost two centuries ago. They were hardy and insular, and while not necessarily hateful to outsiders, they had a pretty good tendency to stick to and trust the locals, rather than the summer people, when push came to shove. Though I lived there year-round now myself, I was a newcomer by the eighteenth-century standard and would still have to serve my time as an outsider for a while. Being both in and out, I kept wondering what would happen if a woman from the outside were to suddenly die without telling anyone that she had left a pair of shoes to be repaired in that eighteenth-century house.

This idea, coupled with what I knew about two murders that had occurred in Berkshire County while I was working for the newspaper, gave me a story that was eventually published in *Yankee*, a magazine that has a reputation as a rigid recorder of New England thought. One of the actual murders was of a young schoolteacher from Provincetown who had come up to the Berkshires one winter weekend to visit her fiancé's family and who, for some reason no one ever fully explained, stayed in a hotel rather than with the fiancé's family. The other murder was of a high school girl who was abducted in the middle of winter on her way to the library one night and whose frozen body was later found in the woods, intact except for the fact that she wore no shoes. Both stories tugged at my sense of tragedy as I trudged to and from work in the Berkshire cold.

Another story was given me, as Horace has it, by a newspaper article I read while I was living in Albuquerque a few years after that. As I recall, the article reported briefly that a decorated Vietnam veteran had been killed while protecting a saleswoman in a convenience store. I was so moved by the fact that this anonymous man, who could have been in boot camp with my brother, had made it all the way through that war to come home to this, that I couldn't put him out of my mind. And I probably wrote myself into the story because there is a peripheral sister-figure who keeps driving by.

But while, like many writers, I keep a journal, my journals — and a hanging file marked "Story Ideas" in my back-porch desk — are also full of stories I ended up knowing better than to write. Although I have taken story ideas at times from events reported in the various newspapers in the places that I've lived and worked, newspaper clippings are usually a terrible place to get ideas, if only because of the senselessness of so much of the violence of those events. I have just come across, for instance, the following summation I made of an event that occurred while I was living in Michigan:

> (*Detroit News*, Aug. 15, 1989) The badly decomposed body of a 55-yr-old trucker is found in the sleeping compartment of his truck, the motor of which is still running, in a McDonald's parking lot nine days after he is reported missing by his wife.

At this point in time, I have no idea what I ever thought I was going to do with this event, but I seem to have rejected it almost simultaneously with this remark: "Postmodern questions — why didn't anyone notice the truck hadn't moved before they became aware of the odor?" In other words, *Doesn't anybody out there give a damn?* I seem to have known better than to use this idea because all it reports — the whole story — is humanity's to hell with you attitude toward the rest of the human race. And that is not a message I really want to put in print.

Another story idea, taken from a newspaper article on another occasion and penned onto the back of a card, breaks my heart. I keep the card not because I will ever use the idea — I know I won't — but because I want to know why I know I won't use it.

A foster mother cares for an abused child from 8 mos to 2 yrs. At 2 the child is returned to its natural mother, who w/the child's stepfather "potty trains" it by sticking his head upside down in a toilet bowl. The foster mother's words haunt me: *What was that child thinking when he died? Was he thinking, What did I do that they have left me here and don't come back for me? Was anyone there to hold his hand and hug him when they pulled the respirator out?*

I can't bear this story. I break down and cry. And it seems to me that unless I can answer that foster mother's question — *Was anyone there?* — I cannot allow myself to write this story. I would have to write an invisible angel into the story to hug the child, and then no one would believe me. The harder critic in me wants to dig until she finds out why that story cannot be art.

Yet another idea that I wrote down years ago comes from my sister, who told me about a girl with whom she'd graduated from high school:

My sister's friend on her honeymoon in a cabin in the mountains in the rural South. Her new husband lighting the gas stove in the kitchen that explodes and kills him after their "first night."

I think that to have followed through to write this particular story would have been to write with what Primo Levi calls "bathos and revenge." Bathos says, *You see then, don't you, that there is no use,* while revenge asks, *What kind of god would allow a thing like that?* It is true that life is sometimes tragic. It is also unfortunately true that innocent people — especially children — die for no good reason. But that is exactly where literature can intervene, for, as most of us have determined, literature is *not* like life. Literature is not a happenstance but a carefully worked-out construction of words from thought. The writer does not have to be helpless in the face of a particularly violent idea that somehow comes. The writer's voice can be that of the protester. It can point out and protest the injustices and inequities of human life.

A period of quiet or silence while one is working out the proper form for this protest need not necessarily be unproductive to one's work. A period of silence can provide the distance from the pain of involvement in a given experience — whether one be involved directly or indirectly, whether one is the wife in the anecdote about the newlywed couple or whether one has heard the tale from someone else — that allows the writer to be able to treat the subject matter more objectively, not possessively, not as one's own. Clearly, there needs to be some balance between the writer's experience in the world, or the writer's appropriated knowledge of an experience, and the deliberation over the experience — the deliberate turning-into-fiction of that event or thought.

In a chapter of *L'Espace littéraire* that pits an emphasis on action or experience against the writer's innate need for solitude, Maurice Blanchot writes: "L'artiste qui s'offre aux risques de l'expérience qui est la sienne, ne se sent pas libre du monde, mais privé du monde, non pas maître de soi, mais absent de soi, et exposé à une exigence qui, le rejetant hors de la vie et de toute vie, l'ouvre à ce moment où il ne peut rien faire et où il n'est plus lui-même."[64] According to Blanchot, then, writers who offer themselves without reservation to the risks of their own experience (experimentation or adventure here) cannot feel free of the world but rather are deprived of the world. They are not their own masters, but are exposed through these very adventures to that moment in which they can do nothing and in which they can no longer be themselves.

Perhaps, then, if one chooses to go all out for adventure, one will not write. Distance from experience, whether the subject matter one chooses is from one's own life or from observation or imagination, is a prerequisite to the transformation of the experience into art. This may be what William Wordsworth meant when he made the oft-quoted remark that poetry is "emotion recollected in tranquility." Wordsworth may have anticipated the contemporary writer's felt need for distance in his implied decision to distance himself from suffering in order to write about it when, in his preface to *Lyrical Ballads*, he noted with apparent concern "a craving for extraordinary incident which the rapid communication of intelligence hourly gratifies."[65]

This need for distance is at once Wordsworth's "emotion recollected in tranquility" and Blanchot's *oubli*, or forgetting — that which Blanchot ultimately terms "le silence d'une profonde métamorphose," or "the silence of a deep metamorphosis."[66] There is a time of artistic silence that is not necessarily the dreaded black hole or writer's block. This silence can rather be, as Blanchot has said, a profound metamorphosis of act and thought — a time during which the writer contemplates the given till the art takes hold.

Stéphane Mallarmé appears to agree with both Wordsworth and Blanchot when he says, "Poetry lies in the *contemplation* of things, in the image emanating from the reveries which things arouse in us."[67] *After*-thought, the kind of deliberation that is a deliberate rethinking of events, is an important part of the process of writing. Without it, one has experienced nothing.

The most eloquent exploration of the question of artistic silence may be Tillie Olsen's *Silences*. Yet as moving as that great work is, it finally capitulates to the very despair that prompted it and underlines the unjust circumstances in its premise with, *That's the way it is*. When I read *Silences* some years ago — as a seldom-published writer working as a secretary for a temporary agency in order to help pay for a new house out on a God-forsaken piece of desert in New Mexico that was infested with black widow spiders, stink-bugs, scorpions, and prairie dogs — I could read only about one chapter of the book before I became completely despondent and, on at least one occasion, very ill. So if I seem, on first reading, to have sold out on the question of contemplation to more privileged writers who have been able to afford to stop and think every now and then and still have ample time left over to sit down and write, I would argue that since my experience as a working mother forced me into a period of apparent nonproductivity in writing for a while, it was for this particular minor woman writer a matter of survival (*I will still write, I will write anyway*) to reevaluate that silence and to see it more in terms of a profound metamorphosis than as just lost time.

I recall a small and elegant concert given in the home of a friend of ours, who is a professional violinist and who herself does not have children, when our daughter was about eighteen months old. At one point during the recital the baby began to cry, and I took her into a room on the second floor of our friend's house to comfort her, so that her crying wouldn't bother the other guests. With the faint strains of the music somewhere off in the background, I lay down on the bed with the baby for the remainder of the concert, completely rumpling my best concert clothes. The baby quieted down and eventually fell asleep there in my arms. That concert has remained for me, all these years, as one of the few moments of my life when I could have defined in one whisper the feeling *calm*. Yet after the recital, my friend came to me in kindness to let me know that she had pitied me because I had missed the concert and the communion with the other guests. I could not explain to her that I had had with this baby in my solitude an experience that I would not have given over to someone else, not for all the good music and good conversation in the world. The joy that looked to another creative woman like deprivation gave me valuable experience with what literary critics sometimes call the inexpressibility topos, because I could not possibly tell her how I felt. I gained something through that contemplation — enforced though it may have seemed to others at the time — that I have accepted as a kind of influence on my art. Eccentric "old lady" writing in the Maine woods with my German shepherd as my sole companion that I might still like someday many years from now to be, I have learned a particular kind of concentration or contemplation because of, not in spite of, the fact that I had a child.

In my own case, the authorial search for adventure just so that I will have something to write about is over. In the end, dear reader, I got married anyway, just as my mother said I would, to a nice man who said I could stay home for a while in the house he already owned and get my health back and sit on top of his heater all day long and have time to write. Although I eventually had to go back to work, as they say, with all the artistic suffering and lack of time to write my stories that has implied, my point is that, self-conscious reader of my own life as I was, I began at some point to question the entire concept of the writer as romantic adventure seeker. Dear reader, I did marry him. And that, to tell the truth, is my *expériment*. To continue to insist that the subject matter that one's real life has given one somehow isn't interesting or adventurous or rich enough is to ignore the multiple endings that are possible beyond our texts. It is to deny the possibilities of our own lives.

5

Listening

. . . .

My real subject: human relationships.
—*Eudora Welty*

*That is the whole story, hers to tell; yet some part of it is
mine as well. And there is a larger story; I think of where I
am in it.*

*Some of my mother's memories have become my own. This is
the real burden of the blood; this is immortality.*

I invented history.
—*N. Scott Momaday*[1]

I spent my childhood in Atlanta during the late
1950s, and almost every night at the dinner table — especially during those summer nights when fireflies winked
outside the screened porch and my brother and I had grit
inside the creases of our elbows from having played so hard
in the kudzu-draped woods and in the red clay gully down
below our house and it was so hot that my mother had to
put ice cubes in our milk so it would not get warm — my
brother and older sister and I sat and listened to true tales
that had happened in our family's past. My brother, Billy,
and I were usually the ones to set these wonderfully repeti-
tive stories off. We would beg our parents, *Tell us about the
olden days.*

Until recently, it had never occurred to me that this was
not the way with all families. I didn't grasp the meaning of

people's puzzled looks when I asked my friends about their family legends. *Family legends?* they would answer. *What are those?* Yet the family tales I heard on that good screened porch are in my blood.

One story my father told again and again had to do with his father's father, a Texas Ranger during the 1850s, who had to leave his pregnant wife on their ranch near Fort Worth to go on a secret assignment for the federal government in the Embarcadero area of San Francisco. There he single-handedly (or so it went in the story) wiped out the shanghaiers — the villainous men who dealt in the slave-trade of merchant seamen on the wharf. When the Texas Ranger finally returned to his ranch in Texas three years later, he found his wife had remarried because the government hadn't allowed him to tell her where or how he was.

They told me you was dead, Hal. It's why I gone and married. For the child.

And the Texas Ranger tells his wife, *I don't want no trouble, Lottie. I just come to see my boy. I want to see my boy, then I'll be on my way, real easy, no trouble, I won't make no trouble for you, Lottie, none at all.*

The new husband allows the Texas Ranger to stay in town long enough to finish up some business and to see his son. The only condition is that he isn't allowed to wear his guns. Then one day, the Texas Ranger goes into town without his guns, and a cattle rustler sees him and tells him he is going to get him for the time the Texas Ranger sent him up.

The Texas Ranger tells the cattle rustler, *You can see for yourself I ain't got my gun, Mister. Let me go get my gun and I'll face you, man to man, in an even fight.*

But the rustler isn't interested in even fights. *I know if you had a gun I couldn't kill you.* And he hauls off and shoots the Texas Ranger. In the back.

The Texas Ranger crawls back on his hands and knees to the ranch, to Lottie. The Texas Ranger dies out there in the dust in the yard of the ranch, in Lottie's arms.

Some years ago, the Texas Ranger's wedding-day photo came to rest in all its sepia-toned complexity above the piano in my living room. My father gave it to me the day I moved into yet another house. I have done everything I can for the young man in the picture, who gazes down at me from the wall with my brother's eyes. I have kept his name as my own instead of taking my husband's. I have honored and revered his grandson, my father, all my life, even while I detested the military defense machines he was helping to create, even while everyone else I knew in my generation referred to their parents as *my old lady* and *my old man*. And so one would think, from the calm in the young man's face in the picture on my wall, that the Texas Ranger would settle down one day into some sort of western setting sun — *just beyond those hills, ole timer, Biff, Bill, Shorty, mind those dogies, don't take too much of that water now, ole timer, easy now* — and get his peace at last, and give me mine.

But even though I have published the Texas Ranger's tale full-length in one short story, in a nutshell as part of another, and then again as a longer poem, I have found myself making notes on the tale again and again just to see if I can't include it in just one more place, tell it one more time. When a friend's ten-year-old son, a budding composer, asked me to write a libretto for an opera, there *he* was. It will not rest, that story. My passion for the story is so great that I can't even write *about* it without beginning to write the story all over again just for itself, in the exact, unpunctuated rhythm of my father's voice.

Eudora Welty has observed that as a small child out for a drive in the car with her mother and father and a family friend she would "ask to sit in the middle, and say as we started off, 'Now *talk*.'"[2] Like Welty's parents, mine were willing to talk, and it was because of this willingness that I eventually came to cherish the act of listening as a vital ingredient in art. In fact, after all the theoretical discussion about source and appropriation and adventure has been sorted out, it is still possible that the best way to get experience is just to listen — to listen as an artist and to listen well.

The writer has not only the privilege of listening but the responsibility as well. The ethical aspect of this listening lies in the participation it implies in a dialogue with the human community — the kind of dialogue or two-way communication that Narcissus failed to see in the ancient myth when he cried out, "Is anyone here?" and mistook the source of Echo's responsive "Here!" as his own image or self-reflection in the pool.[3]

Yet writing is not always seen as a two-way conversation with the world. On one level, the creative writing student in one of this country's many writing programs may agree that writing is a dialogue with the reader, in that the writer is sending out words to some ideally receptive reader who will like the words — and who may even in turn write admiring letters back. But this particular concept of the writer's artistic solitude, while it admits of the writer's appreciation for the "ear of the Other," as French critic Jacques Derrida puts it — and while it may even admit the writer's dependency (like that of Narcissus) upon that ear as a repository for its own words and thoughts — undervalues both the duty and the rewards of listening back. The establishment of this dialogue between the Self and the Other might even be, as some critics already suggest, the ultimate purpose of all writing, for all *écriture*. As Derrida explains it (in reply to a question put to him regarding Nietzsche's

Ecce Homo, "What happens when Nietzsche writes, finally, to himself?"): "When [Nietzsche] writes himself to himself, he *writes himself to the other* who is infinitely far away and who is supposed to send his signature back to him."[4]

The nonwriting public has wonderful stories that deserve to be told and that are worth listening to, not only because this is the nice or ethical thing for the writer as a human being to do but because this is also a legitimate way to avoid the atrophy of art. The German philosopher Walter Benjamin may best sum up the peculiar influence of certain kinds of listening upon the writer's art in his essay "The Storyteller," when he writes, "This process of assimilation, which takes place in depth, requires a state of relaxation which is becoming rarer and rarer. . . . Boredom is the dream bird that hatches the egg of experience."[5] It was perhaps more possible, in that slower-to-progress South of the fifties where I grew up, to experience the boredom that Benjamin refers to here — that willingness to sit still and listen — than in other parts of the United States or, for all I know, even in the South in this postmodern age, since I left Atlanta when I was twelve and did not go back.

The nineteenth-century Italian novelist Giacomo Leopardi comments in his *Il testamento letterario* that this kind of passion for listening to a story, or *entusiasmo*, as he alternately calls it, is the single most important element of all art:

> Si abbandona come ad una forza estranea che lo trasporta, non è capace di raccogliere nè di fissare le sue idee, tutto quello che vede è infinito, indeterminato, sfuggevole, e così vario e copioso che non ammette nè ordine nè regola nè facoltà di annoverare o disporre o scegliere, o solamente di concepire: in modo chiaro e completo, e molto meno di *saisir* un punto (vale a dire un soggetto)

intorno al quale possa ridurre tutte le sensazioni e immaginazioni che prova, le quali non hanno nessun centro.[6]

[The writer] abandons himself as if to a foreign force that transports him. He cannot recover or fix upon his ideas. All this that he is seeing is infinite, undetermined, fleeting, and so varied and abundant that it doesn't allow either for order or rule or for the ease with which to renew or disperse or choose, or even to conceive of, in a clear and complete fashion — much less to seize [*saisir*, a word Leopardi borrows often from the French] upon — a point (that is, a subject) around which he can reduce all the sensations and images that he is experiencing, which have no center. (translation mine)

Leopardi brings together the quality of listening with passion. The overheard story "seizes" the listening writer with all its "sensations" and "images" and embeds itself in the writer's heart.

A number of American writers — particularly those who have grown up in the American South — seem to have had this passion for listening. At least one anthology of stories by southern writers, Ben Forkner and Patrick Samway's *Stories of the Modern South*, bears out the impression that listening — particularly as it relates to family narratives — has proven to be a potent source. Madison Jones's "The Fugitives," which tells of a young architect's brief encounter with an escaped prisoner, hints to the reader that the main character might not have been so fascinated by the escapee (who in the end is killed by law enforcement officers only a few feet away from the astonished main character) had he not listened as a child so intently to his Uncle Tad's "recounting over and over violent tales of the days when he had been a railroad engineer."[7] Likewise, the main character of Hunter Kay's "The Fifth Generation" knows very well how he came to be this watered-down version of a man. One can imagine the tales passed down to the narrator when he tells the reader, "The old outlaw robbed by main force and his grandson seized through cunning, sleuth, guile; but not my father."[8] Again, in Elizabeth Spencer's "The Finder," a family that has inhabited the same hill country for generations talks about its members "with such clarity and wit . . . you would think the dead were still right there and about to come in any minute."[9]

Oddly enough, the stories by Katherine Anne Porter and Eudora Welty included in the collection — "Holiday" and "The Wide Net," respectively — are perhaps the least representative of these two authors' dependence on family narratives and the oral tradition as a kind of source. In invoking Porter's name, one cannot help but think of the now-classic *Pale Horse, Pale Rider*, which many readers consider her most powerful work. Of the tales included in that collection, "Old Mortality" bears the strongest traces of the influence of family legend — tales Porter had heard frequently, and with passion, during her early life. As the critic Enrique Hank Lopez puts it, "'Old Mortality' was about as autobiographical as anything she ever wrote." Lopez points out that the character Miranda is "Katherine Anne Porter herself."[10]

Another critic, Jane Krause DeMouy, asserts, "The significance of Miranda's character to Porter's work can hardly be overstated. She is the identified center of consciousness in fully half of Porter's short stories and the implicit narrator in *Ship of Fools* and at least six other stories, including the most psychologically complex ones."[11] Miranda, De-

Mouy remarks, is above all an observer, and we might extend the definition of an observer to include a listener — one who has an acute aural, as well as visual, sense of the surroundings.

In *Conversations with Katherine Anne Porter*, Lopez brands Porter's father as a "gifted raconteur" who took great pleasure in telling his young daughter Miranda/Katherine Anne, among other family tales, romantic stories about his dead sister, who would in turn very clearly become the beautiful and rebellious Aunt Amy in "Old Mortality." It is this passion for listening as a child to family tales, Lopez claims, that eventually caused the adult Porter, just returned from Europe in 1936, to write "Noon Wine" and then "Old Mortality" in only seven days each, alone in an inn in Pennsylvania, "unraveling sequences of a story that had been gestating in her mind for twenty or thirty years."[12]

DeMouy also labels "Old Mortality" as a "fiction of memory."[13] The story contains the jumbling of events and the juxtaposition of time and tense that are reminiscent of the kind of tangled family storytelling I heard around my dinner table as a child.

In *Tapestries of Life: Women's Work, Women's Consciousness, and the Meaning of Daily Experience*, Bettina Aptheker goes so far as to suggest that this tendency toward oral storytelling — and, one would assume, the passion for listening to oral tales — is particularly strong in women, even though the story told (and retold) may never be written down. She writes, "Many of women's stories have never been written. They form an oral tradition, passed on from one generation to the next. Sometimes they are just seen as anecdotes about family 'characters' and their antics. Sometimes they are teaching stories. They are about having respect, about having decent values, about how to live properly, about how to survive."[14]

But family legend, or any other kind of oral tale that the writer receives through the listening process, must undergo some sort of metamorphosis before it can properly be termed art. Part of the attempt to determine the possibility of success as fiction for any given legend or oral tale may lie in a study of how like fiction certain parts of the family legends are. Only the parts with storylike elements to them — those with plots, with a beginning, a middle, and an end — become successful short stories that those outside the family will want to read.

On the other hand, of course, someone else, such as the French poet Stéphane Mallarmé, may very well come along and undercut the concept of beginning, middle, and end by saying that the writer should "always omit the beginning and the end of what you write. No introduction, no finale."[15] In any case, the qualities that allow for certain family narratives or oral legends to lend themselves well to fiction and/or poetry extend far beyond the issues of beginning, middle, and end, and some of those essential qualities are extremely difficult to pin down. One expert on oral storytelling speaks of the "tiny grain of truth somewhere in the most improbable yarn."[16] But we are then left with poor Pilate's immortal question in the New Testament of the Bible, "So what is truth?"

In the case of the story that derives from family legend, truth might only be that part of the legend that is universal, that speaks to the ears and hearts not only of one's own family but of the human race. The extraneous material — that which remains after this dissection takes place — can only properly be termed *memoir*. As Walter Benjamin puts it, "It is not the object of the story to convey a happening *per se*, which is the purpose of information; rather, it embeds it in the life of the storyteller in order to pass it on as experience to those listening. It thus bears the marks of the storyteller much as the earthen vessel bears the marks of the potter's hand." [17] Benjamin is reflecting here upon the differentiation among the *mémoire pure*, *mémoire volontaire*, *mémoire involontaire*, and *mémoire d'intelligence* of Marcel Proust, and in doing so he attempts to show the movement from memory into art.

In "Old Mortality," Katherine Anne Porter has the two sisters, Maria and Miranda, accomplish this delicate operation — the excision of fact from fiction, the movement from memory into art — for us. The girls listen to family lore, "all ears and eager minds, picking here and there among the floating ends of narrative, patching together as well as they [can] fragments of tales that [are] like bits of poetry or music, indeed [are] associated with the poetry they [have] read, with music, with the theater." Their discernment of what makes a good story — of what is most like "bits of poetry or music" in the family legends — serves to distinguish between the truly fictive story and the mere memoir. From the start, the girls are very aware that the story of their Aunt Amy belongs "to the world of poetry" and that it is also, as Porter will prove, the stuff of fiction. The girls note that "the romance of Uncle Gabriel's long, unrewarded love for [Aunt Amy], her early death, was such a story as one found in old books; unworldly books, but true, such as *The Vita Nuova, The Sonnets of Shakespeare* and *The Wedding Song* of Spenser, and poems by Edgar Allan Poe." [18]

If one views the unfolding of the Aunt Amy legend in terms of some of the reader-response theories bandied about today (and in this case it would be more correctly in terms of a listener/observer response), one is impressed with the multiple versions of the Aunt Amy story, its openness to interpretation by other members of the family. In a very literary sense, if one accepts Wolfgang Iser's partial definition in *The Act of Reading* of greatness in a work as the ability of the text to withstand multiple readings and to resist closure, the particular greatness of the root legend of "Old Mortality" can be seen in its ability to withstand closure by its onslaught of listeners in the generations of family members like Maria and Miranda who are yet to come.[19]

But the growth from borrowed legend to original story in the writer's mind can come only with the frustration of the knowledge on the writer's part that the person telling the story cannot possibly get the story right. We are convinced, after only one generation of Porter's family characters has passed, that there is no right interpretation of the Aunt Amy tale in "Old Mortality." Having somehow accepted her immediate family's version of Aunt Amy's courtship, elopement, and fatal illness, Miranda is appalled, upon meeting the dry, unattractive, older Cousin Eva on a train many years later as she returns for Uncle Gabriel's funeral, to find that Eva's version of the story (that is, her *reading* of it) is completely different from her own. In Eva's version, the Creole suitor Raymond (who was an exsuitor according to Miranda's version) persuades the romantic Amy to elope with him, and, in Eva's version, Amy's brother Henry actually shoots Raymond. Eva's version contains more violence than Miranda can accept. She says, "Cousin Eva, my father shot *at* him, don't you remember? He didn't hit him. . . ." To which Eva replies, as though it clearly doesn't matter to her whether she's right or wrong, "Well, that's a pity."[20]

We are further led to believe that Gabriel's second wife, Miss Honey, may have *her* version of Amy's story and that other family members may have *their* versions as well. In the end, as Cousin Eva and Miranda's father begin to swap family tales, Miranda rebels against the limitation the stories seem to have bred in her. Porter writes, "Miranda could not hear the stories well, or stories like them. She knew too many stories like them, she wanted something new of her own. The language was familiar to them, but not to her, not any more."[21]

As Robert Penn Warren describes Miranda's reaction to the retelling of the old familiar family tales, "Miranda will find *a* truth, as it were, but it, too, will be a myth, for it will not be translatable, or, finally, communicable. But it will be the only truth she can win, and for better or worse she will have to live by it. She must live by her own myth." Listening to Eva and her father talk, Miranda ultimately rejects the legends which have in some very real way given birth to what she is at this point in her life. Porter tells us, "Her blood rebelled against the ties of blood."[22]

Unlike Eudora Welty, a writer whose work also depends largely on the oral tradition, Katherine Anne Porter (like her character Miranda) seems to have felt limited in the end by her marriage "for better or worse," as Warren puts it, to family lore. There seems to be some elusive difference in the way the two writers move autobiographical experience, or the oral retelling of it, into story, and it is a difference which appears to have proven somewhat fatal to Porter's art. That is, she seems ultimately to have run out of stories to tell.

But a close reading of Welty's comment upon her own writing in *One Writer's Beginnings* tends to suggest that the difference between the prodigiousness of the one writer and the small output of the other may lie in something as fundamental as attitude toward the oral material with which the writer works, particularly if that material depends on family lore at least in part. The oral tradition, inasmuch as both of these writers were southern, was there in their youths to provide abundant material for writing. But one has the feeling, reading biographical sketches of Porter, that, like Miranda, she rebelled against both her personal history and the oral narratives foisted upon her and that she would like to be quit of them entirely if she had a choice.

For Porter, the oral narratives may have become what might be called *obsession tales*. In a number of photographs taken of her in Hollywood during the 1950s, she can be seen trying to create some sort of authorial persona, as if to overthrow that "refugee from Indian Creek," as she once called herself. The family prototypes for her heroines create themselves as fiction, in perhaps much the same way Porter creates the beautiful but ultimately untruthful image of herself as Hollywood star, on the order of a Jane Froman or some other *vedette* of that essentially fictitious milieu. On returning home from her adventurous trip to Mexico with her brother and Gabriel, Miranda remarks, "Mammy, it was splendid, the most delightful trip I ever had. And if I am to be the heroine of this novel, why shouldn't I make the most of it?"[23] Like Miranda, Katherine Anne Porter seems unable, in the end, to have distanced herself from the stories she heard as a child and to continue to write beyond them.

Eudora Welty speaks of the need on the part of the author to put distance between oneself and the factual source of the writing so as to view the story with an impartial eye and thus not to be obsessed with it: "My temperament and my instinct had told me alike that the author, who writes at his own emergency, remains and needs to remain at his private remove. I wished to be, not effaced, but invisible — actually a powerful position. Perspective, the line of vision, the frame of vision — these set a distance."[24] It is no mere coincidence that Porter wrote an introduction to Welty's *Selected Stories*, seeing in Welty's stories the same oral roots that had fed her own. But Welty treats the oral nature of the source of her storytelling in a very different manner than does Porter. While Miranda/Katherine Anne Porter rebels against the stories, wanting something new and "of her own," Welty rejoices continually in her family's inclination toward tale-telling and in her part as listener and recorder of events. The joy she has taken in the oral tradition, not only as it reflects the retelling of family lore but also the overheard conversations in train stations and in beauty parlors, is evident in such early stories as "Lily Daw and the Three Ladies" and "Petrified Man."[25]

Furthermore, Welty's delight in observation and listening does not seem to have dimmed through the years. The abundance of her work seems to imply that, while family lore and the oral tradition may provide the writer with a wealth of material, the writer needs to have a limitless compassion for the human spirit — particularly as it is evidenced in love of family — in order to continue to delve into the regions of tale and myth. The writer needs to continue to desire to listen.

But the writer who feels a relentless impulse to turn a particular oral legend into art may have to struggle against the will of the narrative as history to tell itself. One may have too much passion or enthusiasm for a given tale and find oneself in the position of writing, over and over, a single piece. As the contemporary writer Nancy Hale has remarked of her own work, there have been times when she has feared "that I'm just drawing on the life . . . that I really and fully lived . . . before I wrote much. Well, you can't draw on that forever. One reason there are so many one-book authors is that they used up the living years in the one book. And you do feel, if you write, that you are not so wholly involved in situations that come along as you once were."[26] The writer needs to keep listening so as not to be limited to the obsession tale. Some family narratives, as obsessed as the writer may become with them, may in fact not be conducive either to poetry or fiction. For one thing, in family narratives in particular, there are at least as many versions of any one incident as there are tellers of the plot, and one's human sense of family justice, never altogether objective in the first place, may interfere when it comes to deciding on the story's slant.

Margaret Walker's novel, *Jubilee*, about a black family just prior to and after the Civil War, is clearly a novel that struggles against the exigencies of the obsessive tale. Walker has said that she never had a choice whether to write this novel. She had heard the story as a child from her grandmother, and the need to write it down was overwhelming. She writes in *How I Wrote "Jubilee"*:

> Long before *Jubilee* had a name I was living with it and imagining its reality. Its genesis coincides with my childhood, its development grows out of a welter of raw experiences and careful research, and its final form emerged exactly one hundred years after its major events took place. Most of my life I have been involved with writing this story about my great-grandmother, and even if *Jubilee* were never considered an artistic or commercial success I would still be happy just to have finished it.[27]

Vyry Ware's struggles in *Jubilee*, as a black woman in the antebellum and Reconstruction South, needed to be told. Readers, both black and white, needed to see that Scarlett O'Hara's will to survive as a southern white princess no matter what the consequences of her acts in Margaret Mitchell's *Gone with the Wind* was not the only southern story to be told. Vyry — or the historical figure she really was — could not have spoken for herself, could not have written her own story, because the pre–Civil War and Reconstruction South had seen to it that the real Vyry never even learned to write her name. Janet Sternburg has noted in her introduction to *The Writer on Her Work* that "against the silence of the past and of immediate forbears, we are speaking for those who did not speak."[28] In *Jubilee*, Margaret Walker is certainly speaking for those who did not speak, and the work cannot be read outside the context of the historical oppression of which it speaks.

Yet as necessary as the existence of this novel is in view of the enormous absence of black women's voices in written texts during and about the Civil War, there is a peculiar lack of lyricism in *Jubilee*. This may be due in part to the influence of secondary material on the original tale — research perhaps ironically overdone precisely because of the felt burden of the responsibility to get it right. There is no other way to account for this lack of lyricism in *Jubilee*, since Walker's lyrical voice in her first collection of poems, *For My People*, is rich and strong.

Walker herself alludes to her difficulty with the facts of *Jubilee* in her discussion of her attempt to turn the oral material of her childhood into fiction while she was still a student at Yale. She states, "I had a major flaw in my fiction. I knew what it was, but I did not know how to correct it. So, I left Yale with Professor Pearson's criticism in my ears. 'You are telling the story, but it does not come alive.'"[29] The "flaw" Walker is alluding to here may lie not so much in her fiction-writing abilities as in her completely understandable absorption in — her passion for — this obsessive tale.

One may need, in the end, not only to have the predisposition for listening but to be aware of the relative dangers of this passion for listening as well. It is possible to have heard good stories as a child and to incorporate them successfully into the body of one's short stories as an adult. But one cannot then tune out, in adulthood, all the other stories or narratives that continue to be told and to abound. Through an ongoing, active participation, the author avoids the possibility of the atrophy of art. Henry James writes in *The Art of the Novel*, in his discussion of the oral tale that was the source for "What Maisie Knew," that he would not let his host ruin the story for him by completing it in the wrong direction, but that he listened up to a point and then tuned out.[30] Listening "up to a point" seems good advice.

The quality of listening is not without its humorous aspects as well, particularly when someone wants to get the writer in question to turn off the writerly listening mode long enough to legitimately just sit down and talk. In an interview that a newspaper reporter was attempting to have with the writer Gail Godwin — also considered a southern writer even though she has lived and written for some time in the North — the interviewer's good-natured frustration was evident when she reported that every time she asked Godwin a question, Godwin answered by trying to get the reporter to talk about *her* life.[31]

E. M. Forster found this kind of overpowering curiosity about other people's affairs to be "one of the lowest of the human faculties." In *Aspects of the Novel*, he is very hard on aggressive listeners, saying of them: "You will have noticed in daily life that when people are inquisitive they nearly always have bad memories and are usually stupid at bottom. The man who begins by asking you how many brothers and sisters you have, is never a sympathetic character, and if you meet him in a year's time he will probably ask you how many brothers and sisters you have, his mouth again sagging open, his eyes still bulging from his head." But then Forster adds to this somehow very uppity British-sounding remark, almost as an afterthought, "Curiosity by itself takes us a very little way, nor does it take us far into the novel — only as far as the story. If we would grasp the plot we must add intelligence and memory."[32] So while perhaps the quality of listening, in and of itself, is not necessarily an artistic one, in that good listeners don't inevitably become good writers, Forster does imply that good storytelling has something to do with the addition of "intelligence and memory" to listening, the end result being that we can "grasp the plot."

The difference between the blatant curiosity Forster seems, perhaps justifiably, to loathe and simple listening may ultimately lie in the motive behind the writer's desire to hear the tale. If one is only providing one's ears with good stories to write down, then the very power that gives the story its capacity to have universal relevance and to transcend the human condition may be lost. While the artistic reward for listening may be rich, one cannot legitimately listen merely for the reward. To play just a little upon Horace's stated two-fold purpose for literature to entertain and to teach, the writer needs to ask if he or she is there to be entertained by the oral story or because there is something abiding in the tale that teaches and that can be written down and left behind for others.

But the writer still has to listen all the time, to keep listening, because it is impossible to know what will ultimately be worth listening to when the speaking starts. I remember — in fact, for some reason I am unable ever to forget — standing in the corridor of a crowded, steamy, second-class train car somewhere in France some years ago and listening to a group of disheveled, unwashed American backpackers who had just met each other in that corridor and who, in fact, all looked a lot like me, as they discussed their impressions of the Europe they were seeing for the first time. As it happened, one young woman felt she could sum up all she had to say about this experience if she described her first reaction to the Eiffel Tower. *And there it was, you know, just this stupid wire structure. Just this stupid wire structure that was really tall. And, like, I don't know what it was I was expecting, but it wasn't that.*

This particular overheard gem has stayed with me ever since that moment on the train as a kind of emblem for disappointment. What was it that young woman was expecting, if it wasn't *that*? I have come to suspect that what she wanted, what she was expecting, was to see herself as the girl in the travel poster she had seen at home. Tidily dressed, pretty, smelling not of sweat and of dirty jeans but of discreet cologne, she would stand in front of the Eiffel Tower, *an American in Paris*, looking up. Something wonderful would happen when she saw that tower. She would never be the same again. People would say of her, *She has been to Europe. Yes, she went to Paris and saw the Eiffel Tower. She has seen so much!*

Sometimes, as a minor woman writer, I think my dreams and expectations have been just a little bit like that dirty, disappointed backpacker's Eiffel Tower. That is, if I were to get what I thought I wanted someday — recognition, one book in the college canon, *that* success — would I suddenly be the woman in the travel poster? Or would my success turn out to be *just another stupid wire structure* — something that I thought would make me happy, *but it wasn't that*. The joke would be that in the aftermath of this success, I wouldn't know exactly what it was I had been expecting all this time. But it wasn't that.

This *stupid wire structure* that has kept me busy thinking about the nature of artistic expectation and disappointment all these years originally came to me as something I overheard. I wasn't, at that point in my experience, even capable of making up an emblem as rich as that. And even now, as I use it, it isn't mine. I don't own it; I didn't make it up. The image that I overheard was there because I listened, and it stayed with me until I needed to give a name to disappointment, to misplaced desire.

And so *everything* is worth listening to. Even human gossip cannot be categorized as unworthy or unserious. The writer, as a member of humanity, is not free to say, *I can't stand listening to all these people, how they go on and on. These stupid middle-aged women who have done nothing but raise children and stay home all their lives can have nothing of interest to say to me.* I am convinced that all writers, with no so-called experience of their own, could sit in one of those orange-plastic coin television seats in the waiting room of a Greyhound Bus depot and have stories that would last them all their lives, if they could only be meek enough to sit still and watch people and listen and to relate people's joys and sorrows to the joys and sorrows they must have felt themselves. It is only through this human connection, this participatory observation, that the writer can ever become, as Henry James repeats in so many ways in *The Art of the Novel*, an observer who misses nothing, someone on whom nothing is lost. The same power that wants to listen is also the power that needs to write. As one writer on women's personal narratives puts it, "Reading and listening are skills; they are also arts. They can be taught, and they must be honored."[33] One can no more say, *All I want to do is write*, than one can say, *All I want to do is talk*. Just as writing and reading are two parts of the same action, so the writer has to read and listen as well as write and talk.

In a speech delivered before the American Academy of Arts and Letters, Isak Dinesen spoke of a motto she took from the crest of the English Finch-Hatton family, *Je responderay*, or I will answer. She liked, she said, "the high valuation of the idea of the answer in itself. For an answer is a rarer thing than is generally imagined. There are many highly intelligent people who have got no answer at all in them. . . . And how, then, will you yourself go on speaking?"[34] It is only as the writer listens that he or she begins to find the answer. And responds.

6

A Sense of Place

Geographic Flux and the Writer's Work

. . . .

Recently I have begun to wonder if my mother and father would have told us such richly embroidered family narratives had it not been for the passion for the past that my brother and I absorbed while we were growing up in the still-preurbanized 1950s' South. History in that Georgia was not just something one learned in the Fulton County schools; it was all around. If I borrowed the neighbor's horse and set out riding, I was bound to come across a brass plaque along Mt. Paran Road marking some event that had occurred during what was known simply as Sherman's march through Georgia. My older sister still claims that in five years of high school history classes — grades eight through twelve — her teachers never got beyond the Civil War. *The South should have won*, they told us. Then, while the slow bees droned in the dogwood trees outside the old brick buildings, they told us why. Our villains were historical, and they were much more real to us than the ones we might have seen while watching reruns of westerns on Saturday morning television.

The South, as has been borne out in its rich literature, has kindled in its writers what the English novelist D. H. Lawrence would term a particularly strong "spirit of place."[1] But a writer may also have to struggle against the adverse influences of such a place. If this particular white middle-class daughter, as I was then, were now to go into the guilt and shame that my preintegration southern childhood has cast like a shadow upon me, I would need another book. If Eudora Welty's southern childhood gave her plenty to write about, mine, once I started going to a California high school and reading *real* history, left me furious for the holes my southern education had left in my humanity. I seem to believe that that particular sense of place was adversely influential enough that I had to leave the South before I could come to terms with it — had to teach my tongue new ways to move in my mouth so that my Georgia cracker accent would be erased.

The German writer Christa Wolf deals continually in her work with a similar kind of guilt over her geographic and generational upbringing. At times, she is almost obsessed with the question her autobiographical character Nelly in *Patterns of Childhood* asks her father, "Is it really possible to turn every human being into an animal?"[2] Her fundamental question here is the age-old metaphysical query, *What is man?* However, this is a question that not only German writers whose compatriots passively looked the other way during the Holocaust must try to answer but one that any writer who has grown up as a member of a privileged race or class must rethink as well. It is just possible that too rigid a sense of place, and of one's own place within it, may stultify and limit one's humanity and therefore one's writing — especially in terms of subject matter and characterization — rather than enrich them both.

In order to come up with some sort of artistic framework for both the posing and the answering of that age-old question — particularly for the writer who has been brought up in an environment that answers this question with an adverse response, as in, well, people are white or

Aryan or Israeli or male or any other noninclusive type—the writer has to have an affection for humanity, a felt responsibility for the affectionate representation of the Other in one's own art. It is only through this larger consciousness that the writer can begin to counteract the adverse geographic influences on his or her art.

While a writer cannot ignore the importance of having some fixed geographic source or background in order to be able to create a fictional sense of place, there may be a simultaneous need for distance, a term that is by no means relegated entirely to the mental realm. Mme. de Staël suggests in *De l'Allemagne*, her critical comparison of French and German literatures, that a balance should be struck between the neoclassicism that was the rigid status quo of the French literature of her time and the exuberance she was discovering in German music, literature, and philosophy as she traveled through an as yet diverse and folktale-oriented Germany—through an innocent, prenationalistic-rhetoric, pre-Vaterland.[3] The writer needs to draw back and look at his or her geography as one apart.

American literature in particular is full of journeys away from and back to the fictitious home in this regard, the implication being that one needs the perspective that moving away provides. American writers, especially, have tended in comments upon their writing to stress the importance of getting into perspective the real place that inspires the fictional setting. Henry James, whose status as an exiled American is now so established that an editor working on a bibliography of English and American literature often cannot decide where to place him, speaks of this need for distance in his preface to *The Americans*, when he describes the strength of the view of Paris outside his window:

My windows looked into the Rue de Luxembourg . . . and the particular light Parisian click of the small cab-horse on the clear asphalt, with its sharpness of detonation between the high houses, makes for the faded page to-day a sort of interlineation of sound. This sound rises to a martial clatter at the moment a troop of cuirassiers charges down the narrow street, each morning, to file, directly opposite my house, through the plain portal of the barracks occupying part of the vast domain attached in a rearward manner to one of the Ministères that front on the Place Vendôme; an expanse marked, along a considerable stretch of the street, by one of those high painted and administratively-placarded garden walls that form deep, vague, recurrent notes in the organic vastness of the city.[4]

The picture James paints of the Paris he sits contemplating at his window is vivid and enduring, like the settings in his fiction. But that view both inspired and distracted him at the same time. He immediately goes on to warn the budding writer about the dangers of this kind of all-encompassing looking out:

I have but to re-read ten lines to recall my daily effort not to waste time in hanging over the window-bar for a sight of the cavalry the hard music of whose hoofs so directly and thrillingly appealed; an effort that inveterately failed — and a trivial circumstance now dignified, to my imagination, I may add, by the fact that the fruits of this weakness, the various items of the vivid picture, so constantly recaptured, must have been in themselves suggestive and inspiring, must have been rich strains, in their way, of the great Paris harmony.[5]

James seems finally to come to the conclusion that, while his impression of Paris was deep because of this daily contemplation, he had to remove himself from the real setting entirely in order to write about it:

> I have ever, in general, found it difficult to write of places under too immediate an impression — the impression that prevents standing off and allows neither space nor time for perspective. The image has had for the most part to be dim if the reflexion was to be, as is proper for a reflexion, both sharp and quiet; one has a horror, I think, artistically, of agitated reflexions.[6]

It is sometimes very difficult for the writer to separate experience from the strong impression, or "agitated reflexion" as James has it, of a sense of place.

As a southern writer, Erskine Caldwell found that he needed to leave in order to find a perspective. One interviewer says of him, "He decided to settle in Maine, for a number of reasons. One was that there he could view the South from afar, an aid to perspective. Another, he thought the life there would be simple and cheap. Another, he anticipated that his neighbors would let him alone while he worked."[7] Here, the New England population's reputation for aloofness attracts a writer who needs to be alone and at a distance from the original sense of place.

Perhaps, with all this writerly need for geographic as well as spiritual distancing, the writer, whether or not he or she is considered regional by someone else, is always an outsider, or should be — even an outsider to his or her own place. Eudora Welty, who left the South long enough to go to college at the University of Wisconsin, devotes an entire chapter of *One Writer's Beginnings* to the question of creative nonbelonging, arguing for a more detached, observant sense of place. She notes in the chapter she calls "The Angel of Departure" that "travel itself is part of some longer continuity."[8] As she describes in the journal her coming home from college for vacations, one feels that her exodus and her coming back are both alike. As an artist, even when she comes home, she's still away. Welty's distance, then, is not solely geographic but is also a transcendent one; she sees the writer's perception as coming from apart, though not from above. That ability to distance herself from her geography may in the end be the grace that has saved her from the historically less attractive aspects of coming from the South.

Although, like Erskine Caldwell and Eudora Welty, many a southern writer has taken the distancing journey north, and although any number of other American writers during the twenties, such as Hemingway, Fitzgerald, and Gertrude Stein, believed they needed to escape eastward to Europe in order to reflect, quite often the distancing process has taken American writers on a journey west. Ever since the Lewis and Clark expedition to the Pacific Coast, the idea of going west in search of escape and renewal has been one of the white American romantic's prevailing themes. Even though newer historical works, such as Dee Brown's *Bury My Heart at Wounded Knee*, expose less romantic, more brutal aspects of the opening up and settling of the American West by eastern whites, this stubborn American metaphor for self-expansion still hangs on.[9] The western novelist and essayist Wallace Stegner has written, "Americans have a centuries-old habit of dreaming westward." He goes on to quote Henry David Thoreau: "Eastward I go only by force; but westward I go free. The future lies that way to me, and the earth seems more unexhausted and richer on that side."[10]

Willa Cather devotes an entire quarter of her novel *The Professor's House* — the main narrative of which, as the title might suggest, follows an aging professor's losing battle with his wife's plans to build a larger, more comfortable house that is supposed to mirror what she believes is his success — to the story of the professor's alterego, Tom Outland, a self-taught young man who long ago came to the professor with a story about a lost mesa and its ancient civilization that he discovered in the West. Though physically bound to his home on Lake Michigan, Professor Godfrey St. Peter progressively escapes from his own flat and inward-turning midwestern landscape by rereading and pondering the western journals of the long-dead Tom Outland, who, through an ironic twist of events, is ultimately responsible for Professor St. Peter's current comfortable financial position. The lure of Tom Outland's escape to the West ends for Professor St. Peter — as it did many years before for Tom — with the lesson that total avoidance of some sort of personal responsibility for modern civilization's evil is impossible.

A character's pursuit of the myth of the great wide West in a narrative can probably take only one of two directions: either the character's abandonment of an established existence in a permanent sense of place in order to pursue the romance of the West ends in the exploitation of other people (as Tom Outland's inadvertently did) or the character, humbled by the enormity of western space and sky, ultimately reestablishes a relationship with the rest of the human race. This reestablishment is often literally marked in the narrative with a geographic return to the starting place.

For the character Jack Burden in Robert Penn Warren's novel *All the King's Men*, going west provides a temporary and much-needed escape from the brutal picture of life in the kingpin politics of a corrupted South. After reflection, Burden returns from his trip out West, and a decided change occurs in the direction of the narrative in the novel from this point on. As Burden reports at the end of the contemplation scene that takes place out West: "So there is innocence and a new start in the West, after all." [11] After a new start, Burden returns to participate in his established, geographic place as a sort of reformed character — a contributor to what the reader is led to hope may become a renewed South.

The dichotomy of this idea of going/returning is also often quite evident in Warren's poems. Two poems in particular from *New and Selected Poems* — "Arizona Midnight" and "Far West Once" — seem to reflect a desire on this southern poet's part to escape the burden of mortality and corruption during a period of self-imposed isolation on a journey West; a third poem, "Immortality Over the Dakotas," by contrast, seems to show the poet working out of that desire for isolation, toward a return to communion with his fellow beings. In most of his western poems, Warren as poet is alone with nature, contemplating its immensity, coming to terms with mortality and immortality, listening to the sound of his own inexpressibility. But the poet in the airplane of the poem "Immortality Over the Dakotas" — he who has seemed so convinced that he is beyond his fellow beings, so above — becomes by the end of the poem in some way answerable for the specific mortality of the imagined fellow on the ground. [12]

The fact that all the going and returning in these works may serve as metaphors for escape and renewal depends upon our observation that the characters do have, or have had at some point, a sense of geographic belonging. They have a homeland, even if it is an undesired or undesirable one. They are not in a state of geographic flux. One might well wonder about the impact that the incessant relocation of corporate America in the postmodern era may have begun to have upon American writers' traditional sense of place. It may be one thing to be the artistic outsider or observer in a place the writer knows well, or once did know well. The writer who goes away from a fixed point is probably still on solid ground. Mimetic fiction in particular needs a setting in which to take place — a kind of chosen atmosphere — and unless the genre in which one is working is fantasy, one cannot call a sense of place that which is really only a description of the labyrinths of the human mind.

In short, it is difficult to write about a geographic setting if one never did belong in it in the first place, and at the end of the twentieth century in America, there are more and more writers who never did belong. My own geographic biography, as the daughter of a man who worked for an aerospace corporation, is a case in point. My father started out on the line in the late thirties helping to build airplanes with a box of tools. A native Californian, as he always said, he moved our family to the treeless, mossy, flat stretches of Iceland when I was three, so that he could help build an airport in Keflavík. His company moved us again to Atlanta when I was five. We were not, then, by any means, truly southern — a debate that went on between me and the *real* southerners in my schoolroom until we moved to the San Francisco Bay Area at the end of my seventh grade.

Meanwhile, as my father was bringing me up on *his* family narratives from the West, my mother, a staunch New Englander, brought me up on *her* family narratives

that centered around the Connecticut/Massachusetts bor-
derline. My older sister was conceived in St. Paul and
brought forth in Seattle, but whenever she has had to fill
out the place of birth section on any form, there is no place
that lets her add that her parents only lived in her place of
birth for eighteen months. I myself was born in California,
as was my younger brother (*A rare California native!* people
would always say to us in a kind of awe), but only because
my gypsy parents happened to be passing through there
when they were on their way to somewhere else. By the
time my father got transferred to Northern California after
the stint in Georgia, I had to enter school right in the middle
of their junior high school — junior high school not being
something we Georgians had. I got transplanted to that
Sunnyvale bubble-gum-snapping, tight-skirted junior high
school as a prissy outsider who wore full skirts and rust-
colored lipstick and got taken by all the other California
imports for a southern belle. Four years later, I went off to
college in Oregon, then transferred back to Berkeley where
things were going on, but then trekked off to Switzerland
with all my worldly belongings and got a job. When I came
home to the United States, I landed in Massachusetts, and
from the letters I received in my mailbox on Boston's Fen-
way from all my mother's Massachusetts relatives that said,
Welcome home!, I suppose I should have felt once and for
all that I was on ancestral bluestocking territory and that
I was settling down. But by then I had grown used to that
question people inevitably ask each other the minute they
meet — *where are you from?* — and the truth was, very
simply, I didn't know.

And I still don't. Since getting married, I seem to have
displaced my formerly stationary native Californian husband also, so that we have now lived together in a total of

fourteen different houses in twenty-two years, in two foreign countries and six different states. So which "spirit of
place," out of all these geographic places, would D. H. Lawrence say belongs to me?

The question of place for many postmodern writers is
very much bound up with just these kinds of major and
frequent moves from east to west, even from continent to
continent, whether the moves are the result of family relocation by the corporation or of the *Siddhartha*-style migra-
tory moves one may go on making, as I have, out of a kind
of habit, an unconscious choice. (I'm referring here, of
course, to Hermann Hesse's *Siddhartha*, perhaps the most
influential novel of the sixties, as it justified an entire generation's collective need for the *Wanderjahr* and wanderlust.)
Maybe the only possible geographic setting for postmodern
American writers is going to be this not necessarily always
benign geographic flux. Our spirits of place may have become the islands of interstate highways, the observation
decks of airline terminals, the muffled interiors of automo-
biles, and the hard vinyl seats of Greyhound buses and
commuter trains. As the poet Carolyn Forché puts it, "For
non-Native Americans, America is a nation of exiles in
search of a homeland, and now that this need for homeland
has become interiorized, and is experienced as interior exile, the homeland sought has become figurative."[13]

But there may be some sort of unwritten limit to all this
coming and going, some *place* at which the American
writer must finally stop. Quite aside from the fact that a
writer needs to sit down in some place, any place, with a
typewriter, a table, and a chair at least long enough to produce a poem or a story (even if it's short), physical stillness
might also be considered both the outward manifestation
and the accompanying characteristic of a contemplative or

listening state of thought. The attitude of listening is one that may become more and more difficult for the writer in the postmodern era to sit down long enough to grasp. While futurists John Naisbett and Patricia Aburdene report in their *Megatrends 2000* that spirituality, along with a resurgence in the arts and literature, might be the order of the nineties, the stillness that makes room for spirituality must be present first.[14]

I have no idea where the answer for this postmodern evil as it affects the artist in particular may lie, but I think that we might begin to look for the answer in the kind of work the writer must do for a living. Since the question of place for the present-day writer in America, especially the minor one, cannot be separated from the need to have an income, the right kind of work might even provide another source of subject matter, if one adopts the quality of listening no matter where one is and if one is careful not to appropriate for fiction what does not belong.

The question of work is one that has been troubling writers for a long, long time. Unfortunately, despite some legitimate book-length attempts by writers to answer some of these questions about financial needs, such as *Starting from Scratch* by Rita Mae Brown, most employment that any writer undertakes outside writing is treated as a painful necessity, something that the writer does grudgingly and preferably part-time. I have a feeling that this attitude must change. The hard facts are that the unknown or minor writer's occupational identity has rarely been defined in the sole phrase, *I am a writer*. In all likelihood, the author who does not have what French critic Michel Foucault would call a name probably makes most of his or her income doing something else.[15] But having something else to do outside writing can give the minor writer a sort of protective shield of privacy for that awkward moment when the casual *So what do you do?* question inevitably comes up.

I was extremely grateful, for instance, after I went back to graduate school at the University of New Mexico some ten years ago to be able to tell people *I teach*, because this meant I did not have to answer the questions that inevitably follow the minor woman writer's statement, *I am a writer*, if that's all she does. The declaration *I am a writer* always leads the unsuspecting other person to the next response. The individual who has just posed the identity question *What do you do?* now wants the self-proclaimed author to define herself. *What sort of thing do you write?* the individual asks innocently. Then, *Have I heard of you? Has history recognized you? Do you possess a name?* And the minor writer must answer in all honesty, *No I don't.* I have learned that if I can avoid this conversation altogether I am better off.

I remember driving out into the countryside in San Diego County on a trip to California with my husband once and stopping on a crazy whim at a new housing development called the Something-or-Other Ranch. The minute we entered the clubhouse where the salespersons were housed, we both saw that we were in the wrong place, as this was obviously a housing development for the horsey and the rich and not for the lower to middle class. But we proceeded to write down our occupations anyway on the visitors' register, prompted by the beautifully groomed saleswoman's smooth request. The saleswoman looked down and saw that I'd written *Writer*. So she asked me politely, *Is it possible I might have read something that you wrote?* Then, of course, I had to answer, *I don't know.*

Do you read literary magazines? To which she, uncertain now what to do with either one of us, replied, *Not very often. No, I don't.*

I've come to believe that if I hadn't felt particularly stubborn about my identity as a writer at that time (this followed a long spate of rejection slips), I might not have subjected that basically innocent salesperson to what was really a sort of put-down of her on my part. I made the very bigoted assumption that, because she was well dressed and bejeweled, doing a money-making job, I was superior to her as a thinker, and she couldn't possibly have the depth of character to read. But if I truly thought that, I might just as well have written on the ranch's guest register, secretary (or salesclerk or free-lance journalist or telephone operator or whatever else it was I happened to be doing to make money at the time), and been done with it and not tried so hard. What did it matter whether this innocent stranger validated my unrecognized artistic suffering? In spite of her nice hairdo, suit, and flashy rings, she most probably had problems of her own. A little humility might have been in order. I didn't really need to tell that woman about my writer's persona, and I'm sorry now. I gave her a hard time. A willingness to accept a little anonymity can help others out.

For Plato in the *Republic*, the concepts of being and doing are inextricably linked. People are what they do. They are their work. But little-known writers are among the few people I know to have a split occupational identity — to in fact work twice. Writers, unless they repeatedly produce best-sellers or are independently wealthy, need to find jobs that at the very worst will not be detrimental to what they probably believe is their *real* work. And what they do in that case will most probably not be what they really are.

Yet what one chooses to do or must do to make the kind

of money that will pay the bills can still provide just enough of a living to leave time to write. An occupation outside writing may itself serve as a source of ideas for stories.

I've had plenty of menial occupations. As a result, most of my characters work, and I respect them for it. In fact, while Eudora Welty has said that she keeps plumbing the depths of her southern childhood for events and characters, I still find that I go back to sift through my reflections about those jobs. The main character in one of my published stories finds herself sitting one day in the waiting room of a Southern California telephone company personnel office, since she worked as a telephone operator near San Francisco during a summer once, and she needs a job. Ultimately, she gets up and leaves before the personnel director of the phone company comes to interview her because she remembers *all the Mr. Balls in the hall* during her summer job. Well, there really was a Mr. Ball during the summers I worked as a long-distance operator for Pacific Bell, and he and his career phone-company lookalikes really did frighten me enough to convince me that I wasn't ever going to stay in any one job, no matter what it was, for all my life. That experience was eventually put onto my fictional character, who goes on to sell junior sportswear at Joseph Magnin's, as I have also done.

My work experience seems, likewise, to have made me acutely aware of some of the characters in my reading who don't have to work. In her collection *The Burning House*, Ann Beattie hovers over her baby boom generation characters like a child who has invented a realistic twentieth-century dollhouse of her very own. She sells off their antiques, pushes the buttons that run their marvelous made-to-scale technological machines, and turns on their miniature stereos so that they can listen to Judy Collins's *Wildflowers* or

Bob Dylan's *Self-Portrait* or sixties' rock. Although it could very well be that what these characters *do* matters less to them than what they *are*, in a Platonic sense, I often find the ennui that results from their privileged leisure more spoiled than sad.

But the lack of characters with everyday occupations in Beattie's stories may be ironically linked to the question of authorial success. Often the work of a less well known writer, such as Anthony Stockanes's *Ladies Who Knit for a Living*, which won a University of Illinois Press short fiction award some years ago, seems to be laced unself-consciously with details from the various jobs the author has had to do in order to make a living. Even the title of Stockanes's collection shows the writer's commiseration in this particular human need. While he has himself never been a waitress (so that the question of appropriation of experience for the purposes of fiction again looms here), the character in the title story of the collection has the kind of job that allows him to frequent a working-class diner every day and thus to observe the waitress who works there. Perhaps Stockanes had a laborer's job that enabled him to go in to the diner and to meet the waitress and to listen to her as she talked. He writes, "The waitress, celery-green smock with carrot-orange pockets, orange insets on the sleeves, orange piping on the lapels, stands with boy hip canted, pencil poised over a small green pad with orange lettering. Between 'toast' and 'coffee' she always pushes a frizzy comma of cement-colored hair away from her eyes with her wrist. Then she always says, 'Juice?'" [16]

Stockanes may in the end prove to have been privileged in a special sense, in that through the very financial deprivation his status as a minor writer has caused him, he has had the opportunity to make the kind of participatory observations that a more materially successful writer cannot. I never had a waitress job, but I would think one could participate in the rest of humanity's conversation in that particular occupation fairly well, just as I think the job of parenting might be good (even required) working experience for someone who wants to write about children, whether that be in children's books or in fiction for adults.

Ultimately, the writer is at times a professional eavesdropper, if a kindly one, and work — the kind the rest of the world does most of the time without the option of writing about it — may provide the needed key. A Los Angeles writer once said in a talk I heard that he'd never been a bartender but that if he hadn't suddenly found himself with a movie contract for his novel (and ergo wealthy), he thought bartending would have been an excellent job because of the conversations he would have overheard. Likewise, since I was always good with hair, as my family put it, I occasionally considered going to beauty school (as they always called it), so that I could cut and blow dry all the Maudes' and Junes' and Jennys' and Elizabeths' hairdos and listen to their gossip to my heart's content. The Michigan writer Janet Kauffmann in her *Places in the World a Woman Could Walk* has in fact written a wonderful story, "The Alvordton Spa and Sweat Shop," in which the main character rejoices in the bizarre creations her friend, the "stylist," accomplishes on her hair while they talk and talk.[17]

All this jumping from one menial job to another that I seem to be supporting here only works, of course, if a writer can really participate on the job, can feel an equality with co-workers. The writer can be the observant outsider, perhaps, but without the feeling of having a superior vantage point. In any case, it is difficult to do this kind of menial work for very long and remain a snob. And the artistic rewards of this kind of work are too little talked about. Ingrained in my mind now, because I have heard and spoken it almost all my life, is what Wordsworth — who did not do for a living in the sense I'm advocating here — longingly referred to as the "language of conversation of the lower to middle class."[18] At its best, any higher education the writer with working-class roots eventually acquires can help that writer to mediate between the academy, as it is called, and the fictional characters that the working-class writer is capable of creating from a real, lived past.

But if the writer finds the jobs of secretary, telephone operator, salesclerk, or beautician a challenge to self-esteem, there are other jobs that may, while offering the needed monetary compensation, also offer the ideas and some leisure with which to write. Up until maybe forty years ago, one of the most obvious jobs for an American who wanted to write but who needed to work was newspaper reporting. Ernest Hemingway, Sherwood Anderson, Willa Cather, Katherine Anne Porter, and any number of other American writers of this century made their living at writing newspaper copy. Much of Hemingway's work is peppered with tidbits he got as a free lance for the *Toronto Star*.[19] And it is generally agreed that the narrator-journalist in Sherwood Anderson's *Winesburg, Ohio* is Anderson himself. Willa Cather's feature articles and reviews, while they contain little resemblance to events of her fiction, suggest that her journalistically learned talent for research and her involvement in the small-town atmosphere she had to cover for her newspaper certainly gave her subject matter, while deepening her sense of place.[20] Katherine Anne Porter's main character in *Pale Horse, Pale Rider* gets her start at the local paper during World War I writing advice to the lovelorn.

Margaret Walker, the author of *Jubilee*, eventually went

into university teaching, but she first toyed longingly for a while with the idea of making a living at newspaper work. She reflects in *How I Wrote "Jubilee"*:

> [In 1939] . . . I decided I must go back to Graduate School and work towards a Master's degree in English so that I could go South and teach in college. I wanted more than anything else to write, but as my father warned me, I would have to eat if I wanted to live, and writing poetry would not feed me. I knew from experience that I would not make a good newspaperwoman, and I could not free-lance in the bohemian world. Both worlds produce excellent writers, but by then it was clear that with three generations of forebears who had taught school, I was not going to be able to escape my traditional academic background. (I have now been in the teaching harness for twenty-seven years and as much as I love the profession I have always rationalized that it was only a means to an end, since the chief goal of my life was to be a writer.)[21]

Walker chose teaching instead of writing newspaper copy, just as many writers, with the added option of the university creative writing programs, do today. But journalism is still a viable occupation for a fiction writer or poet.

In any case, newspaper work happens to be one way to make a living that I know a lot about. When I came home from my secretary's job in Switzerland to a job as a copy-kid (an all-around errand runner) for the *Christian Science Monitor* in Boston, I also began to write free-lance feature articles for the paper on the side. I poured my off-work hours into writing articles about draft counselors, Vietnamese boat people, and the injustices of nuclear waste, suddenly dreaming (after having actually gone to bed hungry in Geneva several times) that one day I might be a foreign correspondent. But the fatherly British editor who befriended me gently observed out loud that my bent (as he lovingly called it) was a bit too literary and that the chances of my becoming a foreign correspondent were already a little slim anyway since I was not a man. I have ended up being grateful for that advice, since it kept me from seeking an exciting career just at the point in my life when I was the most vulnerable to that kind of occupational success. *Foreign correspondent* sounded to me at twenty like intrigue, danger, adventure, travel, and renown. But this kind of career journalism can be in itself all-consuming, leaving no time for a serious commitment to writing or to any other art. One can get very accustomed to seeing one's name in print, even when it isn't at the top of a short story or a poem, and thus settle for what one knows is not what one really wants to write. That's a very subtle danger that a fiction writer or poet can't overlook.

I finally learned to distinguish between this kind of full-time career journalism that becomes the only writing that one does and a good old clumsy newspaper job, preferably a part-time or free-lance one at that. When my husband and I settled in the Berkshires a few years later, the pre–foreign correspondent copykidding experience on my résumé got me another job that I am not through plumbing the possibilities of even yet.

As a regular features writer and photographer for a local weekly, I was charged to write at least one magazine-length story a week either about the locals or about the various new-to-the-area characters who had come to the Berkshires because, like me, they thought it would be a pretty place to do their creative work. Though I had some definite points of difference with the editor, the job itself seemed cut out for me just then. For one thing, I could set my own hours. If I overproduced feature articles for a while, I could bend the truth a little and call in to say I was working at home. I was in fact working at home, but I was writing fiction at my desk and not the cover story for the tabloid of two weeks from then.

It was at least in part through the required research into the lives of the locals that I began to get a sense of place that hasn't left me yet. In discussing *Ethan Frome*, Edith Wharton says of the Berkshires, where we lived, "In those days the snow-bound villages of Western Massachusetts were still grim places, morally and physically; insanity, incest and slow mental and moral starvation were hidden away behind the paintless wooden house-fronts of the long village street, or in the isolated farm-houses on the neighboring hills; and Emily Brontë would have found as savage tragedies in our remoter valleys as on her Yorkshire moors."[22] In my traveling from one end of Berkshire County to the other, I came to know the "insanity, incest and slow mental and moral starvation" of those "grim places" firsthand.

One day I took the company van to interview an old man who claimed to have found an ancient Indian civilization in a creek bed in his backyard. *Go humor this old geezer*, my boss told me, *because he reads our stuff.* When I arrived at the old man's bleak, makeshift shack, his wife showed me into the kitchen. Her long, uncombed black-and-gray hair hung down loosely over her all-black dress. An enormous black cat sat on the kitchen table, to which it was attached by a heavy chain. Surrounding the cat were stacks and stacks of dollar bills, thousands of them, and by my quick estimate I knew, even if those were all one-dollar bills, that was a lot of cash. I suddenly felt that, having come to do an interview about some questionably ancient Indian rocks, I had instead walked into something else — something dangerous and illicit. Gambling? Witchcraft? Drugs? Meanwhile, though it was mid-February — *cold* in a region where the winter regularly lasts a full nine months — big, black, nasty flies buzzed at the plastic that had been tacked to the kitchen windows over the sweating glass. Something moist, odorous, and hot was hidden somewhere in that house. I was scared.

A short while later, while the old man was showing me the rocks that he'd supposedly found in an ancient site (and that I could see for myself had been scratched and engraved with children's crayons to look like artifacts), two very large, pale teen-age boys came inside from an underground cave that served as their quarters behind the house. For the first twenty minutes of my stay there, I had been hearing the steady *dum dum dum* of heavy metal rock. Learning that I was a newspaper reporter, the two boys decided I had to be some kind of celebrity and therefore rich. They kept looking back and forth at each other as they asked me, *You make a lot of money as a newspaper writer, huh? Bet you make a lot of money doing this?* I swore up and down that I didn't (it was the truth), as I scribbled bogus notes about the ancient Indian civilization in my trusty stenographer's notebook with a shaking hand.

As soon as I could, I told the old man that I was finished with the details, adding, *Thank you very much my editor will get back to you very soon*, and I ran down the hill to the company van I had borrowed for the day. I was convinced that if I hadn't repeated my litany over and over into the unseeing vacuity of those two boys' faces — *The newspaper knows I'm up here, the newspaper, you see, has loaned me their van to drive up here, and they are therefore expecting me, you see, they will notice if I disappear or if I am late or don't return the van* — I would not have escaped from that place of "insanity, incest and slow mental and moral starvation" with my life.

I could be wrong, of course. I probably am. But while I have never been able to write that particular incident up as fiction, the sheer terror I felt that day gave me the sense of place for a story that was eventually published. My experience on that job in the Berkshires convinced me that there really were witches and ghosts and hobgoblins in Nathaniel Hawthorne's Berkshire woods and that I knew them well enough to write them down. Because of the way I made my living, I also became a better reader of that place.

Part of that particular sense of place, as it has been presented by Berkshire writers such as Hawthorne, Melville, and Wharton (all of whom, like me, were more or less imports from some other place), has always included what I believe Victor Hugo may have meant by the word *grotesque*. In his preface to *Cromwell*, Hugo declares that his new character will be both grotesque and sublime. He assumes that we know the term *sublime* through a familiarity with Longinus's *On the Sublime*, but he tells us that the grotesque separates *les modernes* from *les anciens*. The grotesque takes two forms, he says. It is either that which is deformed and horrible, like the gargoyles on the spires of the cathedral at Rouen, or it is all that is weirdly funny, as in some of the minor demonic figures in an otherwise harmless painting by Rubens. Hugo suggests that the grotesque grows mainly out of the romantic sense of *mélancolie*, as a direct result of the *pitié* inspired by Christianity in the modern period (his own romantic period), the third of the three eras he schematizes for humankind.[23]

Hugo's grotesque seems particularly applicable to the

Berkshire writers' sense of place, in that his grotesque is closely linked with a sense of derision or of *ironie*, not necessarily as it is directed at the dramatic character in question but as it points to the absurdity of his universal *condition humaine*. It is perhaps only within the context of this irony that one can ever succeed in discussing the sort of mindless evil I imagined in the kitchen of that Berkshire hovel — the kind of gross, ignorant cruelty with which most people have no idea quite how to deal.

In his preface to *The Aspern Papers*, which contained the shorter piece "The Turn of the Screw," Henry James, also a Berkshire writer of a sort, specifically discusses the difficulty of describing and dealing with evil in the text. He writes, "What, in the last analysis, had I to give the sense of? Of their being, the haunting pair, capable . . . of everything — that is of exerting, in respect to the children, the very worst action small victims so conditioned might be conceived as subject to. What would *be* then, on reflexion, this utmost conceivability?" James concludes that he finally cannot describe his particular evil and still necessarily convince the reader of the horror that he glimpsed. He decides that he must describe the evil in general enough terms so that, in the end, the particular horror invented is the reader's own. As James puts it:

> There is for such a case no eligible *absolute* of the wrong; it remains relative to fifty other elements, a matter of appreciation, speculation, imagination — these things moreover quite exactly in the light of the spectator's, the critic's, the reader's experience. Only make the reader's general vision of evil intense enough . . . and his own experience, his own imagination, his own sympathy (with the children) and horror (of their false friends) will

supply him quite sufficiently with all the particulars. Make him *think* the evil, make him think it for himself, and you are released from weak specifications.[24]

Or as a postmodernist theoretician might more succinctly put it, we must problematize the subject. The evil is identified not with the character but with itself.

My job on the weekly was not without its bizarre accents of humor, though. I would much prefer here to speak of humor as good, clean fun — the kind of humor that provides for me, in real life, what one aspirin a day seems to provide for others. That kind of humor is the raft that I hold on to with my fingernails when I'm about to go under, the laugh that keeps me alive, my saving grace. But as a writer I have found that humor, while it may be abundant in the spontaneous events of my hourly life, is far more difficult to bring out in the carefully created world of fiction than it is in life.

At one point while I was working for the tabloid, I had an assignment that allowed me to do a little investigative reporting, even if I knew that I wasn't ever going to be a foreign correspondent. The town library — an old, staid institution whose circulating books still bore the signatures of local noteworthies from earlier times — had reported that several rare books and some salt shakers that had once belonged to Nathaniel Hawthorne had been stolen from a glass display case. The entire affair was written up in the daily paper (both the daily paper and the weekly were owned and operated by the same family) as a question of big city disrespect for little country folks. The local police had complained to the daily paper that they'd found the identity of the books-and-shakers robber, but that when they had told the New York City police that the thief had gone there to sell the items, the New York City police had let this small-town robber get away, because our little town in the Berkshires didn't matter in the overall Big Apple scheme of things. Donning my sunglasses and the new London Fog raincoat I had just purchased on a bus trip to Boston (in order to write a how-to-go-to-Boston-for-the-day travel article for the local folks), I began my investigation. I also had my editor's blessing: *Go out there and find out what these local idiots are really doing and show 'em up!*

First, I called up the local police department and asked to speak with the police chief, just to get my facts straight before starting out. The police chief's name was spelled R-o-m-e-o. I'd already noted that in the phone book and on local voting posters there were Romeos living and running for office all over Berkshire County, north and south, but since I didn't know anyone from the vast branches of this family (insanity, incest, starvation?), I'd never heard the name pronounced aloud. So I was careful to pronounce the police chief's name the way (since I spoke Italian) it looked to me. *Ro-MAY-o*, I said nicely into the telephone, with the accent on the second syllable. *May I speak to Chief Ro-MAY-o*, I politely asked.

The police officer on the other end of the line chuckled, but soon Chief Romeo himself came on the phone. *Yeah? What is this? I already talked to the paper.*

I began my conversation with a greeting I thought polite. *Good morning, Chief Ro-MAY-o, this is . . .*

But the chief interrupted me. *RO-me-o*, he said. *RO-me-o. It's pronounced RO-me-o. You got it wrong.*

Ah, yes, I said. *Excuse me. Yes. Of course. Romeo. Romeo.* (And, *wherefore art thou, Romeo*, was what I thought.)

I then asked Chief *RO-me-o* my questions. But after getting the facts from the police chief, I began to see that something was missing. Did Police Chief Romeo know, I asked, that his story didn't quite fit with the one the New York State police had just given me? And why hadn't the chief talked to the alleged thief's girlfriend, who lived around the corner from the police department and who had just told me over the phone that her boyfriend would be coming back from New York City that very night?

After a few more of my questions, the police chief let me know he didn't have any more time for the likes of me. And anyway, he said, he'd already told it all to the daily paper. *You go read the paper*, he told me. *It's those New York City police guys. They got too much to do down there t' bother 'bout some ole books and salt shakers. Those guys down there got killers and drug dealers, not just yer petty stuff.*

Then he hung up on me.

In the end, after a few calls to the rare book store in New York where the thief had managed to sell the stolen goods and after a few conversations with both the New York City and New York State police, I found that what in fact had happened was that the local police, apparently unaware of the writ of habeas corpus and not wanting to work over the weekend (the robbery had occurred on a Friday night), hadn't asked the New York City police to make the official arrest of the thief in question within the required statute of limitations of three days. Therefore, the police in New York City had to let him out.

I decided to confirm this with Chief Romeo.

The police officer who answered put his hand over the telephone and called out with a laugh to Chief Romeo, *Hey, Chief, it's Police Reporter!*

Police Chief Romeo told the officer to tell me he was too busy to talk right now.

When my story came out in the weekly, reporting that

the police department had let this clever New York robber get away, it was determined that the weekly, always a poor cousin until now, had scooped the daily. The summer people who lived in New York City loved it. *I laughed and laughed*, one summer resident wrote me in one of my rare pieces of fan mail as a reporter. *That was really great!*

But the locals weren't quite so happy with my scoop. *This is a small town*, one resident told me soberly. *You can't just go around telling the truth like that and expect to stay around town afterward yourself with nothing changed.*

The investigation did in fact have its frightening consequences, in that the police, offended by the story, let me know that if I ever got in trouble, *Lady, don't call us, you're on your own.* And they proved to be as good as their word, when they shrugged off the dead body that a walker discovered on the forest trail behind our house.

The scary part of this experience, if coupled with the wisecrack reactions of both the summer people and the locals to my small-town investigative piece, provided the possibility for the kind of discontinuance, or juxtaposition of the ludicrous with the serious, that the nineteenth-century critic William Hazlitt may have been talking about in his *Lectures on the English Comic Writers*.[25] But this kind of humor, which, like Faulkner's humor in *The Rievers*, focuses on a small-town mentality and a kind of local-color sense of place, poses an ethical question of its own. It is generally assumed that the lost "second book" of Aristotle's *Poetics* contained a lengthy explanation of humor, the moral of which was that being funny in literature usually means that someone is being mocked. Umberto Eco pursues the traces of Aristotle's second book to a monastery in northern Europe during the Dark Ages in *The Name of the Rose*, and the consequences of that moral conflagration have become well known. But Aristotle has left us, in his discussion of *eutrapelia*, or ready wit, in the *Nichomachean Ethics*, at least the broad frontiers of an ethics of laughter, when he writes, "In agreeableness in social amusement the man who hits the mean is 'witty' and what characterizes him is 'wittiness.' The excess is 'buffoonery' and the man who exhibits that is a 'buffoon.' The opposite of the buffoon is the 'boor' and his characteristic is 'boorishness.'"[26] For Aristotle, the *eutrapelos*, or humanely humorous man, is the one who can successfully strike the difficult balance, or mean, between buffoonery and stolidity — the one who can, in keeping with the Aristotelian concept of catharsis, provoke an audience to purge itself of its vices through the laughter that is a direct result of ready wit.

In other words, in order to put Chief Romeo into fiction on Aristotle's ethical basis, I would have to find something in my readers — and in myself — that deserved to be purged through ready wit. I would have to include myself as the butt of the joke. Otherwise, I would be mocking my fellow humans — making myself superior to them — through my so-called wit. The truth was that both Chief Romeo and I were capable of painting ourselves into a corner in order to avoid a little work. The shared element of human fallibility just may allow humor in fiction to be humane.

Jean-Jacques Rousseau, in *Reveries of the Solitary Walker*, lets us see what he thinks of laughter on the whole, and he does not suggest that he believes in any kind of Aristotelian mean. He says that the Other's humor — the Other's laughter at Rousseau's expense — has given him the moral stance of the victim, because this humor mocks. Rousseau positions himself as the universal victim. "The most sociable and loving of men," he writes, "has with one accord been cast out by all the rest."[27] The reader becomes increasingly uncomfortable with this messianic stance, as Rousseau stakes out his territory and claims to be the one who is universally shunned by all others and who, although blameless himself, is willing not only to suffer for the sins of his mockers but to forgive them all.

A writer will probably have less time for this kind of self-indulgence if he or she has to work. If small-town investigative reporting isn't available on a full- or part-time basis, then free-lance book reviewing is also an avocation that the writer might consider doing for a while.

Shortly after my husband and I moved to Albuquerque, with our daughter just four at the time, I turned my skills as a reader, along with the ability I'd learned in features writing to keep my sentences small and tight, into the work of book reviewing. Book reviewing of fiction and poetry, at least as it appears in most newspapers, is a job that has fallen onto people who write fiction and poetry themselves, rather than to academic critics who may be more interested in the kind of reviewing that allows them to explore theoretical and philosophical questions to the full extent. I began to review new fiction in Albuquerque at a time when there was an enormous need — one might say even an odd kind of market — for free-lance book reviewers in the West. I found out only after going back to graduate school that I happened to have been in good company. Poe's now-legendary coining of the specific genre of the short story as the "brief prose tale" was at its inception a book review of Nathaniel Hawthorne's *Twice-Told Tales*. Flannery O'Connor's *The Presence of Grace and Other Book Reviews*, a collection of reviews she wrote for *Commonweal*, presents a devout Catholic's incisive comments on the complicated question of trying to be true both to one's most cherished inner beliefs and to one's art. And Louise Bogan's *A Poet's*

Alphabet, a collection that spans over forty years of her reviews in the *New Yorker*, begins to offer us almost a working basis for defining greatness in contemporary literature as new works come out.[28]

Considered thoughtfully, the job of what I came to call reading for a living can give the writer a basis for working out a personal theory of writing, because theory is exactly what is at work when one contemplates with any degree of depth the question of what one does or doesn't like. But the book reviewer who also writes creative prose or poetry has a special obligation, since he or she knows the labor involved in the act of writing, to present this working theory with a special tact. The book review is no place for the smart comment, however clever the reviewer's purple prose may be. That way of writing, if we are to believe Edith Wharton, who herself wrote any number of reviews, belongs only to a "subjective class" of critics — those to whom "writing is no sacred, no reverend employment." Those kinds of reviews, she says, are "often mere records of impressions."[29]

In the reviews I've written, I have tried to do what I finally found myself doing for students in fiction workshops and what I have come to appreciate from decent editors, even in rejection letters, and that is to try to make helpful comments, in the case of what I might have considered a failed novel or short story collection or book of poems, as to why, for me anyway, that particular project did not quite work. Reviews don't really need to hurt in order to do their job.

I have always been particularly touched when I have come across a reaction from a writer to what he or she apparently considered an unjust review. When Sainte-Beuve wrote his vicious attack on Gustave Flaubert, Flaubert's close friend and mentor George Sand rushed to his side in a letter, as she usually did. She admonished him to ignore the comments, which she considered not only merciless but inaccurate as well, and she urged him not to be distracted from his writing goal:

> L'artiste est un explorateur que rien ne doit arrêter et qui ne fait ni bien ni mal de marcher à droite ou à gauche, son but sanctifie tout. C'est à lui de savoir, après un peu d'expérience, quelles sont les conditions de santé de son âme.[30]

> The artist is an explorer whom nothing can stop, and who accomplishes nothing by going first to the right and then to the left; his goal justifies everything. It is up to him to know, after a little experimentation [in the sense of trying out], what are the healthy conditions of his soul. (translation mine)

Sainte-Beuve accomplished nothing with Flaubert as far as suggesting changes in his writing. What then was the point of all that caustic rage on Sainte-Beuve's part? Maybe a little artistic envy was at work. In the end, it may not be enough, in an ethical or humanly communal sense, to be working out some kind of theory that excludes any possibility of dialogue between reader/critic and writer — a theory that says, in effect, *Here's what I think of your book, you fool, and there's nothing else.*

The question of brutal reviews, and their effect on the author, is made even more relative when we consider Maurice Blanchot's implied theory that the act of reading and the act of writing provide two aspects of what is essentially the same act. Such a theory would have the reader/critic actually performing an act of self-destruction in the cruel review. Blanchot admits he cannot help feeling wounded by harsh criticism of his work. In a discussion of the writer's or artist's bitterness that his or her work will be subjected to a casual reading or glance, he comments, "Such effort, such sacrifice, such calculation, a life of solitude, centuries of meditation and seeking — all this is appraised, judged and annihilated by the ignorant decision of the first person to come along, by a chance mood."[31]

Hurt feelings aside, the reader/critic might argue, sometimes a work is bad enough to deserve what may amount to a scathing review. History may eventually vindicate the worth of misjudged works by a Flaubert, a Sand, or a Blanchot, this reasoning goes, but certainly not every book printed by commercial publishers these days is great — or even good. What does the writer/reviewer do with all the honestly poorly written books he or she may get?

Once I became trusted by a book editor as a reviewer, I received any number of books with a hasty slip attached that said, *Let me know if you think you want to review.* Eventually, it came down to a kind of choice. I've come to believe that unless a book is downright pornographic — not in any proscriptive moral sense (such as that tied up with the debate over funding for the NEA in recent years) but in the sense of being written so stupidly on purpose that it denies even the intelligence of its intended reader — the best review I can give is a silent one. I learned to turn down books for this reason, knowing that my remarks weren't going to change the writer's apparent will to make a living (even get rich quick) through the exploitation of bigotry or lust. By choosing not to review it, I was in some small way denying it recognition, even though that be done in a Texas-newspaper-omission sort of way.

I don't mean to suggest that just anyone can start reviewing books for a living. A recent *Writer's Market* — despite all its articles on point of view and character, on poetry and fiction and articles markets, and even despite its several listings of places where one can sell Valentine's Day doggerel to the makers of greeting cards — for some reason didn't even mention book reviews. Perhaps that's because they know how hard it is to build up a clientele. The mechanics may look simple enough. The writer talks the local paper into letting him or her do one review, then sends fifty photocopies of the published review, along with fifty letters of introduction, out to newspapers that boast a circulation of the next biggest size. Two or three of those answer . . . and up and up.

But reviewing as a way to earn a living, especially if the reviewer also writes poetry or fiction, has its drawbacks. For one thing, if one is good at it, one may become too busy writing reviews to have time to write anything else. Or one may become well known — one may gain a name — as a reviewer, instead of for the work one is much more passionate about. Then one may find oneself in sympathy with someone like, say, Sainte-Beuve, chopping away at other writers out of one's own sour grapes.

By the time I came to graduate school at the University of Michigan, I had been writing two to three book reviews a week for various newspapers around the country for about four years. I was at the point where blurbs from my reviews appeared on the jacket of the author's second book. In the meantime, I had continued to write my stories and to send them off and to publish them at what I've since learned is considered a fairly decent rate. (The National Endowment for the Arts, as a rule of thumb, currently requires that in order to be eligible for a fiction grant a short story writer must have published at least five stories in three different journals over the last ten years.) One day a visiting writer looked up at me when he heard my name and said, *Hmmm. Gail Gilliland. There's a critic who calls herself by that name. Could that be you?* My name had begun to be known in connection with written work I had only taken on to support my other writing. My name as a fiction writer had been usurped by my need of winning bread. And that, for this short story writer anyway, was a bit too much. I quit reviewing completely for a little while.

As a final drawback to reviewing for a living, one need only look at the financial end of things. The pay for a single review is usually quite minimal, even if one's fiction or poetry is widely enough published that one can eventually work up to doing an occasional short review for the *New York Times*. Obviously, there are only so many reviews any one book editor is going to want to print by the same reviewer. Then, too, most editors pay on publication — a practice I found very hard on our finances. I remember one month in Albuquerque when we had second notices on all our credit cards and I could count that I had written, but not been paid for, $1,300 worth of book reviews. At $75 to $100 each, that's too many reviews for any one human being to have written in a single month. It was during one of those three-to-five-book weeks that I happened to go into the English Department of the University of New Mexico to talk. *God, Gail*, the professor who became my mentor said when I told him what I'd been doing. *Three to five books a week plus your own stuff?* He promised me a job teaching freshman composition, tuition toward a Masters in English, and time to write. All I had to do was decide to teach.

But teaching — especially as it applies to the creative writing workshop — can cause its problems for a writer, too. Teaching doesn't provide the same kind of participation in a world of diverse people that other kinds of employment can provide. (Nor, I suppose one could once again argue, does reviewing books.) In the end, work — the kind that may make for dirty fingernails and sweaty armpits and quickly spent paychecks, the kind in which the phony persona of being a writer is challenged every time the minor writer has to stare at his or her own unmasked reflection in the boss's eyes — makes for good poems and stories, not only in terms of helping the uprooted American writer to gain a sense of place but in terms of providing an active participation, a dialogue with other members of the human race, most of whom also have to work at something other than writing to earn their pay.

7

Diction

Searching High and Low for the Common Man

. . . .

In the fall of 1985 I took a ride down the Seine in a Bateau Mouche with my seventy-five-year-old mother-in-law, who was visiting Europe for the first time in her life, wearing her Rockports and raincoat. Though I felt the Seine ride was an excursion almost exclusively taken by tourists, I managed to marginalize myself from that group of foreign-city consumers according to the following criteria:

- I lived here once. That makes me superior to these tourists, who have not.

- I speak French. That makes me not only separate from these others but even perhaps superior to them, especially when most of the others are Americans, and everybody knows that Americans rarely speak anything other than English.

- I, of course, would not normally lower myself to take this tourist excursion, but I have to, in order to keep peace in the family. Therefore, I am once again superior to these other people, because their motive for taking this trip is not a moral one, like mine. They are only taking this trip to have some fun.

Both my self-conscious self-marginalization on the boat trip and Christo's gold silk "wrapping" of the Pont-Neuf which I then saw (apologetically getting great shots of it with my Kodak Instamatic from underneath) I now believe in a very real way are indicative of an unattractive intellectual exclusivity that is strangely peculiar to the postmodern age. This conclusion may seem altogether startling if one accepts the premise that the single most important ethical drive of the postmodern period has been to democratize everything from foreign travel to art. But this new democratization must be seen to stem from the romantics' love affair with their concept of what they uniformly termed the *common man* — a desire that nevertheless had an entrenched definition of an opposing Self and Other at its heart.

When Wordsworth stated, in his "Advertisement" for the *Lyrical Ballads* of 1798, that the poems he and Coleridge included in the volume were "experiments written to ascertain how far the language of conversation in the middle and lower classes of society is adapted to the purposes of poetic pleasure," he was proposing a theory that was apparently revolutionary to the historical literary preference for high and great character and diction over low.[1] But the literary dispute over the use and abuse and/or boundaries of high and low begins at least as early as Aristotle, who in a characteristic attempt to be balanced in all matters, calls for a "mixed diction." He tells us in the *Poetics*, "What we need is a mixed diction. On the one hand, the use of unusual, metaphorical, ornamental words . . . avoids commonness and colloquialism; current vocabulary, on the other hand, makes for clarity. Lucid yet noncolloquial language results in large part from using nouns in lengthened, shortened, or altered forms, for these, while avoiding the colloquial by being unusual, yet remain near enough the usual to retain clarity."[2] Although Aristotle is giving us here, through his expected mean, the basis for an argument for a literary diction that, while heavy with metaphor and "ornamental words," is still close enough to the "usual" to "retain clarity," he can by no means be seen to be advocating a language of poetry that derives from the language of the common man. He is clearly calling to beware of "ordinary language," even while he warns against exclusivity in language — against a literature that would prefer one class of readership over another.

Likewise, when Horace claims in his *Ars Poetica* that "my aim shall be a poem so moulded of common materials that all the world may hope as much for itself," he by no means wants to identify his as a common voice. Horace goes on to imply that the process by which he will "mould" his poem of "common materials" will make the poem appear deceptively easy, so that "all the world may hope as much for itself, may toil hard, and yet toil in vain if it attempts as much: such is the potency of order and arrangement; with such dignity may things of common life be clothed." Thus, while Horace may admit finding the germ for his poem in "common materials," in "things of common life," his genius as a poet is to order and arrange these things with a dignity that will elevate them beyond the common life. His diction, we are given to understand, will not be common, because he plainly says, "I shall not be content with the plain nouns and verbs of common life."[3]

It is probably safe to say that most of the early theoretical discussion about diction, even when it appears not to want to exclude certain readers through a contrived level of language, still assumes that the language of poetry is on a higher plane than the language of the common man. Even a literary voice as disparate as that of the Christian apostle Paul appears to accept this assumption, when, after delivering a sermon in what was considered the straightforward language of his time, he repeats the same message to his listeners in a language he clearly considers to be on a higher plane, referring to the diction of "certain of your own poets."[4]

But if William Wordsworth was perhaps one of the first to attempt to say that the language of poetry and the language of the common man could sometimes be the same, Samuel Coleridge concluded in his well-documented split with him that Wordsworth failed to define, and so, perhaps more important for Coleridge, to place even imagined limits upon, exactly what he meant by the "language of conversation." Ideally, such a language would have to deal with three main areas of everyday speech — with subject matter, diction, and cadence. While Wordsworth's theory clearly proposes a departure from "what is usually called poetic diction," he seems in practice to limit his own revolution to the question of subject matter and not to alter to a great degree either the diction or the traditional metric patterns of his poems.[5]

For instance, the subject matter of the poem "Simon Lee" may be in keeping with Wordsworth's plan, in that we hear of the life of a poor rural character who must continue to labor even though he is old and ill, but the tale is obviously told by an educated, genteel observer — a sort of well-dressed country squire off for a Sunday stroll in the woods, who comes upon some charming little people of the lower class and essentially impersonates them in a poem so that people of his elevated station in life might appreciate them more. There is as yet really no revolutionary change in the diction of the poem. The narrator records the history of the Other from a plane apart — and maybe even from a plane above. We still have the very literary convention, "My gentle reader," and the educated inversions of subject and verb, as in "He all the country could outrun," as well as the use of genteel words like "ere."[6]

Occasionally, Wordsworth carries through his "experiment" to some degree when he clearly delineates or admits his role as narrator and allows the Other (albeit within quotation marks) to speak. We see this begin to work in the poem "We Are Seven." When the narrator first sets the scene for the poem, his diction is that of the educated observer. In his polite address of the child as "Little Maid" and "Sweet Maid," and in his use of the subjunctive form of the verb, as in "How many may you be?," he sets himself apart from her in class. However, when the child herself is allowed to speak, we begin to hear an appropriate (if appropriated) simplicity of diction in her voice, as in the insistent, oft-repeated refrain of the title itself, "We are Seven."

Yet even when Wordsworth lets the child speak for herself, his experiment in language ultimately falls short of our expectations because of the demands of the meter and rhyme scheme on the persona of the Other he would take on. The child ends by employing Wordsworth's own, more complex diction at times, as when she says, "So in the churchyard she was laid," in place of the much simpler (and, I would assume, more authentic), "We laid her in the churchyard." Also, the child reports, "Together round her grave we played," instead of the more common, "We played together around her grave."[7]

Wordsworth appears to have begun a revolution, in terms of expanding the subject matter of literature beyond the great subject matter systematically argued by neoclassicists such as Pierre Corneille. In "Three Discourses on the Dramatic Poem," Corneille had taken the Aristotelian idea of pity and expanded it, telling us that the falling of two characters (and he named Rodrigue and Chimène from his play *Le Cid*) was only justifiable when this pity could make us afraid we might fall into a like situation: "Cette pitié nous doit donner une crainte de tomber dans un pareil malheur, et purger en nous ce trop d'amour qui cause leur infortune, et nous les fait plaindre."[8] Corneille's use of *nous*, the we, assumed that the viewer or reader was as aristocratic as the characters in the play and could identify with them. "We" might feel an excess of romantic love that would make "us" forget our "higher" duties. He insisted that characters were only dignified by their inner conflict between romantic passion and their greater interest in the state, between love and some more noble passion such as ambition or revenge. To be a *major* character, according to Corneille, one must be above common human desires. One must be, or behave, like royalty.

If Wordsworth seems at first to be going beyond this treatment of noble characters to finally include the common man, he left to his poetic successors the task of questioning the necessity for employing existing forms of rhyme and meter. For one thing, he neglected to deal with at least one very important aspect of the "language of conversation" — the inherent cadence of this common voice.

Some fifty years after Wordsworth's "Preface," Walt Whitman again took up the question of the appropriateness of the language of the common man. As with Wordsworth, subject matter was at the base of Whitman's new theory of poetics. Whitman wrote in his preface to *Leaves of Grass* that the "genius" of the United States lay "always most in the common people," in "the fluency of their speech." In terms almost precursory to French postmodern linguistic theories about signs and signifiers, he aligned speech with the significance of democratic gesture ("The

President's taking off his hat to them not they to him") and saw in the combined diction and gesture of the common people an "unrhymed poetry."[9] His theory of "unrhymed poetry" translated, in practice, into what must be seen as one of the earliest examples of what we have come to call free verse.

Whitman recognized, as Wordsworth apparently had not, that if the subject matter in a new poetry taken from the common people were to differ from earlier literary convention, allowing for a language hitherto only heard in oral ballads or in the lines of popular poets like Robert Burns, the dropping of formal metric patterns would be necessary to release the poet to record the natural cadences of common speech. But if in giving us free verse Whitman released further possibilities for a poetry that would reflect the genius of the common people, it can hardly be said that the poems in *Leaves of Grass* succeed in employing their diction. This may be due in part to the fact that Whitman's narrator is the personal *I*, who, like Wordsworth, is only a fascinated observer outside the Other's life. Whitman rarely lets the common people speak for themselves, as Wordsworth seemed instinctively to know he would have to do. So while in Whitman we occasionally hear the actual patterns of common speech, such as "Where are you off to, lady?" in "Song of Myself," the emphasis is on a higher diction — Whitman's own. His is a song of myself indeed and not a song of the Other.[10]

A somewhat successful combination of the simple subject matter of the common man, a diction more native to a still untutored voice and the free-verse cadence of spoken speech, does not in fact seem to occur in America until the poetry of Robert Frost. In his preface to *A Way Out*, Frost speaks of "the speaking tone of voice somehow entangled in the words and fastened to the page for the ear of the imagination. That is all that can save poetry from sing-song, all that can save prose from itself." Though Frost was perhaps less apt to propose, as had Wordsworth and Whitman, a formal theory of his poetics, he nevertheless often spoke publicly and in letters to interested friends of the "sound of sense." In a letter to John Bartlett he writes of a sound that is even at times independent of meaning but which always depends on the cadence of the spoken voice. "The best place to get the abstract sound of sense," he says, "is from voices behind a door that cuts off the words." Two years later he writes to William Stanley Braithwaite in more detail, as though in the meantime he has been further working out this "sound of sense" for himself, "We must go out into the vernacular for tones that haven't been brought to book. We must write with the ear on the speaking voice. We must imagine the speaking voice."[11] Still, Frost is recording the voice of another, an overheard sound that the poet will deliver for someone else.

The language of the common man is at last evident in poems such as "The Death of the Hired Man," in that in this poem Frost removes his own voice to let the common man speak for himself. In doing so (this time without Wordsworth's quotation marks), Frost achieves not only the inclusion of the common man's subject matter but also the appropriate simplicity of his diction and the actual spoken cadence of his voice.[12]

But even this new call for the simplicity of the common man's diction and cadence in both poetry and prose might be seen to fit within a historical pattern of protest against obscurity in literary language, a kind of challenge that Tolstoy was also making in Russia in the nineteenth century when he complained in "What Is Art?" that Baudelaire's

Les Fleurs du mal "contained not one poem which is plain and can be understood without a certain effort — an effort seldom rewarded, for the feelings which the poet transmits are evil and very low ones . . . always, and purposely, expressed by him with eccentricity and lack of clearness." Tolstoy further implies a division in the language of poetry and prose when he states that he is particularly annoyed with the "obscurity" of Baudelaire's prose, noting that, in prose, the author "could speak clearly if he wanted to."[13]

Wordsworth, Coleridge, Whitman, Tolstoy, and Frost may all be seen to be contributing to a literary argument as old as Aristotle and Horace. It is one that has most recently led us into an era in which the historical protest against obscurity and for commonality has taken on such proportions in our art in general that the theory of simplicity, as reflected not only in literature but in Christo's wrapping as I saw it with my mother-in-law from the Pont-Neuf, has acquired a rigid and indisputable, even a superior, intellectual authority of its own.

Evidence that the simplicity of a work of art such as Christo's *Pont-Neuf* still manages to elude, even exclude, the comprehension of the common man, in spite of all its apparent overthrow of authoritarian convention and the oppressive limitations of existing genres, can be found in a conversation I had with a Paris taxi driver shortly after my mother-in-law and I finished our Bateau Mouche ride. *Pffffft!* he said. *If that is art, then I will drape my taxi in some gold cloth and park it in front of the Louvre and stand there and collect the proceeds instead of drive.*

One cannot help wondering at times if the kind of critical adulation publicly afforded to the simplicity of a work such as Christo's wrapping might be due to a kind of inner fear on the part of the critic that these movements still may have very little, or nothing at all, in common with the common man. This may be the same fear that kept the crowd of onlookers from telling the king he was strutting around his kingdom stark naked in the fairy tale about the emperor and his brand new clothes. Being simple, even being common, does not necessarily mean being easy-to-do or obvious. It just may be that under the gossamer guise or wrapping of simplicity struts the naked truth of much that is dehumanized and essentially vacuous in postmodern art.

Likewise, writing that purports to be simple or minimalist is not always necessarily good. Robertson Davies, best known as the author of *The Diary of Samuel Marchbanks*, comments that he distrusts the general advice he so often hears being given to novice writers to keep it simple in terms of style. Simple, he says, is too often confused with mediocre, since the ultimate motive of being simple is often confused with the historical desire not to be obscure. Davies asks, "What is the point of holding up mediocrity as a model? What is gained by urging-aspiring writers to be simple and direct, choosing the concrete word in preference to the abstract, and avoiding complexities of structure? Of course real simplicity can be great writing, but few writers achieve it; what they attain is not simplicity, but flat-footed, drudging simplemindedness."[14]

Of all the dangers inherent in the peculiarly American phenomena of the creative writing workshop as it now exists, the tendency toward literary mediocrity that Davies is decrying may be the one that thoughtful monitors of creative writing programs should be most wary of. Not all the secondary short stories that have evolved out of the popular literary movement called minimalism — a movement that is most often reflected in the workshop environment with the advice to avoid complexity of sentence structure (too often universally termed Jamesian prose) and instead to keep it tight — have the depth of compassion or the writerly genius that is reflected in the stories of Raymond Carver, the movement's earliest exemplar. The problem may lie, as it does with the perpetuation of any kind of school in literature or the other arts, in a kind of cloning as it is technically mastered by a lesser artist who has neither read nor contemplated life enough.

Curiously, the rush to set up schools for writing seems to be one that European writers have avoided up to this point. This avoidance has at times been very self-aware. In his essay "Idealismo e cosmopolitismo," the Italian novelist Luigi Capuana essentially praises Italian literature for its absence of *scuole*, or writing schools, and argues against the writer's hopping onto any existing literary bandwagon:

> Ogni grande opera d'arte è un simbolo. . . . Il *cosmo-politismo* . . . toglie via, o tenta di toglier via, tutti i caratteri particolari, e per ciò intende ridurci al *simbolismo* forzato, al *simbolismo* artificiale.[15]

> Every great work of art is a symbol. . . . *Cosmopolitanism* . . . takes away, or would attempt to take away, all of the traits that are peculiar to us, and thus to reduce us to a forced *symbolism*, an artificial *symbolism*. (translation mine)

Capuana concludes that the writer who writes with a sense of regionalism — whether that regionalism is geographic or spiritual — can't help but turn the particular into the universal. The particulars of the individual writer's region then become the symbols for the world.

The painful truth just may be that there are far more human beings with stories to tell than there are genuine writers to write them down and that creative writing workshops, while they can provide the reasonably coherent novice with a kind of technical polish he or she may lack, don't in the end make writers. I don't pretend to know how to draw the line between the person who has a good story to tell and the person who has the creative talent to write it down, but I have yet to meet a talented writer who was born in a creative writing workshop. Even the good writers in those workshops — the ones who don't fit into some kind of literary mold or succumb to the style of a successful mentor when the rewards are right — were already writing, usually prodigiously, before they got there.

Most of them were inveterate readers, too — not just readers of current copies of the *Paris Review* or the *New Yorker* (the unspoken motive often being, *I'd like to be in there*), but of Tolstoy and Dostoyevsky, of Sartre and Camus, of O'Connor, Porter, Cather, Fitzgerald, and Hemingway, as well as of more recently discovered non-Western writers or some of the minor writers of earlier times. Quite often, after carefully reading a piece of work in a writing class, I have suggested that, say, Chekhov once wrote a short story about, say, a lady and a dog, *just as you have here*, and that the student might want to take a look at that story, just to see what Chekhov did. But the reactions to this kind of advice in a workshop can sometimes be volatile. *What?! Me read a story about something I thought up all by myself and end up being influenced by that guy? No way, man, no, not me.*

There are times when one is tempted as a workshop leader to be less than polite and kind to this response. *You could do worse than be influenced by Chekhov*, I want to counter on behalf of my more caustic self. *You could, for instance, find yourself writing no better than this for all your life.*

This particular form of exclusivity (as in *I don't want to be influenced by nobody, thank you very much*) comes under the guise of what the critic Harold Bloom might call the anxiety of influence.[16] These students claim to be afraid that they will end up writing more like William Faulkner or Anton Chekhov than like themselves. Harold Bloom would argue, of course, that students cannot avoid being influenced by their forebears, even if they haven't read them, since the literary imprint of those precursors has remained, in a way, in the very air.

The argument over the problem of influence, though, by no means begins or ends with Harold Bloom. The Italian novelist Umberto Eco, in response to a similar theory of influence put forward by Benedetto Croce, notes that

> quanto all'esecuzione musicale, Croce l'assimilava alla rimemorazione che il poeta fa della propria poesia; non traduzione in opera nuova, quindi, bensì *ri-creazione* dell'opera originale.[17]

> as to the musical execution [of the poem], Croce accredited it to the poet's committing his own poetry to memory; thus, not a translation into a new work, so much as *re-creation* of the original work. (translation mine)

Nor is Ezra Pound the least anxious that students who are heavy readers might be so influenced by another writer that they will not be able to discover their own originality. Indeed, as though referring to the European artist who learns to paint by copying a masterpiece in a museum for many hours, Pound asserts in a statement that resonates with Croce, Capuana, Bloom, et al.: "The first phase of anyone's writing always shows them doing something 'like' something they have heard or read." The signs of real talent, he says, must lie in the work that follows the apprenticeship, because the truth is that "the majority of writers never pass that stage."[18]

The point to be made here is that all work to some degree — whether creative or critical — is somewhat derivative, and not necessarily to the detriment of the work. According to Bloom, Keats would derive from Shakespeare and Milton. But then Bloom would derive from Benedetto Croce and Ezra Pound. In the end, arguments over the derivation of a work tend to be tedious and circular. What may matter most, as one sits down to write, is that one be well informed enough about what has come before to have the possibility of choosing the derivation of one's work, or at least to have an inkling of where it might fit in the overall literary scheme of things.

Most European writers don't seem to have this bizarre fear of being influenced, and perhaps that is why their education is usually in the traditional university setting as informed readers (of history, philosophy, or literature) rather than as writers in a creative workshop — a term that suggests a kind of technical trade school. Cesare Pavese remarks at least once in *La letteratura americana* that close attention to an established writer's work (in his case, through multiple translations of other authors) can hardly be considered a danger of the trade. In fact, he says, the influence of this kind of writerly reading tends to go the other way. That is, the act of translation tends not only to provide a model but, in some cases, to teach the novice writer what *not* to do. Pavese writes:

> Il tradurre ... insegna come *non* si deve scrivere. ... Alla fine di un periodo intenso di traduzione — Anderson, Joyce, Dos Passos, Faulkner, Gertrude Stein — *io sapevo*

esattamente quali erano i moduli e le movenze letterarie che non mi sono consentiti, che mi restano esterni, che mi lasciano freddo.[19]

> Translating . . . teaches how *not* to write. . . . At the end of an intense period of translation — Anderson, Joyce, Dos Passos, Faulkner, Gertrude Stein — I *knew* exactly the models and literary movements that do not agree with me, those that remain external to me, those that leave me cold. (translation mine)

The trouble with writing within the workshop mode without this kind of readerly expertise is that one ends up not by being original but by being influenced primarily by the fledgling writers in the workshop. One tends to be bullied into overlooking some fairly substantial grammar and spelling tics as well. *Spelling, for God's sake? Comma splices? What are we doing here, anyway? I didn't come here to take a goddamn grammar or spelling lesson, I came here to write!*

While some of the foremost writers of the American modern era have sometimes been seen to prophesy toward, even approve of, some sort of institutionalized writing workshop program, those who bring up the issue at any length — those who have tried to propose a format or to suggest readings for such a workshop — ultimately end their polemical discourse by backing off.

The main problem with the workshop phenomenon in America involves the same kind of question that is testing most departments of literature these days: What should the curriculum be? In *ABC of Reading*, Pound devotes several chapters to suggested readings and to the problem of teaching student writers how to write. He suggests, for one thing, that novice writers read tracts by other writers on writing. He cites Henry James's collected prefaces, *The Art of the Novel*, as "the one extant great treatise on novel writing in English."[20]

Pound seems, however, to become more and more confused about setting up any given workshop as he goes along. Having begun a good reading list for the student writer, he then suggests that it isn't enough only to read American literature. "You cannot learn to write by reading English," he concludes rather testily, ultimately arguing that other languages have richer literatures. He adds, almost in response to an imagined suggestion from the American workshop student that there are, after all, translations of all these things, that the novice writer should learn how to read these texts in the original language. Consequently, we find ourselves adding an extensive language requirement to the rigors of the creative writing workshop degree — a degree that as it now exists in America is usually granted after only two academic years. In the end, Pound prescribes course requirements that are much more likely to be found today in a doctoral program in comparative literature. But then, just as though he had reread what he'd written and discovered how very discouraging his suggestions might sound, he makes another stab at being helpful. "The way to learn the music of verse," he sets out again, kindly and confidently to tell us (so that we think, *Yes?* and, *Yes?*), "is to listen to it."[21]

Pound's words of wisdom turn out to be almost a caricature of the old joke, *Want to know how to get to Carnegie Hall, kid?*, with its inevitable, *Practice, practice, practice, ha ha ha*. In part, his answer to becoming a writer, and only if you already are one, is to read. He finally concludes, "In the main I don't see that teaching can do much more than expose counterfeit work, thus gradually leading the student to the valid."[22] The "valid" in writing, one begins to see after reading through even a limited number of the almost countless tracts on writing that have been passed down to us by writers through the years, eventually proves to be a very elusive quality — something that, while it can be nurtured, cannot be learned. One is ultimately led to draw the conclusion that the "valid" lies within.

Annie Dillard remarks, with no apparent attempt to be humorous, that when someone comes to her to ask her the breathy question, "Do you think I can be a writer?," she responds, "I don't know. Do you like sentences?"[23] And sentences seem to me to be exactly what writing is all about. The student writer may be able to learn technique in a workshop, but technique can be learned in an English composition course as well, along with indispensable rules about spelling and grammar and mature sentence construction, and where to interrupt dialogue scenes with he said/she said when characters are meant to be speaking for themselves. My own fear is that America's literature is fast becoming an illiterate one — not so much because of the proliferation of creative writing workshops but because of an inherent, perhaps even historical, distrust we seem to have for education and even for its linguistic result of speaking right. At times, the provincialist American assumes, in an odd redefinition of the quality of humility, that since much that has come before in literature has been high, then everything he or she has to say as a commoner about everyday occurrences in contemporary life must of necessity be wholly original, never said before — and that therefore no rules exist. *This is my voice, folks, entirely mine.*

This kind of solipsism is only a new cloak for the old argument of the untutored genius. The original coiner of the *ars poetica* himself caricatured the myth of the untutored genius, saying it was not possible to be uneducated and to write. Horace writes, "For my part I do not see what study can do without a rich vein of native gift, nor what the native gift can do without culture: so much does each ask of the other and swear eternal alliance with it."[24]

Horace does not believe in the parentless baby, the literate surprise. Nor, I am still discovering, do I. But while Horace shows great distrust here for the old adage, *Genius will out, no matter what*, his remarks should serve as a comment upon our public educational systems as well — and upon our responsibility to improve them, to make them fertile soil for new writers as they come along, no matter what their ethnic or racial origins. Only in this way can "study" be made available to "native gift."

Virginia Woolf, of course, has something to say in *A Room of One's Own* about the relationship between genius and education and the rare likelihood that one's talent as a writer will ever come to fruition if one is poor. She quotes Sir Arthur Quiller-Couch as saying, in his "The Art of Writing":

> It may seem a brutal thing to say, and it is a sad thing to say; but, as a matter of fact, the theory that poetical genius bloweth where it listeth, and equally in poor and rich, holds little truth. . . . In our commonwealth, the poor poet has not in these days, nor has had for two hundred years, a dog's chance. . . . A poor child in England has little more hope than had the son of an Athenian slave to be emancipated into that intellectual freedom of which great writings are born.[25]

But if Woolf was decrying the lack of educational opportunities for the English poor, the French philosopher and author Jean-Paul Sartre actually saw the myth of the untutored genius as a peculiarly American temptation — and one, we are given to believe, that would hide the importance (and so the availability) of formal education for the writer behind a kind of misdirected plebeian pride. He notes the tendency on the part of American writers to set themselves up in a kind of superior isolationism when he remarks, "The American writer . . . writes blindly, out of an absurd need to rid himself of his fears and anger. . . . He does not invent his manner against tradition, but for want of one, and in certain ways his most extreme audacities are naïvetés. . . . He has no solidarity with other writers. . . . Nothing is more remote from him than the idea of college or clerkship."[26]

Sartre assumes here a choice on the part of all American writers to keep themselves isolated. Much more remains to be said about the argument for the untutored genius that would perpetuate the very lack of education that has kept the common man (or anyone separated from the mainstream by gender or ethnicity or race or class) an outsider all this time.

Ultimately, all our literary talk about the common man, at least as it has continued into the postmodern era and particularly in the United States, may have more to do with an ironic sense of pity (and with keeping the common man common) than any of us has wanted to admit so far. In "Essay on the Origins of Language," Jean-Jacques Rousseau asks the question, "How are we moved to pity?" He immediately answers his own question by responding, "By getting outside ourselves and identifying with a being who suffers."[27] Jacques Derrida in one place undertakes an extensive discussion of Rousseau's essay, which he plays off Lévi-Strauss's research on the Nambikwara, a South American tribe. He appears to come to the eventual conclusion that both Rousseau's image of the uncorrupted child in *Émile* and Lévi-Strauss's image of the uncorrupted (in this case, meaning nonwriting) Nambikwara are romantic and hopeless identifications with the Other. Derrida constructs a certain "economy of pity," in which the act of writing distances the Self from the Other and the Other's suffering, mainly so that the Self can survive. That is why a Faulkner's appropriation of a Dilsey's voice, major as that mimicry is made to be, contains an ethical question that conscientious critical theoreticians cannot avoid.

While I can suggest that only the voice of the Other can speak with any integrity of itself, to play any further upon the question would make me guilty of the same kind of appropriation here myself, in that I would be presuming to write the *ars poetica* for some generically defined common man. In the future, the *ars poetica* of some minor woman writer of color may also take up these questions. In the meantime, as Derrida comments:

> We neither can nor should feel the pain of others immediately and absolutely, for such an interiorization or identification would be dangerous and destructive. That is why the imagination, the reflection, and the judgment that arouse pity also limit its power and hold the suffering of the other at a certain distance. One knows this suffering for what it is, one pities others, but one protects oneself, and holds the evil at arm's length. This doctrine — which could further be related to the theory of dramatic representation — is formulated in both the *Essay* and *Émile*. The paradox of the relation to the other is clearly

articulated in those two texts: the more you identify with the other, the better you feel his suffering as *his*: our own suffering is that of the other. That of the other, as itself, must remain the other's.[28]

It is far too easy to isolate Derrida's concept of the economy of pity to the academic arena and to ignore the political and ethical ramifications inherent in a system which implies self-conscious distancing from the Other. If the language of literature has supposedly become more and more the language of the common man, the language of academic theory that validates the authenticity of the common voice — that is, the language of the pieces that are discussing this so-called literary language of the common man — has become more and more the language of an intellectual and highly educated elite. If we were to produce a sort of linear Aristotelian scale of the levels of language, we might find the spoken conversation of the undergraduate who is talking to his friends (*And my father was I mean like there I was and ba-oh he's standing there saying when I was your age and I'm there thinking oh god you oh you know what I mean, like, here he comes . . .*) at one end of the spectrum, with the more educated language of the professor's written academese (*We can therefore deduce from Rousseau's implied, although perhaps somewhat intentionally obscured, construct, in which the self distances itself from the other through what Derrida, in a perhaps unintentionally Marxist mode terms an "economy of pity," that . . .*) at the other. If there is a postmodern language, it is more likely that it is this highly obscure academese rather than the slang-riddled and fragmented everyday conversation of the undergraduate — or of the uneducated poor, of the common man.

One wonders what Tolstoy, with his annoyance for the

premeditated obscurity of Baudelaire, might have made of a Derrida. The language of academic journals may premeditatedly distance itself from the language of the Other in order to prove the superiority of the educated middle to upper classes over the as yet uneducated lower classes and in order to perpetuate literary exclusivity. *Like, we the educated know what the hell you common-man writers are trying to say, you know what I mean, but you guys're just the proverbial untutored geniuses, and so you can't possibly be intelligent enough to realize what you've just said.* Whether stated simply or in the obscure language of academese, the message of usurpation is the same.

Everyday spoken language, while it may seem limited in its scope to the academic, is nevertheless a language — like that of Rousseau's Émile or Lévi-Strauss's Nambikwara — that has a certain integrity or innocence of its own. As indistinct as this spoken language sometimes seems to be, it still has at its root not so much a willful self-distancing from the Other as a need or desire to belong with him or her — to find some common ground of feeling in which individuals try to understand each other without words. *I mean, you know what I mean, I was standing there and I was, you know* . . . And in the end, *the thing is*, the *you* being addressed with all those *you knows* really does, or at least does try to, know what the *you know* means.

My suggestion that much of the critical language of the postmodern era — including Derrida's — differs from the language of the romantics in that it willfully distances itself from the common man obviously does not originate with me. George Orwell's oft-taught "Politics and the English Language" is very apropos to the argument in that it, too, focuses on the language of professors, with their use of the "passive voice," of "pretentious diction" (he is in fact particularly unfond of terms like apropos), and of "mean-ingless words."[29]

But there may still be some unwritten limit to the use in literature of common prose. It is only when the writer with an initial talent is provided with the option of education that he or she has a choice between what is termed common, or low, diction and a higher voice. The untutored genius must be allowed to make a conscious choice. Only through edu-cation can the common man become a kind of mediator between the Self and the Other, both the observed and the observer, at once the common that is expressing itself and *knowing better than* the level of the language out of which it comes.

The common man who becomes a writer should know what Derrida likes to call the *différance*.[30] Without even a passing feeling for the kind of critically historical dialogue between high and low that began with Aristotle and Hor-ace, the writer knows only one side of the story. He or she is ignorant of Aristotle's call for mixed diction — of the full range of the language of literature, of the kinds of heights and depths that can be accomplished through the delicate balance of traditional concepts of high and low.

Wallace Stegner touches upon this question in his collec-tion of essays *One Way to Spell Man: Essays with a Western Bias*. In an essay entitled "Good-bye to All T——t!" he deplores the overuse of profanity in contemporary fiction — not, he insists, because he is a prig or a puritan or because he thinks this language is common, but because it is used to excess and because it is used in ignorance of any other modes of speech. Stegner writes:

Words are not obscene: Naming things is a legitimate verbal act. And "frank" does not mean "vulgar," any more than "improper" means "dirty." What vulgar does mean is "common"; what improper means is "unsuitable." Under the right circumstances, any word is proper. But when any sort of word, especially a word hitherto taboo and therefore noticeable, is scattered across a page like chocolate chips through a Toll House cookie, a real impropriety occurs. The sin is not the use of an "obscene" word; it is the use of a loaded word in the wrong place or in the wrong quantity. It is the sin of false emphasis, which is not a moral but a literary lapse related to sentimentality. It is the sin of advertisers who so plaster a highway with neon signs that you can't find the bar or liquor store you're looking for. Like any excess, it quickly becomes comic.[31]

Becoming comic, as Stegner puts it — that is, laugh-*at*-able, not *with*-able — cannot be the goal of an artist who purports to be on the side of or even equal to the common man, when becoming comic hurts rather than helps the human plight of that common man. Becoming comic — making that only laughable which should affect to change — may ultimately be a literary act that is at the sleazy end of Derrida's economy of pity. Admittedly, Stegner is talking here about a specific form of common language, profanity, and not about the breakdown of high or high-class language altogether, but the point is the same.

For instance, while I was teaching introductory composition courses at the University of New Mexico, where a high percentage of my students were labeled nontraditional (over thirty), minority (Native American or Hispanic), and marginal (or poor), we had a discussion about the then-current slang phenomenon called Valley Girl. I had an instinctive dislike of this language (*I'm like, oh wow, totally, tubular, I mean fab*), but I was not sure why. I distrusted myself as a language snob. So I asked my students what they made of the whole argument. They pointed out to me, almost unanimously, that I didn't owe the language of the Valley Girls one moment of my support. It wasn't the language itself that bothered them, they said, but the lack of human values behind it, the lack of thought. Valley Girls, my students concluded, were people who had every available opportunity to be educated and literate, if they chose to be, because they or their parents were rich. Given a choice, they had chosen the possession of material things over the things of mind. *I mean, they're not standing there in the supermarket line, right, with all their food stamps, like some of us (laughter).*

These were the sentiments of people whom William Wordsworth would probably have put under the appellation of common man. Because of their poor educational backgrounds, they could not write well. Yet they had the intelligence — and some of them had the writing talent — that deserved the kind of education that would have enabled them to tell the stories of their home lives and family narratives in a voice that knew the difference. They could have told those stories themselves, rather than leaving them to be told by a more educated (and usually white and middle class) observer/writer on their behalf. Literature is enriched, not through some takeover by a falsely produced language of the common man, but through a language, supported by a better public education system, that allows the common man to speak honest, inherited dialogue, unhampered by the veil of Wordsworth's quotes. The common man would then be observing genuine origins in a lyric voice.

But there can also be, at times, a kind of revenge on the

part of the formerly unheard voice that may prove detrimental in the end to the production of a great literature by the common man. For example, in light of William Faulkner's recurring theme of rejection of the unprivileged from the respectable front door of the big white southern house, particularly as it is encountered in *Absalom, Absalom!*, one might very well take note of a similar preoccupation with rejection at the white front door as it occurs in Alice Walker's memoir, *In Search of Our Mothers' Gardens*. A Georgia sharecropper's daughter who was noticed in the public school system as being bright and who eventually received a scholarship to go to Sarah Lawrence College, Walker admits that she has had much to be grateful for. But, she adds, she still could never read the texts her teachers selected for southern literature classes in the same way she might have read them if she had been white. "One reads Faulkner," she says, "knowing that his 'colored' people had to come through 'Mr. Williams's' back door, and one feels uneasy, and finally enraged that Faulkner did not burn the whole house down. When the provincial mind starts out *and continues* on a narrow and unprotesting course, 'genius' itself must run on a track." Later, she calls him the "eloquent but morally befuddled Faulkner."[32]

In a historical sense, she and other African American women writers have been rejected from the traditional male Anglo-Saxon writer's big white publishing house and from the academic reading list it still in part decides. At one point in the narrative, she learns that as a five-year-old child she lived not ten minutes from the home of Flannery O'Connor, whom she has come to admire through her literary studies at Sarah Lawrence. When she goes with her mother to visit the O'Connor house, her feelings of anger at rejection surface. As she knocks on the front door of the house for the black caretaker to come to let her and her mother in to look around, she notes:

> What I feel at the moment of knocking is fury that someone is paid to take care of her house, though no one lives in it, and that her house still, in fact, stands, while mine — which of course we never owned anyway — is slowly rotting into dust. Her house becomes — in an instant — the symbol of my own disinheritance, and for that instant I hate her guts. All that she has meant to me is diminished, though her diminishment within me is against my will.[33]

This passage might be seen in one way as a cruelly ironic rewriting of Faulkner's offensive "monkey nigger" sequence in *Absalom, Absalom!*, in which the servant of the white male authority figure continually rejects the ambitious Thomas Sutpen from the front door of the big white house. But this time, in a revenge such as Sutpen will never know, a female African American author returns to the white author's door and knocks on it as a Pulitzer Prize–winning novelist. It can only be a comment upon the unrewarding nature of revenge that Alice Walker feels only more fury, rather than satisfaction, at this point.

I am not suggesting, by any means, that just because, all of a sudden, the literary scene in America is finally open to women and to people of color, we forget the past, as some so-called revisionist historians suggest that we forget the Holocaust. An entirely historical view of literature can sometimes find room to excuse or to make too little of certain lapses in literary representation of particular groups of human beings over time. Some European critics of American literature, for instance, have failed to see the fundamental inseparability of ethics from literature. Their critiques of

American literature seem to be entirely too historically con-
textual at times, allowing them to forgive or overlook the
hard evidence of authorial bigotry in some texts. One of the
foremost French Faulknerian critics, André Bleikasten,
calls *Absalom, Absalom!* "son roman le plus admirable à tous
égards" ("his most admirable novel in every way"). Bleikasten prefers, like a growing number of contemporary
French critics, to underplay the more recent American
trend toward ethical readings of the work, such as Alice
Walker makes in her commentary. Bleikasten suggests that
Faulkner is only "self-ironizing." After all, he adds, there is
little that Faulkner could have done to change the historical
circumstances under which he wrote. Bleikasten suggests
that Faulkner is neither a racist nor a misogynist but merely
a "realist."[34]

Nevertheless, just as there was a popular call a few years
ago among religionists for a liberation theology that might
make the things of God, as the New Testament has it, more
visible in the lives of human beings — particularly in regard
to human rights issues in South and Central America — so
the writer in any historical era might have the opportunity
to participate in a kind of liberation literature of his or her
own. The concept could have particularly far-reaching possibilities in the postmodern world.

Perhaps it would be helpful to once again consider here
Victor Hugo's concept of the grotesque. Hugo applies this
concept to characterization as well as to subject matter. In
his preface to *Cromwell*, Hugo clearly states that the main
character of the play has none of the traditional prerequisites for a major tragic hero as depicted in the classicism of
Racine or Corneille. Cromwell is not royal. He is not grand.
He does not subordinate his life to the noble goal before
him because he is full of doubts and contradictions about

that goal. He differs from the classics-derived French tragic hero in that he is existentially uncertain. By his own admission, he doesn't know anything. Hugo describes this new dramatic character at length:

> C'était un être complexe, hetérogène, multiple, composé de tous les contraires, mêlé de beaucoup de mal et de beaucoup de bien, plein de génie et de petitesse . . . sobre, simple, frugal, et guindé sur l'étiquette; soldat grossier et politique délié; rompu aux arguties théologiques et s'y plaisant; orateur lourd, diffus, obscur, mais habile à parler le langage de tous ceux qu'il voulait séduire; hypocrite et fanatique; visionaire dominé par des fantômes de son enfance, croyant aux astrologues et les proscrivant; défiant à l'excès, toujours menaçant, rarement sanguinaire; rigide observateur des prescriptions puritaines, perdant gravement plusieurs heures par jour à des bouffonneries; brusque et dédaigneux avec ses familiers, caressant avec les sectaires qu'il redoutait; trompant ses remords avec des subtilités, rusant avec sa conscience; intarissable en adresse, en pièges, en ressources; maîtrisant son imagination par son intelligence; grotesque et sublime; enfin, un de ces hommes *carrés par la base*, comme les appelait Napoléon, le type et le chef de tous ces hommes complets, dans sa langue exacte comme l'algèbre, colorée comme la poésie.[35]

> [Cromwell] was a complex, heterogeneous, and diverse being, made up of many opposites, a combination of much that was good and much that was evil, full of both genius and pettiness . . . sober, simple, frugal, and well-grounded in rules of etiquette; both a disgusting soldier and a delicate politician; a being who had broken away from theological disputes and yet who used these

disputes to his own advantage; a base and diffuse orator, yet one who was capable of speaking the very language of those whom he meant to seduce; a hypocrite and a fanatic; a visionary who was obsessed with the dreams of his childhood, who believed in astrologers at the same time that he told them what to predict; defiant to excess, always menacing, rarely compassionate; a rigid observer of puritan pretexts who nevertheless wasted several hours each day in frivolities; brusk and disdainful with his friends, obsequious with the sectarians whom he feared; a man who could trick his own sense of remorse through subtleties, and deceive his own conscience; indefatigable in adroitness and resourcefulness, a clever inventor of snares; mastering his imagination through his intelligence; grotesque and sublime; finally one of those men who are *obstinate by nature*, as Napoleon described them, himself both the type and the forerunner of all these complete men, in his language that was at once as exact as algebra, as vibrant as poetry. (translation mine)

So Cromwell is both good and evil, kind and mean, at once a defiant rebel and a rigid observer of the status quo. He is a compilation of contradictions, neither high nor low. Though Hugo gives us a sense of the origin of the grotesque (he finds traces of it in antiquity but says that it grows mainly out of *mélancolie*, a direct result of the *pitié* inspired by Christianity), we are for the most part left, as we are with Wordsworth's "language of conversation," to narrow down the criteria for the quality of grotesqueness on our own.

The grotesque seems to be closely linked with a sense of derision or of irony, not necessarily as it is directed at the dramatic character in question but as it points to the absurdity of the universal human condition. This combination or interplay of opposites — of, for instance, the tragic and the comic at the same time — that Hugo sees as the genius of Shakespeare is what separates us (*les modernes*) from them (*les anciens*) and what makes us new:

> Ainsi voilà un principe étranger à l'Antiquité, un type nouveau introduit dans la poésie; et, comme une condition de plus dans l'être modifie l'être tout entier, voilà une forme nouvelle qui se développe dans l'art. Ce type, c'est la grotesque. Cette forme, c'est la comédie.[36]

> Thus here is a principle not found in Antiquity, a new kind of character introduced into poetry; and, since any condition added to existence modifies existence as a whole, here is a new form developing in art. The type is that of the grotesque. The form is that of comedy. (translation mine)

We can, as Hugo invites us at the end of his preface, study the character of his Cromwell as an example of the grotesque. But Hugo also offers us another literary example. We can find the grotesque, he says, in the common man's literature in the romantic period, and we will find that it is always linked with what Hugo terms *le beau*. He points us to a particular fairy tale, originally formed in the oral tradition but written down just prior to the era which he calls *moderne*. "L'antiquité n'aurait pas fait 'La Belle et la Bête,'" he tells us.[37] ("The classic period could not have produced 'Beauty and the Beast.'") Hugo is referring here, of course, not to the 1990s' Disney movie nor to the 1940s' movie directed by French filmmaker Jean Cocteau, from which the Disney version so clearly originates, but to the original seventeenth-century story by Madame Leprince de Beaumont.[38]

Throughout the tale we hear an overriding tone of *ironie* in the running commentary by the narrator. The two sisters, for instance, while *très belles,* are neither as beautiful nor as good as Belle, and they have much pride which the narrator exploits with *ironie*. It is pointed out, in this tone, that the older sisters refuse to receive the visits of other merchants' daughters because they only accept persons of quality as their friends. But obviously, they, too, are only merchants' daughters. They are, in a way (after all, they are only secondary or supporting characters, whose evil stands in contrast to the goodness of *la Belle*), like Hugo's Cromwell, who commits regicide in order to free England of its tyrant king, then seeks to have himself, a commoner, set up as king.

Hugo sees this sin of pride as very much linked with the grotesque. It is what makes a great person's fall funny and what allows us to see Belle's sisters as buffoons. Hugo says of the grotesque as it applies to Cromwell:

> Il y a surtout une époque dans sa vie où ce caractère singulier se développe sous toutes ses formes. Ce n'est pas, comme on le croirait au premier coup d'oeil, celle du procès de Charles Ier, toute palpitante qu'elle est d'un intérêt sombre et terrible; c'est le moment où l'ambitieux essaya de cueillir le fruit de cette mort. C'est l'instant où Cromwell, arrivé à ce qui eut été pour quelque autre la sommité d'une fortune possible, maître de l'Ecosse dont il fait un pachalik, et de l'Irlande, dont il fait un bagne, maître de l'Europe par ses flottes, par ses armées, par sa diplomatie, essaie enfin d'accomplir le premier rêve de son enfance, le dernier but de sa vie, de se faire roi.[39]

There is above all a period in his life in which his singular character is seen to have developed under all its forms. This moment isn't, as one might expect at first glance, the period of Charles I's trial, as rife with somber and terrible interest as that might be; it's the moment in which this ambitious man attempted to gather the fruit of this death. It is the moment in which Cromwell, having arrived at what would have been for anyone else the summit of possibility, as master of Scotland, of which he made a type of fiefdom, and of Ireland, of which he made a penal colony, and as master of Europe through his naval fleets and armies, and through his diplomacy, finally tries to accomplish the utmost dream of his childhood, and the ultimate goal of his life, to make himself king. (translation mine)

Belle's older sisters, too, wish in a way *de se faire roi*, to make themselves king. As commoners who want to be more than they are, they commit the sin of searching for satisfaction in a selfhood framed only on material values — a sin that is all too often common to us all.

Belle's older sisters are perhaps most representative of the grotesque in the fact that their ugly personalities are at odds with their attractive physiognomies. This is a contrast that later English versions of both "Beauty and the Beast" and "Cinderella" remove, by making the older sisters as ugly as they are mean, as if to perpetuate the nineteenth-century concept that the body is the extension of the mind.

To go perhaps one step beyond Hugo's grotesque, I'd like to suggest that we need more than a too-good Belle and her all-bad stepsisters if we are going to provide for a range of characters and diction in the postmodern era that will be truly mixed. While Belle lacks the possibility of ever falling into sin or self-corruption with that all-pure heart, her step-sisters also, sadly, lack the possibility of falling into grace. A more street-smart Belle — one with a sense of humor — might be the only kind of fictional character who would have the power to tame a postmodern beast.

I read an offhand anecdote from a starlet once, in one of those magazines that come free with the local Sunday paper, which, while I threw it away with the rest of the paper at the time, keeps coming back to me as the kind of tale that might very well contain the seed for this fictional post-modern Belle and her postmodern Beast. In this brief inter-view, the starlet told of her first visit to New York as an as yet un-street-smart, pretty (and, we are given to believe, innocent) young Belle. Just after she got off the bus in New York City, where she'd come to visit her sister, two men drove up in a taxi and accosted her, throwing her inside. As they drove through the streets discussing all that they were going to do to her, she said, she was scared to death. Per-haps it was for that reason that she kept a perfectly ri-diculous running commentary going on all the sites the men were driving past, which she probably thought she wouldn't live to see. After a while, to her utter amazement, one of the men said, *You know what? She's funny. Let's let her go.*

What I would add to postmodern subject matter, and to the violent experience it sometimes depends upon, is a post-modern *la Belle* — one with a sense of humor a bit like this. We don't believe in fairy stories anymore. We are far too experienced for that. And so what we may need, if we are going to survive the historical outcome of Victor Hugo's grotesque, may be a Belle who is wacky and whimsical, as well as a Beast who has the possibility of saying, *You know what, this girl is funny, I will set her free.*

I can think of one other grotesque story that I clipped out of the local paper, knowing that I would probably do something with it at some point. It is the story of a woman whose young daughter tells her that a stranger has tried three times to get her into his car at the corner where she catches the bus for school. The mother stakes out the bus stop, armed with her binoculars and a camera with a zoom lens. Eventually, she takes a picture of the suspect that leads to his arrest. Now this story and this mother, the Belle figure, are both just crazy enough to interest me. The Beast figure — the man in the car — may be beyond my comprehension as a reasonable person, and perhaps that is why I cannot seem to get him right as a character in my mind.

So I begin to expand on the mother. I see her as a quiet woman who might have a hobby of watching birds. (Hence the high-powered binoculars and the camera with the zoom lens.) She feels no ill will for anyone in the world, has more interest in trekking alone through high bulrushes looking for scarlet tanagers than she does in the men who are arguing back and forth about troop reductions in a crazy, post–power struggle modern world. News, in short, doesn't interest her.

But then her daughter gives her the words every mother fears. *He offered me money, Mom. Lots of it.*

The mother becomes a tigress. She is magnificent, her soft ears bright orange as she listens, all alert. Once she honestly believed, during the process of childbirth, that *the lion shall dwell with the lamb*, and that if she were a cat, any kind of feline, she would watch the less powerful creatures only to admire them, only to protect them. She would not catch birds. There was nothing left in her, during the pain of childbirth, that would want to hurt.

But suddenly, all that has changed. A stranger has *offered* to molest her daughter. And she is wise enough to know that this stranger is no lamb. Before he can catch her daughter, she will catch him. All of her sharpened claws are out to save.

So she stakes out the bus stop. She hides in the bushes with her camera and binoculars. She will not even tell her daughter that she is there. Finally, he shows up, this stranger, this man in the car with the money every mother fears.

And then I took after him, maybe seventy, seventy-five, miles an hour.

In this instant, as a writer, I don't care anything about this character's class or diction, whether someone thinks her culture is pop or high, what she does for a living, or her sense of place. I only know that when I see her take off after that stranger's car I want to cheer. *Get him, honey!* I yell from above my hands that are madly playing at the keyboard of the word processor as I write. *Faster! Faster! That's it, take a picture! Write down the number on the license plate and turn him in!*

Perhaps this homemaker/mother is the kind of human being we are looking for when we say we are looking for the common man. Perhaps we are looking for a human who is like ourselves, perfectly ordinary on almost any given day but who somehow, because of circumstance, is transformed into greatness overnight.

8

The Moment of the Subject

Motherhood and Authorship in a Deconstructive Age

. . . .

*There you have three short unambiguous words that share a
sound, and the sound they share is this:*

I.

I.

I.

—*Joan Didion, "Why I Write"* [1]

Sentence diagraming as it was taught in the grammar
school I attended in Georgia while I was growing up was a
tool for learning the names of the different parts of speech
in the English sentence. To diagram a simple sentence, the
pupil drew a straight line with a perpendicular line through
the middle, then found the subject of the sentence and entered the noun or pronoun that served as the subject on the
first half of the line that had been cut in half. Next, the pupil
found the predicate or verb with which this subject did its
acting and wrote that word down on the other half. The
subject of the sentence had the primary position. What the
subject did or was got the second slot. All the direct objects, adjectives, adverbs, and prepositional phrases came
after that.

I became very adept at diagraming sentences, even the
compound and complex ones. I could use bending legs to
neatly attach the prepositional phrases to the main part of
the sentence, as well as make the straight line of dashes for

a little *for* or *and* that connected the two otherwise completely different sentences of a complex or compound sentence. Whenever we went on field trips, I could be found at the back of the bus, making up sentences that were sure to keep at least two or three other grammatically minded pupils busy for most of the rest of the jouncing ride.

But the sentence that interests me now is a simple one. *I write.* In that sentence, *I* am the subject, and what I as the subject do as my activity is *write.* Deconstruction as a literary theory stems from a highly intellectualized study of linguistics that questions the central position of the subject in that sentence. The subject is not necessarily *I* now when *I write.*[2]

Owing its importance for the most part to the French theoretician Jacques Derrida, deconstruction is extremely attractive in terms of its almost miraculous ability to go to work on any text. Yet the highly complex sentence structure and elitist vocabulary inherent in any discussion of postmodern criticism, and in particular of deconstruction, have made it difficult for the very groups whose literatures might be most affected by the possible consequences of deconstruction's problematization of the subject to attempt to answer the many ethical questions that this peculiarly postmodern philosophy leaves unresolved. The novelist and critic Charles Newman, in *The Post-Modern Aura: The Act of Fiction in an Age of Inflation*, repeats the underlying distrust many contemporary writers express toward literary theory of any kind when he says, "At the very moment the artist has lost his traditional prestige and privilege, the critic arrogates them to himself."[3]

Even though I am in agreement with Newman on this point, his insistence on the masculine pronoun as the traditional-universal one leads me one step beyond. Both the traditional position of power (if we eventually agree to call it that) originally occupied by the artist-as-romantic-hero as *subject* and the new power of the usurping postmodern critic to become the subject instead, basically reflect power struggles between educated white males — struggles that exclude by their very language the identities of the individuals and groups who are at stake.

Edward Said describes the language of postmodern criticism as a convoluted, exclusive language that, as a representative Third World critic himself, he fully loathes. Nevertheless, he says, he ultimately must take part in that same language to make his point. He writes, "You have to pass through certain rules of accreditation, you must learn the rules, you must speak the language, you must master the idioms and you must accept the authorities of the field — determined in many of the same ways — to which you want to contribute."[4] As feminist literary theory, once marginalized by all but a few female English professors, becomes more and more relevant to theory reading-lists, feminist critics, along with Said, may also have to buy into the *man-guage* of critical academese to some degree, if only to continue to be taken seriously — to take part in the discourse, as academic jargon has it now. One can only hope that this participation, while it is obviously necessary, will not also mean a change in early feminists' simple, at times almost colloquial, writing style, or in their unabashed use of the *I* (Didion's "I. I. I.") of personal experience in critical tracts.

One of the most valuable contributions of feminist theory is its reluctance to give up the subject entirely. It is only in a study of the construct of the apparent subject that the literary critic can attempt a discussion of the idea of source. As the sources for feminist theory continue to grow, one might well hope that feminist theory's concern with identity and subjectivity will not allow it to forget its own congruent quality of originality, along with its symptomatic distrust of so overquoting the earlier theoretical discourse of its "mothers" that it will eventually become derivative itself.

One might well consider here the idea of source in Jacques Derrida's essay "Qual quelle" in *Marges de la philosophie* as it has affected his writing on Rousseau in his "Genesis and Structure of the 'Essay on the Origin of Language'" in *Of Grammatology*. Although Rousseau, the ultimate romantic, makes very little reference to his erstwhile precursors (*he* is the original subject) in his "Essay on the Origin of Language," Derrida, whose negative theology must deny that the Self can in any way be the source or origin of something new, not only depends on a plethora of footnotes while writing about Rousseau's essay but interrupts his own critical commentary to repeat whole passages of the Rousseau.[5]

While earlier feminist critics may have offended more traditional critics with their emphasis on the injustices done to women artists and writers as these critics went meticulously over the ground of lost genius, of paintings and poetry and novels conveniently channeled into quilts and raspberry jam or into tapestry for cigar-smoking male visitors' parlor chairs, the assertion of originality in early works such as Elizabeth Abel's *Writing and Sexual Difference* or Elaine Showalter's *The New Feminist Criticism* or Sandra Gilbert and Susan Gubar's *The Madwoman in the Attic* has also added to critical discourse a delightful alternative to the writing style of a Derrida.[6] It is no doubt due at least in part to a refreshingly simpler, more accessible writing style that these anthologies, however much their moral outrage may have alienated the very ears it needed to address, are beginning to find themselves as respected as the Fryes and Blooms they're currently sitting next to on academic shelves.

The reasoning individual who sets about to deal with the problematization of the subject in the theory of deconstruction might well ask why, just as women's work is gaining some respect, this hard-won subjectivity should be suddenly put into question — along with, one would have to note, its dependent female identity (the "I. I. I.") — at precisely this point in history. The systematic deconstruction of subjectivity in a text can ultimately mean a de-emphasis, even a complete collapse, of the difference between the Self and the Other — between white and black, male and female, rich and poor, educated and illiterate. This difference was the one that the predominantly male academy was only too happy, up until recently, to recognize and to point out.

The deconstructionist might argue, of course, that *all* subjectivity, and not just feminine or Third World, has been de-centered, and that *all* authors, not just female authors or those of color, must now be pronounced dead or, at the most, partially alive. But one wonders about the timing of this death. It is almost too coincidental, too convenient, this death of the subject, this death of the author, coming as it did just when women and other long-suppressed writers were about to enjoy creating some sort of authorial persona of their own. (Remember the be-cloaked and bereted Byron? Remember the cigar-smoking, womanizing, toreador-admiring Hemingway? Remember the multi-married, wife-beating Norman Mailer?) One almost hears a sort of ironic voice speaking at the back of one's usually rational critical consciousness: *Don't take it personal, girls. Nobody's the subject anymore.*

The conscientious critic, male or female, should be at least a little distrustful of the attempts by some theoreticians to imply that the entire debate over authorial responsibility and subjective authorship has little relevance today. The underlying historical tendency to minimize feminine subjectivity or to regard women as either unimportant or comical still needs to be seriously addressed. For instance, alluding in what he must have thought was a comical way (meant perhaps to put what was originally his lecture audience at ease) to the unavoidable connection between feminism and the new argument over authorship, Harold Bloom remarks off-handedly in his otherwise important *Sacred Truths: Poetry and Belief from the Bible to the Present* that "authorship is somewhat out of fashion at the moment, because of Parisian preferences, but like short skirts authorship always does return again."[7] The remark tends both to trivialize the question of authorship and, perhaps not uncoincidentally, to trivialize women. Don't *trousers* change?

Simultaneous with the new debate over the old authorial intention, a new quest for critical accountability can begin. One of the greatest by-products of deconstruction's questioning of the subject has in fact been the devaluation of the author's intentionality, the writer's responsibility for the original conception of the text. The author can no longer be the only origin or source, since the subject is constituted not by the author but by the reader or by existing societal constructs or by previous discourse or by all three. Derrida argues in *Of Grammatology* that the absence or nonpresence of the author in the text (because the author-as-person cannot be both *alive* and *in* the text at the same time) causes a terror or disorientation on the part of the reader. The Derridean concept of absence necessarily means a devaluation of the historical moments in the author's life, of his or her personal biography. In the beginning was the word. Therefore, nothing — no life, no substance, no subject — can exist but the text.

Maurice Blanchot, whose metaphor for writing, particularly in *L'Espace littéraire*, is a kind of death (the author dies *as* he or she writes), is also interested in the idea of absence, though in a slightly different way. For him, that absence is only an apparent one, even though he admits that he cannot find proof of the author's presence in the text. Still, he is not willing to turn over all intentionality to the reader or to something else. His chicken-or-the-egg reasoning reminds the critic who too summarily takes the idea of source entirely away from the author, to place it either in the reader or in previous discourse, that some power of authorial intention still has to put the idea into word:

> Apparently we only read because the writing is already there, laid out before our eyes. Apparently. But the first person who ever wrote, who cut into stone and wood under ancient skies, was far from responding to the demands of a view that required a reference point and gave it meaning, changed all relations between seeing and the visible. What he left behind him was not something more, something added to other things; it was not even something less — a subtraction of matter, a hollow in the relation to the relief. Then what was it? [8]

Then what was it? What *it* was is what the subject leaves behind. Blanchot prefers here to problematize the subject, as current theoreticians say, rather than to deny it or to posit (put) it in a specific place. For him, the search for the subject, like the theologian's search for God, may not have an end in itself. Still, the possibility that the subject may be found in some as-yet-undiscovered *espace littéraire* — the possibility that the subject may to some degree define itself through the writer — allows Blanchot to go on writing even as he continues to question whether the ultimate source of the writing can be himself. *I will sing while I have any being. I will still write anyway.*

If one considers the gaps of productivity in an entire nonhistory of women writers' texts, *absence* may take on a completely different meaning than either the one specifically coined by Derrida or the less closed one that so clearly troubles Blanchot. In *L'Espace littéraire* Blanchot speaks of his "*besoin d'écrire,*" his "need to write." His hand, he says, "doit prendre le crayon, il le faut, c'est un ordre, une exigence impérieuse. Phénomène connu sous le nom de 'préhension persécutrice.'" The need to write is a tyrannic force for him, a creative force outside the writer, demanding that he produce. Blanchot admits that any number of writers "périssent silencieusement" and that "nul qui a regardé le risque en face n'en peut douter."[9] ("No one who has faced the risk of perishing silently can doubt that risk.")

But he could even have gone a little farther, it seems to me. In order for the author-as-subject to be dead, or to perish, as Blanchot has it here, he or she must first exist. He or she must have a name, as Michel Foucault puts it. In order to be an author, the individual who writes must be found to be a definite historical figure in which a series of events converge.[10] Yet historically, for a woman who has felt this need to write, her daily existence, her biography, has determined the very real absence of her text in the written world. She did not write — history did not bestow its name upon her — because of the very subjective existence that a deconstructive reading of her nontext would deny. It is precisely her biographical presence that has determined her documented absence in the collective text. As Jean-Paul Sartre points out in *L'Etre et le néant*, "Il serait impossible . . . de définir l'être comme une *présence* — puisque l'absence dévoile aussi l'être, puisque ne pas être là, c'est encore être."[11] ("It is impossible to define being merely as presence, since absence also reveals being.") Therefore, not to be there — or hardly to be there, until fairly recently, in an entire history of literature — is (still) to be.

A woman's biography, her real-life existence, has often forced her to oppose her need to write. As Tillie Olsen in part describes it:

> Motherhood means being instantly interruptible, responsive, responsible. Children need one *now* (and remember, in our society, the family must often try to be the center for love and health the outside world is not). The very fact that these are needs of love, not duty, that one feels them as one's self; *that there is no one else to be responsible for these needs*, gives them primacy. It is distraction, not meditation, that becomes habitual; interruption, not continuity; spasmodic, not constant toil. Work interrupted, deferred, postponed makes blockage — at best, lesser accomplishment. Unused capacities atrophy, cease to be.[12]

The tendency to deny in herself the need to write in favor of the felt responsibility to look after the needs of others has often had the potential of carrying the creative woman to the frontiers of her death. This danger — the impossible choice that either kills the individual physically (she dies through exhaustion or suicide) or creatively (she does not produce her art) — is one that the study of biography will show us has only been experienced by marginalized groups such as women (of all races), nonwhite men, and the extremely poor.

This is not the place to go into the rediscovery of lost texts by women, the publication and promotion of which have been admirably undertaken most recently by such publishers as the Feminist Press and Alice James Books. Various feminist critics have pointed out that any number of texts by women did in fact exist much earlier but that they were subsequently smothered or dismissed. Yet the evidence is overwhelming that the hardships of women's lives, and not only the historical disinterest of men for the female writer's text, still account for most of the black holes in the canon of literature by women authors, and we need to be as wary of the dismissal of these lacunae as merely the doing of unappreciative male editors and professors in the artist's time as we are of the all-too-timely denial of authorial subjectivity. Otherwise, we may miss the opportunities to make educational and social reforms for women and for minorities and for the ethnic poor so that these texts continue to be present in our time. Some of the combined burdens of child-rearing and housework and the financial need to work outside the home at menial jobs need to be lifted from the unknown or minor artist, whether that artist is a woman or a man. But historically, the writer who does all these jobs at once, and still attempts to write, is not a man but a woman.

In *A Room of One's Own*, Virginia Woolf decries the historical absence of a fictitious author called "Shakespeare's sister." That "Shakespeare's sister" appears to be Woolf's preferred appellative for this neo-fictitious creature — rather than the specific name "Judith" she gives her almost as an afterthought — is particularly relevant to a discussion of absence and subjectivity, if one considers Foucault's concept of the author's name. Foucault explains, "The author's name is not a function of a man's civil status, nor is it fictional; it is situated in the breach, among the discontinuities, which gives rise to new groups of discourse and their singular mode of existence. Consequently, we can say that in our culture, the name of an author is a variable that accompanies only certain texts to the exclusion of others."[13]

In a neat ironic reversal of Foucault's concept of the function of the author's name, the text of Shakespeare's sister, as it might have represented "new groups of discourse and their singular mode of existence," has been excluded because Judith's name, as a symbol of the acts that have made up her existence or as a symbol of her identity or as a way she might have signed the unwritten texts, has been erased. That is, the absence of her text occurs because of the historical denial of her name, except in relation to her brother. She is less Judith than she is Shakespeare's sister.

Virginia Woolf tells us what would have become of a woman of that period in history who was a writer. She says of Shakespeare's sister:

> The force of her own gift alone drove her to it. . . . She had the quickest fancy, a gift like her brother's, for the tune of words. Like him, she had a taste for the theater. She stood at the stage door; she wanted to act, she said. Men laughed in her face. The manager — a fat, loose-lipped man — guffawed. He bellowed something about poodles dancing and women acting. . . . He hinted — you can imagine what. She could get no training in her craft. . . . Yet her genius was for fiction and lusted to feed abundantly upon the lives of men and women and the study of their ways. At last . . . Nick Greene the actor-manager took pity on her; she found herself with child by that gentleman and so — who shall measure the heat and violence of the poet's heart when caught and tangled in a woman's body? — killed herself one winter's night

and lies buried at some crossroads where the omnibuses now stop outside the Elephant and Castle.[14]

Clearly, it is the absence of a text by this author that begins in Woolf the fictive invention of a life for her. Woolf feels this dead author's nonpresence like a cry. For Woolf, the tragic biography of Shakespeare's sister has become more important than the text this poor Elizabethan woman could not have written. Here, the critic in fact needs the biography of Shakespeare's sister in order to deny her text, since it is because of her biography that the text of Shakespeare's sister does not exist. Woolf further writes:

> Yet genius of a sort must have existed among women as it must have existed among the working classes. Now and again an Emily Brontë or a Robert Burns blazes out and *proves its presence*. But certainly it never got itself on to paper. When, however, one reads of a witch being ducked, of a woman possessed by devils, of a wise woman selling herbs, or even of a very remarkable man who had a mother, then I think we are on the track of a lost novelist, a suppressed poet, of some mute and inglorious Jane Austen, some Emily Brontë who dashed her brains out on the moor or moped and mowed about the highways crazed with the torture that her gift had put her to.[15]

In thinking about the subject, particularly in the context (or nontext) of the subject-that-is-not, one cannot help but put some importance back onto historicity and specifically back onto the author's life (in this case, her nonbiography) as it shapes or influences or entirely eradicates the text.

If the subject is to be found as ever having had any real existence of its own, perhaps it is to be found in moments of experience rather than in the historical sense of time.

Walter Benjamin speaks of the moment of shock experience (*Erlebnis*) and by inference of the reflection that turns the moment into lived experience (*Erfahrung*). One feels a sort of anxiety of usurpation in some of the essays collected in *Illuminations*. Benjamin fears storytelling will be usurped by mechanical information and that reader-oriented sensation (as a sort of ironic reversal of the author's moment) will replace the lived experience of the subject:

> The replacement of the older narration by information, of information by sensation, reflects the increasing atrophy of experience. In turn, there is a contrast between all these forms and the story, which is one of the oldest forms of communication. It is not the object of the story to convey a happening *per se*, which is the purpose of information; rather, it embeds it in the life of the storyteller in order to pass it on as experience to those listening. It thus bears the marks of the storyteller much as the earthen vessel bears the marks of the potter's hand.[16]

Poetic language might thus be taken as evidence of the reflection by some subjective consciousness upon the moment of the lived experience — or "emotion recollected in tranquillity," as Wordsworth put it.[17] While the authority of the utterance of the subject may be in the moment, in the unmediated, transcendental, or wordless moment outside the introspection of the self, it is only through lived experience — seen in strong emotion, pain, or ecstasy as it takes place — that the moment finally finds its way through reflection into the poetic language of the text.

This moment might very well be compared to what religionists refer to as a conversion scene. In the last chapter of *Deceit, Desire and the Novel: Self and Other in Literary Structure*, René Girard writes of the inexpressible experience of conversion. The chapter brings triangulation, with its concept of mediation by outside discourse, into question, even after Girard has spent the entire book so carefully building it up. He notes, "If only our prejudices *pro* and *con* did not erect a water-tight barrier between aesthetic experience and religious experience we would see the problems of creation in a new light."[18]

If those of us who cling to our subjectivity can be satisfied with moments outside conventional measurements of time, if we are willing to give up the argument that a name possesses a particular short story or poem or novel throughout some duration of moments that will in turn be called literary history, if we are willing to release the text away from the author into the world that will become its reader in the same way a mother would release a child to its own world in the moment the child is born, then we can begin to know where the subject, if only for the moment, can be found.

Let us get back to Shakespeare's sister, particularly to her experience of having that child by the *kind* Nick Greene. Virginia Woolf, herself childless, essentially tells us that her fictitious author had to choose between her gift and the child. Eventually, as we know, Shakespeare's sister (whose experience I am beginning to become so involved in that I no longer can put her nonexistent name into convenient quotes), killed herself one winter's night, leaving the child by Nick Greene in God knows what sort of repetition of her mother's fate. (I am obviously assuming, with my authorial bent for tragedy, that the child was a *girl*.) Shakespeare's sister's experience is the stuff of plays. I should have liked to have read of her experience, perhaps in place of *The Tempest* or *A Midsummer Night's Dream*.

But Shakespeare's sister would have had, as Woolf points out, no time (and no one to encourage her) to put that experience into poetry or prose. If one looks at the pitifully few books by women authors during Shakespeare's time, or in any period before the twentieth century for that matter, that are included on some reading list, one will find that most of those precious relics of early female experience do not contain the one lived experience (an experience of too great a duration to be categorized merely under Benjamin's concept of *Erfahrung*) that would respond to the experience of a very large number of the women who would have been reading the books, or indeed to anyone who was reading the books who was not white, upper middle class, and male.

The women who could manage to write books were certainly white, most probably rich, and, so far as the evidence tells us, childless. Childlessness is what almost every woman who has managed to write copiously has had in common until perhaps the last twenty years. What is greatly missing in the world's literature, and in most forms of art for that matter, is the lived, biographical experience of childbirth and child-rearing as it finds its way into oil and stone and ink as the artist's text. To an enormous degree, the artistic themes of childbirth and mothering have been largely construed or imagined by men or, though much less often, by childless women.

The French critic and philosopher Julia Kristeva touches briefly on the great gaps in this particular expression of subjectivity in "Motherhood According to Bellini," when she discusses Bellini's baroque sculpture, "Sacra Conversazione."[19] Kristeva laments an art history that is too replete with *man*-made enigmatic mothers, such as Bellini's sculpture, beautiful but distant, the product of cold intellect rather than of joy-as-experience, or *jouissance*.

The *jouissance* of this particular lived experience is missing from most of the world's recorded art. If there are boundaries of appropriation or limits to artistic invention, then childbearing and mothering may well be the experiences whose boundaries would have been most successfully explored by the artist who literally was not there.

Virginia Woolf herself, sensitive as she is to Judith's plight and given as she is in her own fiction to the creation of mother/daughter relationships, still seems to valorize as subject matter, at least in the theory she presents in *A Room of One's Own*, the traditional experience of men, suggesting that only when that traditional definition for worthwhile experience has been opened up to women (including the professions of lawyers, doctors, professors, and soldiers, to name a few) will women *really* have something worthy to write about. It is in fact perhaps one of the greatest ironies of feminist literature that Woolf's poor shunted creature, this Judith, bears the same name as the courageous woman of the Hebrew Apocrypha who slays the monstrous general Holofernes after seducing him in enemy territory in his tent. Woolf laments that Judith cannot have been a warrior — that she is *only* a sister and then a mother. Yet for all her lack of major occupations, Judith has become the indisputable mother of every feminist text that has been written since.

Frankly, I have already read enough books about being a soldier. That subject, that experience, really doesn't interest me anymore at all. On being a soldier, Ernest Hemingway has already told me more than I ever hope to tell again on some postgraduate exam. From what I have learned about being a soldier from Hemingway — or from watching the Huntley-Brinkley report during the sixties, for that matter, since I happened to grow up scared to death my little brother would be killed or maimed in Vietnam — I don't believe I would want that experience, even if I were a male or even if the world, in some warped sense of progress, liberated me enough to allow me to go to war.

No, what I would have liked to have read by Shakespeare's sister (since her brother seems to have known next to nothing about this subject) is a play about her lived experience with Nick Greene's child. I do not wish to see her lived experience — whatever it was — devalued. The intense suffering of that experience alone would have given her plenty to write about, and plenty that very few people have written about before.

A few years ago I was preparing to teach a discussion session for a group of undergraduates reading *Madame Bovary* for the first time. It was also the first time I had reread that book since I had become a mother. I found myself extremely agitated by Flaubert's creation of the relationship between Emma Bovary and her daughter, Berthe. Of course it was only a novel, I told myself. I also knew, with my tidy little B.A. in French from Berkeley, that Flaubert was one of the greatest novelists of all time. But nothing, nothing on earth was going to convince me that the relationship between Madame Bovary and Berthe was believable. This time, when I read the place in the book where the baby Berthe vomits on the shoulder of the elegant robe of her mother and Emma then leaves the nurse's cottage with a careful, deliberate wiping of her feet, I shook my head and whispered, *No.* Flaubert, in attempting to change from *je* to *elle*, is supposed to have said, "Madame Bovary, c'est moi." And in a way that he did not intend, I believe him. Madame Bovary isn't *elle*, she's *lui*. Flaubert did not create a romantic heroine; he created a romantic hero in the body of a woman. He created a woman who is himself, which is to say he created *un[e] monstre*.

Of course it's true, *you idiot*, I told myself, that there are mothers in the world who hate their children and who didn't want them in the first place and who punish them for any little thing at all or who burn them and torture them for pleasure's sake. Medeas, all. But the Medea mother is the exception to the human rule, and that is why we read about her in the newspaper when she gets caught. Yet that mother is the one whose experience in fiction I am most often forced to read, even though, historically, her experience has mostly been the creation of writing men.

Simone de Beauvoir, with her innate ethical sense of giving credit to men where it is due, turns to another romantic, Stendhal, and says of him: "Il est réconfortant d'aborder un homme qui vit parmi des femmes de chair et d'os." This "tender friend of women," as she calls Stendhal, does not idealize women; they are "women of flesh and blood." De Beauvoir goes on to say that because Stendhal loves women in their truth, he does not believe in some unapproachable *mystère féminin*. No single essence can define woman once and for all for him. The idea of an *éternel féminin* strikes him as pedantic and ridiculous, de Beauvoir claims. She is particularly admiring of his Mme. de Rênal, the timid and virtuous older woman in *Le Rouge et le noir* who loves the tempestuous young tutor of her children, Julien Sorel. Mme. de Rênal, she says, loves Julien without self-consciousness. She is a woman who loves Julien in spite of the moral structure imposed upon her by society.[20]

But something still bothers me about Stendhal's woman, who can give her passion to a new man so unself-consciously, so regardless of the consequences, after she has undergone the experience of childbirth — after she has experienced, as Kristeva terms it, "the other in its radical separation from herself, that is, as an object of love."[21] What has this good woman sacrificed herself to? Isn't she just another example of the age-old argument that a woman should be willing to love (have sex with) a man without regard to self? If we would really have a woman in a novel love unself-consciously, we would be willing to write about a woman who loves her child.

What I would object to, if I were Virginia Woolf, is not the fact that Shakespeare's sister wasn't allowed to be an actor or a warrior or a doctor or a lawyer, but that she was not given enough space and time in the world — her own *espace* — to write herself. To be completely fair, I would have liked Shakespeare's sister to have been allowed to write about anything at all that interested her, even if that meant letting her write about being an actor or a soldier. But I would have been intensely interested, as a reading mother, to have been able to read about her and that child and that cad Nick Greene. As Mary Gordon comments:

> It was all right for the young men I knew, according to my specters [the two famous poets who are her ghosts], to write about the hymens they had broken, the diner waitresses they had seduced. Those experiences were significant. But we were not to write about our broken hearts, about the married men we loved disastrously, about our mothers or our children. Men could write about their fears of dying by exposure in the forest; we could not write about our fears of being suffocated in the kitchen. Our desire to write about these experiences only revealed our shallowness; it was suggested we would, in time, get over it. And write about what? Perhaps we would stop writing.[22]

And that atrophy, that stopping writing, seems to me to be the issue that some new Virginia Woolf, with a Shakespeare's sister, should now take up.

It is also closer to the point I think we need to be making about a Foucault or a Derrida. If we are going to liberate Shakespeare's sister, we need to acknowledge her subjective experience, whatever it was. We need to acknowledge her biography — that she was alive. We need to let her write about her married man. Of course Nick Greene was already married. You already knew that, didn't you? The confinement of his marriage would have made the adventurous runaway Judith all the more attractive to the likes of him. Because what a married man does with a Judith, if he can't marry her to get rid of the very rebellion against the status quo that attracted him to her in the first place, is to give her up. *I cannot leave my wife, dear Judith. I love you, but I cannot leave her. We have lost a child together, Judith. She needs me. My wife is a very good woman. And while my passion for you is endless, Judith, you are not.* And then who the hell cares what Judith, let alone her illegitimate lovechild, might be doing after that? For all practical purposes, Nick Greene's departure ends the story; there is nothing left for Judith but to die.

But what if Judith should insist she will keep right on going? Even after that? What if Judith does not stop writing? What if she puts Nick Greene into her fountain pen and writes him out?

In her novel *Occasion of Sin*, the English author Rachel Billington gives a male writer's romantic heroine the opportunity to make another ending for herself. In her rewrite of Tolstoy's *Anna Karenina*, Billington does not have her postmodern Anna, Laura Knight, throw herself under the train but rather allows her to get on the train and head in an unknown direction. Anna is free to seek another ending to the book. Billington doesn't presume to know what will happen to her Anna/Laura but lets the reader imagine all the possibilities. In so doing, she gives Tolstoy's romantic Anna a second chance.[23]

In somewhat the same way, I would like someone to go back in time and wash Judith's dishes for her so that she can write. I would like someone to give her about four hours every morning while Nick Greene's baby is still asleep. I would like the situation surrounding the woman writer to be such that Shakespeare's sister's choice between the child and the gift will not be a choice she will necessarily have to make, because in the end we would still have lost a writer — although a very different one — if the "real" Judith Shakespeare had been allowed to write but had had no child.

Then, after all that miraculous rewriting of literary history has been accomplished, I wish, I really wish, I could read her book. But Virginia Woolf's somewhat benign denigration of the particular experiences of childbirth and family relations — remember that in her "Professions for Women" she is happy to have finally killed off "the Angel in the House" — has continued very much into our own time.[24] It may be somehow suddenly all right now for intelligent, well-educated women to have children. Modern conveniences, an increase in day-care centers, and a growing willingness on the part of fathers to contribute to the raising of their children have made it possible for professional women to have children and to hold a job. Yet we have barely begun to allow women who write to write about the children they only recently were allowed to want to have.

Alice Walker has commented, "The point is, I was changed forever. From a woman whose 'womb' had been, in a sense, her head; that is to say, certain small seeds had gone in, rather different if not larger or better 'creations' had come out, to a woman who had 'conceived' books in her head, and had also engendered at least one human being in her body."[25] If the lived experience of mothering by women writers eventually provides us with subject matter that was previously absent from our art, perhaps that lived experience can also begin to provide us with a metaphor for the act of writing itself. Birthing might serve as an emblem for the process through which the subject is conceived and, in one almost measureless moment, is then brought forth.

Perhaps more radically than any of her contemporaries, Julia Kristeva challenges the Freudian-psychoanalytical base for describing the writing process through the pen/penis metaphor, by replacing the Oedipal stage in human (if predominantly male) development with what she terms in her *Revolution in Poetic Language* the pre-Oedipal or semiotic or thetic stage. According to Kristeva, the basis for analysis should be in the prelanguage period of development in the child.[26] By moving her analysis of the subject to the prelanguage stage, Kristeva has taken the subject almost entirely out of a realm where it can be categorically denied a specific identity. Her subject is one that is in search of its identity, but a subject whose identity is quite surely a possibility in any case. The subject is in process, like a growing child.

It was only after I had a child myself that I began to listen to all those scary stories about childbirth that I had heard in supermarkets, in neighbors' kitchens, and in laundromats. The voices of the women telling those stories finally began to mean something to me, not just as scary stories (or pleasant, quiet stories) about childbirth but as allegories for the process of writing. I had been writing stories and poems since I was a child, but it was only after the experience of childbirth that I realized that writing might find its ultimate metaphor in birth. Although I remember one morning in my seventh month lying on my back and saying (one can only re-member the body of one's thoughts with the limbs of words), *I will never, never tell another woman to go through this*, I cannot remember the actual circumstances that made me say that. I cannot now feel the pain-that-was. At the actual moment in which the baby was born — in that one quick, timeless travel of the whoosh when she jetted out — in that one moment there was honestly no pain. That much I know. In that one moment, the *I* that was me (that "I. I. I.") was sorely needed for the birth of one particular subject or identity, that is, *my child*. Were I to have passed her on to another mother at her birth (as, say, through legal adoption), were I to have died in childbirth (and I have yet to listen to a woman who didn't have that fear), were I to have been separated from her from then on for whatever reason (some affection-starved and childless other woman stealing her from the very nursery that holds her crib), I alone was needed at the moment of her birth. I alone was chosen for that work.

The word for the period just prior to childbirth is *labor*, and I have enjoyed applying Plato's concept of individual work in his ideal city both to the concept of childbirth and to my writing. On some level (though if I am pressed, I will inevitably, even politely, back down), there is only justice in Plato's city of shared work and reward if *my* work, *my* labor is accorded its proper place.

But during childbirth I also had a fleeting sense that something entirely outside of me was taking place. I knew that I could not have done this by myself. Like Kristeva, I cannot be entirely certain that the subject can be closed or that it can be found only in the critic's (mis)interpretation of it. Neither can I believe that the subject is entirely in the author's own experience, in the human self. Perhaps the subject can only be found in a moment, even though that moment be outside time.

Having a child, especially the continuing experience of raising one, has also revolutionized the *way* I write. For one thing, I can't hate any of my characters anymore. Hating them made it easy. All I had to do was to personify *Evil* within some makeshift body and call it quits. My work as a mother has complicated that. The knowledge that I cannot by myself, if she will not listen to me, save my daughter from strangers — no matter how many times I warn her about the Man in the Red Sports Car with the Black Windows you can't see through (*Oh, watch out! watch out!*) — has changed my concept of the setting in which I write. I can foresee problems for my characters, and I can hope that they will choose to avoid those problems. But I cannot solve their problems for them. I can love them, the way I love my daughter (*Oh God, how the angels of my thinking fly out over her fragile body as she leaves my house*), but I cannot completely dictate their actions or be entirely sure how they are going to end up reacting to the situation that is playing itself out for them as I write. I can give my characters friends within the story who will express kindnesses to them, who might help them. I can hover about the margins in the guise of an omniscient narrator and make wise remarks. But in the end I know I don't have all the answers. Like most humans, what my characters are going to learn, they will teach themselves.

In short, evil is no longer in this character or that one for me — the simple Other/Self. Evil is something that is as much at war with my villains as it is with the rest of us. Every one of my characters (like everyone I see on the street since I have become a mother) has to have been at some point some other woman's baby, somebody's child. I seem to have convinced myself that every mother, even if she never saw the child again after the day she bore it, had to have whispered a prayer, if it was only the desperate, thoughtless cry of pain in childbirth that said, *Oh God!* This is the myth of my own creating that I cannot give up.

Just as I work within a framework of responsibility for my daughter's life, even though it is clear to me that she no longer has anything to do with me (that is, I can only be a decent mother if I release her to the process of her growing up), so the continuing responsibility I feel for my daughter's happiness and well-being is very much like what I feel, in my role as a "minor woman writer," for the things I write. I must continue to send my stories to receptive small literary magazines, and when enough individual stories are published, my responsibility to them will be to collect them and to try to place them with some small house.

My text is on its own now, invaluable though I may have been in its coming forth. My daughter is born. She is her own person. I can no more be my text than I can be my daughter. I cannot be another being, nor can I be a book. But neither can I deny the ongoing subject that is myself. In the end, this is the question of being minor, of writing anyway. Singing while one has any being. Giving voice.

Notes

• • • •

Preface

1. Horace, *Horace for English Readers: Being a Translation of the Poems of Quintus Horatius Flaccus into English Prose*, trans. E. C. Wickham (London: Oxford University Press, 1930); Aristotle, *On Poetry and Style (The Poetics)*, trans. G. M. A. Grube (New York: Bobbs-Merrill, 1958).

2. C. O. Brink, *Horace on Poetry: The "Ars Poetica,"* vol. 2 (Cambridge: Cambridge University Press, 1971), pp. 80–81, 521–522.

3. Michel Foucault, "What Is an Author?," in *Language, Counter-Memory, Practice: Selected Essays and Interviews*, ed. Donald F. Bouchard, trans. Donald F. Bouchard and Sherry Simon (Ithaca, N.Y.: Cornell University Press, 1977), pp. 113–138.

4. Josué Harari, introduction to *Textual Strategies: Perspectives in Post-Structuralist Criticism* (Ithaca, N.Y.: Cornell University Press, 1979). For a cogent sketch of structuralist theory, see Cesare Segre, *Strutturalismo e critica* (Milan: Il Saggiatore, 1985).

5. Thomas Mann, "Death in Venice," in *Stories of a Lifetime*, vol. 2 (London: Martin Secker and Warburg, 1961); Louisa May Alcott, *Little Women* (New York: Grosset and Dunlap, 1986), p. 60.

6. Isak Dinesen, "Babette's Feast," in *"Babette's Feast" and Other Anecdotes of Destiny* (New York: Random House, 1986), p. 47.

7. Brink, *Horace on Poetry*, p. 522.

1. The Question of Being Minor

1. Mary Gordon, "Parable of the Cave or: In Praise of Watercolors," in *The Writer on Her Work: Contemporary Women Writers*

Reflect on Their Art and Situation, ed. Janet Sternburg (New York: W. W. Norton, 1980), p. 28.

2. Horace, *Horace for English Readers: Being a Translation of the Poems of Quintus Horatius Flaccus into English Prose*, trans. E. C. Wickham (London: Oxford University Press, 1930); Nicolas Boileau-Despréaux, *L'Art poétique, suivi de l'art poétique d'Horace et d'une anthologie de la poésie préclassique en France (1600–1670)*, ed. François Mizrachi (Paris: Union Générale d'Editions, Editions 10/18, 1966); Sir Philip Sidney, "The Defense of Poesie," in *Literary Criticism: Plato to Dryden*, ed. Allan H. Gilbert (Detroit: Wayne State University Press, 1967); Percy Bysshe Shelley, "A Defense of Poetry," in *Shelley's Prose* (Albuquerque: University of New Mexico Press, 1966); Edgar Allan Poe, "Philosophy of Composition," and "Review of *Twice-Told Tales*," in *Essays and Reviews* (New York: Library of America, 1984); Walt Whitman, "Preface," *Leaves of Grass*, ed. Emory Holloway (Garden City, N.Y.: Doubleday, Page, 1925).

3. Michel Foucault, "What Is an Author?," in *Language, Counter-Memory, Practice: Selected Essays and Interviews*, ed. Donald F. Bouchard, trans. Donald F. Bouchard and Sherry Simon (Ithaca, N.Y.: Cornell University Press, 1977).

4. Ibid., p. 128.

5. C. O. Brink, *Horace on Poetry: The "Ars Poetica,"* vol. 2 (Cambridge: Cambridge University Press, 1971), p. 522.

6. Jean-François Lyotard, *The Différend: Phrases in Dispute*, trans. Georges Van Den Abbeele, Theory and History of Literature Series, vol. 46 (Minneapolis: University of Minnesota Press, 1988), p. 4.

7. Northrop Frye, *Anatomy of Criticism: Four Essays* (Princeton: Princeton University Press, 1973), pp. 8–10.

8. Harold Bloom, *The Anxiety of Influence: A Theory of Poetry* (New York: Oxford University Press, 1973).

9. See Sima Godfrey, ed., *Yale French Studies: The Anxiety of Anticipation*, vol. 66 (New Haven: Yale University Press, 1984).

10. Harold Bloom, *Ruin the Sacred Truth: Poetry and Belief from the Bible to the Present* (Cambridge: Harvard University Press, 1989).

11. Harold Bloom, introduction to *The Book of J*, trans. David Rosenberg (New York: Grove Weidenfeld, 1990).

12. Bloom, *Ruin*, pp. 6–7.

13. Gilles Deleuze and Félix Guattari, *Kafka: Pour une littérature mineure* (Paris: Editions de Minuit, 1975), pp. 29–31.

14. Toni Morrison, *Playing in the Dark: Whiteness and the Literary Imagination*, William E. Massey Senior Lectures in the History of American Civilization, 1990 (Cambridge: Harvard University Press, 1992), p. 46.

15. Léopold Senghor, *Liberté I: Négritude et humanisme* (Paris: Editions Seuil, 1964); Aimé Césaire, *Discourse on Colonialism*, trans. Joan Pinkham (New York: Monthly Review, 1972).

16. Ps. 146: 2.

17. T. S. Eliot, "What Is Minor Poetry?," in *On Poetry and Poets* (London: Faber and Faber, 1957), pp. 39–52.

18. Louis A. Renza, *"A White Heron" and the Question of Minor Literature* (Madison: University of Wisconsin Press, 1984).

19. David Lloyd, *Nationalism and Minor Literature: James Clarence Mangan and the Emergence of Irish Cultural Nationalism* (Berkeley: University of California Press, 1987), p. 19.

20. Horace, *Horace for English Readers*, p.347.

21. Stéphane Mallarmé, "Art for All," in *Mallarmé: Selected Prose Poems, Essays, and Letters*, trans. Bradford Cook (Baltimore: Johns Hopkins University Press, 1956).

22. Lorraine Hansberry, *To Be Young, Gifted, and Black: Lorraine Hansberry in Her Own Words*, ed. Robert Nemiroff (Englewood Cliffs, N.J.: Prentice-Hall, 1969), p. 91.

23. Italo Calvino, *Lezioni Americane: Sei proposte per il prossimo millennio* (Turin: Garzanti, 1988), p. 16.

24. Lawrence Lipking, "Aristotle's Sister: A Poetics of Abandonment," *Critical Inquiry* 10 (September 1983): 79.

25. Horace, *Horace for English Readers*, p. 358.

26. W. H. Auden, "Writing," in *The Dyer's Hand and Other Essays* (New York: Random House, 1962), pp. 21–22.

27. William Pratt, "Missing the Masters: Nobel Literature Prizes in English," Nobel Prize Symposium II: Choices and Omissions 1967–1987, *World Literature Today* 62, no. 2 (Spring 1988): 227.

28. Ibid.

29. Edith Wharton, *The Writing of Fiction* (New York: Charles Scribner's Sons, 1925), pp. 77–78.

30. Carolyn Heilbrun, "Non-Autobiographies of 'Privileged' Women: England and America," in *Life/Lines: Theorizing Women's Autobiography*, ed. Bella Bradzhi and Celeste Schenck (Ithaca, N.Y.: Cornell University Press, 1988), p. 63.

31. Hansberry, *To Be Young*, p. 145.

32. Ibid., p. 219.

33. Annie Dillard, *Living By Fiction* (New York: Harper and Row, 1982), p. 174.

34. Ibid., p. 175.

35. Emily Dickinson, *Letters of Emily Dickinson*, ed. Mabel Loomis Todd (New York: World Publishing, 1951), p. 146.

2. Purpose

1. Jane Spencer, *The Rise of the Woman Novelist: From Aphra Behn to Jane Austen* (New York: B. Blackwell, 1986), p. 87.

2. Alphonse Jacobs, ed., *Gustave Flaubert–George Sand: Correspondance* (Paris: Flammarion, 1981), p. 165.

3. Sylvia Plath, *Letters Home*, ed. Aurelia Schober Plath (New York: Harper & Row, 1975).

4. George Eliot, "Silly Novels by Lady Novelists," in *The Essays of George Eliot*, comp. Nathan Sheppard (New York: Funk and Wagnalls, 1883), p. 202.

5. Gilles Deleuze and Félix Guattari, *Kafka: Pour une littérature mineure* (Paris: Editions de Minuit, 1975).

6. George Eliot, "Authorship," in *Essays and Leaves from a Notebook* (London: William Blackwood and Sons, 1884), p. 358.

7. Ibid., p. 353.

8. Eliot, "Silly Novels," p. 188.

9. Eliot, "Authorship," pp. 359–360.

10. Edith Wharton, *The Writing of Fiction* (New York: Charles Scribner's Sons, 1925), p. 28.

11. Ibid., p. 27.

12. Ibid., p. 174, 171.

13. Flannery O'Connor, *Mystery and Manners*, ed. Sally Fitzgerald and Robert Fitzgerald (New York: Farrar, Straus and Giroux, 1961), p. 118.

14. Flannery O'Connor, "A Good Man Is Hard to Find," in *Collected Works* (New York: Library of America, 1988), pp. 137–153.

15. O'Connor, *Mystery and Manners*, pp. 33–34.

16. Ibid., p. 74.

17. See Jean-François Lyotard, "Answering the Question: What Is Postmodernism?," trans. Régis Durand, in *The Postmodernist Condition: A Report on Knowledge*, trans. Geoff Bennington and Brian Massumi (Minneapolis: University of Minnesota Press, 1984), Appendix, p. 81.

18. Jean-François Lyotard, *Phenomenology*, trans. Brian Beakley (Albany: State University of New York Press, 1991), p. 136; Jean-François Lyotard, *The Différend: Phrases in Dispute*, trans. Georges Van Den Abbeele, Theory and History of Literature Series, vol. 46 (Minneapolis: University of Minnesota Press, 1988).

19. J. Hillis Miller, *The Ethics of Reading: Kant, DeMan, Eliot, Trollope, James, and Benjamin* (New York: Columbia University Press, 1987); Tobin Siebers, *The Ethics of Criticism* (Ithaca, N.Y.: Cornell University Press, 1988).

20. Anna Laetitia Barbauld, "Essay on Akenside's Poem on *The Pleasures of the Imagination*," in *The Pleasures of the Imagination*, by Mark Akenside (London: n.p., 1818), p. 30.

21. Lyotard, *The Différend*, pp. 147–149.

22. Karl R. Popper, *The Open Society and Its Enemies*, 5th ed., rev. (Princeton: Princeton University Press, 1971).

23. Joseph Deiss, *The Roman Years of Margaret Fuller: A Biography* (New York: Crowell, 1969), p. 176.

24. James Carroll, "The Virtues of Writing," *Ploughshares* 15, nos. 2 & 3 (1989): 4.

25. John Winthrop, *The History of New England from 1630 to 1649*, vol. 1, ed. James Savage (Boston: Phelps and Farnham, 1825), pp. 261–262.

26. Ibid., 262.

27. Carolyn G. Heilbrun, *Writing a Woman's Life* (New York: W. W. Norton, 1988), p. 18.

28. Gen. 37.

29. Jerzy Kosinski, *The Painted Bird* (Boston: Houghton Mifflin, 1965).

30. Mary Gordon, "On Mothership and Authorhood," *New York Times Book Review* Feb. 10, 1985.

31. Joan Didion, *Play It As It Lays* (New York: Farrar, Straus and Giroux, 1970).

32. See 1 Sam. 25: 2–42.

3. Why I (Still) Write Stories

1. Herbert Mitgang, "A New Life for the Short Story," *New York Times* Mar. 20, 1985, sec. 3.

2. Ibid.

3. Gayle Feldman, "Is There a Short Story Boom?," *Publishers Weekly*, Dec. 25, 1987, 25, 27.

4. Deirdre Carmody, "The Short Story: Out of the Mainstream but Flourishing," *New York Times* Apr. 23, 1991.

5. André Dubus, "Reading: Fiction and the Facts of Life," *Boston Magazine*, November 1977, p. 58.

6. Edgar Allan Poe, "Review of *Twice-Told Tales*," in *Essays and Reviews* (New York: Library of America, 1984), p. 15.

7. Ibid.

8. Edgar Allan Poe, "The Fall of the House of Usher," in *The Annotated Tales of Edgar Allan Poe*, ed. Stephen Peithman (New York: Doubleday, 1981), p. 62.

9. Aristotle, *On Poetry and Style (The Poetics)*, trans. G. M. A. Grube (New York: Bobbs-Merrill, 1958), p. 16.

10. Horace, *Horace for English Readers: Being a Translation of the Poems of Quintus Horatius Flaccus into English Prose*, trans. E. C. Wickham (London: Oxford University Press, 1930), p. 357.

11. While it is not my intention here to give a full bibliography of the history of the short story or the criticism concerning it, it may be in order to list a few works that I have found helpful in thinking about the short story as a distinct genre. Brander Matthews's *The Philosophy of the Short Story* (New York: Peter Smith,

1931) is one of the earliest book-length attempts to explore the short story as a separate literary entity. For a later general overview of the history of the short story as seen through various essays by short story writers from Poe to Flannery O'Connor to Alberto Moravia, see Charles E. May, ed., *Short Story Theories* (Athens: Ohio University Press, 1976). William Peden's *The American Short Story: Continuity and Change, 1940–1975* (Boston: Houghton Mifflin, 1975) provides useful if somewhat general information on the evolution of the contemporary short story in the United States. William Abrahams's continuing observations about the American short story in his yearly introductions to *Prize Stories: The O. Henry Collection* (New York: Doubleday), as well as the late Martha Foley's and now the guest editor's annual remarks in *Best American Short Stories* (Boston: Houghton Mifflin), provide astute summations of the health of the genre in the United States and English-speaking Canada for any given year. Susan Lohafer's *Coming to Terms with the Short Story* (Baton Rouge: Louisiana State University, 1984), while it may not provide much that is new in terms of genre theory, is a highly readable and entertaining piece of work that should be required reading in short story writing workshops, if only so that budding story writers will know, so to speak, where they're coming from. There remains a great need for a more lengthy critical study of the short story — not only as it has been practiced on this continent but as it has taken form in Europe and beyond.

12. Edith Wharton, *The Writing of Fiction* (New York: Octagon Books, 1966), pp. 50–51.

13. Ibid.

14. Leo Tolstoy, "On Truth in Art," in *Tolstoy on Art*, ed. Aylmer Maude (Boston: Small, Maynard, 1924), p. 33.

15. Carolyn Forché, "An Interview with David Montenegro," *American Poetry Review* (November/December 1988): p. 35.

16. Leo Tolstoy, "What Is Art?," in *Tolstoy on Art*, ed. Alymer Maude, p. 292.

17. Kendall L. Walton, *Mimesis as Make Believe: On the Foundations of Representational Art* (Cambridge: Harvard University Press, 1990). Bruno Bettelheim, in *The Uses of Enchantment: The*

Meaning and Importance of Fairy Tales (New York: Alfred Knopf, 1976), would agree with Walton.

18. Feldman, "Is There a Short Story Boom?," p. 28.

19. Annie Dillard, "Write Till You Drop," *New York Times Book Review* May 28, 1989. The essay was subsequently included in *The Writing Life* (New York: Harper & Row, 1989).

20. Brander Matthews, "The Philosophy of the Short Story," in May, *Short Story Theories*, p. 52.

21. May, *Short Story Theories*, p. 6.

22. Italo Calvino, *Lezioni Americane: Sei proposte per il prossimo millennio* (Turin: Einaudi, 1988), p. 39.

23. Raymond Carver, "A Small, Good Thing," in *Where I'm Calling From: New and Selected Stories* (New York: Atlantic Monthly Press, 1988), pp. 280–301.

24. Frank O'Connor, *The Lonely Voice: A Study of the Short Story* (New York: World Publishing, 1963), p. 18.

25. Ibid., pp. 128–130.

26. Northrop Frye, *Anatomy of Criticism* (Princeton: Princeton University Press, 1973), p. 72.

27. René Girard, *Deceit, Desire, and the Novel: Self and Other in Literary Structure*, trans. Yvonne Freccero (Baltimore: Johns Hopkins University Press, 1961), pp. 294, 309–310.

28. E. M. Forster, *Aspects of the Novel* (New York: Harcourt, Brace, 1927), pp. 144, 241–242.

29. Virginia Woolf, *A Room of One's Own* (New York: Harcourt Brace Jovanovich, 1957), p. 80.

4. Experience

1. Horace, *Horace for English Readers: Being a Translation of the Poems of Quintus Horatius Flaccus into English Prose*, trans. E. C. Wickham (London: Oxford University Press, 1930), p. 346; Anne-Louise-Germaine Necker de Staël, *De l'Allemagne*, 2 vols. (Paris: Garnier-Flammarion, 1967), pp. 194–195.

2. Henry James, *The Art of the Novel: Critical Prefaces*, ed. R. P. Blackmur (New York: Charles Scribner's Sons, 1934), pp. 119–120; R. W. B. Lewis, *Edith Wharton: A Biography* (New York:

Harper and Row, 1975), p. 308; "An Introduction to *The Sound and the Fury,*" *Mississippi Quarterly* 26 (Summer 1973): 413.

3. Jacques Derrida, "Qual quelle: Les sources de Valéry," in *Marges de la philosophie* (Paris: Editions de Minuit, 1972), pp. 327–363.

4. Cesare Pavese, *La letteratura americana e altri saggi* (Turin: Einaudi, 1953), pp. 307–311, 345–351.

5. Giambattista Vico, *The New Science of Giambattista Vico,* trans. Thomas Goddard Bergin and Max Harold Fisch (Ithaca, N.Y.: Cornell University Press, 1948), p. 105.

6. Maurice Blanchot, *L'Espace littéraire* (Paris: Gallimard, 1955), p. 29.

7. Jean-Paul Sartre, *L'Etre et le néant* (Paris: Gallimard, 1943); Jean-Paul Sartre, "Pourquoi écrire," in *Qu'est-ce que la littérature* (Paris: Gallimard, 1948).

8. Immanuel Kant, *Critique of Pure Reason,* trans. F. Max Mueller (Garden City, N.Y.: Doubleday, 1966).

9. Johann Wolfgang von Goethe, "Poetry and Patriotism," in *Goethe's Literary Essays,* ed. J. E. Spingarn (New York: Harcourt, Brace, 1921), p. 251.

10. Jean-Jacques Rousseau, *Reveries of the Solitary Walker,* trans. Peter France (New York: Viking Penguin, 1979), p. 20.

11. Ralph Waldo Emerson, "The Poet," in *Essays,* vol. 3, *Complete Works of Ralph Waldo Emerson* (Boston, New York: Houghton Mifflin, 1979), p. 4.

12. James Russell Lowell, "The Function of the Poet," in *The Function of the Poet and Other Essays* (Boston: Houghton Mifflin, 1920), p. 27.

13. Pavese, *La letteratura americana.*

14. Stanley Kunitz, foreword to *Gathering the Tribes,* by Carolyn Forché (New Haven: Yale University Press, 1976), p. xiii.

15. Carolyn Forché, *The Angel of History* (New York: Harper-Collins, 1994).

16. Carolyn Forché, "An Interview with David Montenegro," *American Poetry Review* (November/December 1988): 35.

17. Carolyn Forché, ed., *Against Forgetting: Twentieth Century Poetry of Witness* (New York: W. W. Norton, 1993).

18. Michel Foucault, "What Is an Author?," in *Language, Counter-Memory, Practice: Selected Essays and Interviews*, ed. Donald F. Bouchard, trans. Donald F. Bouchard and Sherry Simon (Ithaca, N.Y.: Cornell University Press, 1977), pp. 113–138.

19. Ernest Hemingway, *Dateline: Toronto, the Complete Toronto Star Dispatches, 1920–1924*, ed. William White (New York: Charles Scribner's Sons, 1985).

20. Virginia Woolf, *A Room of One's Own* (New York: Harcourt Brace Jovanovich, 1957), p. 116.

21. Mary Gordon, foreword to *A Room of One's Own*, by Virginia Woolf (New York: Harcourt Brace Jovanovich, 1981), p. x.

22. Sara Ruddick, *Maternal Thinking: Towards a Politics of Peace* (Boston: Beacon Press, 1989).

23. Elsa Morante, *La storia: Un romanzo* (Turin: Einaudi, 1974).

24. For a summation of the *terza pagina* (op-ed pages) argument among critics and writers alike on the politics of Morante's novel, see Gregory L. Lucente, "Scrivere o fare . . . o altro: Social Commitment and Ideologies of Representation in the Debates over Lampedusa's *Il Gattopardo* and Morante's *La Storia*," *Italica* 61, no. 3 (Autumn 1984): 220–251.

25. Henry James, *Portrait of a Lady* (New York: W. W. Norton, 1975), p. 146.

26. Edna O'Brien, "'Hers' Column," *New York Times* Oct. 3, 1985, sec. 3.

27. Jonathan Culler, "Reading as a Woman," in *On Deconstruction: Theory and Criticism after Structuralism* (Ithaca, N.Y.: Cornell University Press, 1982), pp. 43–63.

28. Michael Hanne, "Alberto Moravia's *La Romana*: The Appropriation of Female Experience," *Italica* 40, no. 4 (Winter 1983): 351–359.

29. Carolyn G. Heilbrun, *Writing a Woman's Life* (New York: W. W. Norton, 1988), p. 48.

30. J. Christopher Herold, *Mistress to an Age: A Life of Mme. de Staël* (New York: Bobbs-Merrill, 1958).

31. Ann Beattie, "In the White Night," in *Prize Stories: The O. Henry Collection* (New York: Doubleday, 1985), p. 48.

32. Craig Owens, "The Discourse of Others: Feminists and

Postmodernism," in *The Anti-Aesthetic: Essays on Postmodern Culture*, ed. Hal Foster (Port Townsend, Wash.: Bay Press, 1983), pp. 68–69.

33. William Kennedy, "Writers and Their Songs," in *Speaking of Writing: Selected Hopwood Lectures*, ed. Nicholas Delbanco (Ann Arbor: University of Michigan Press, 1990).

34. Plato, *Republic*, Book 3, *Great Dialogues of Plato*, trans. W. H. D. Rouse (New York: New American Library, 1956), p. 190.

35. John Donne, "Meditation 17," in *Devotions Upon Emergent Occasions*, ed. Anthony Raspa (Montreal: McGill-Queen's University Press, 1975), p. 87.

36. Tillie Olsen, *Silences* (New York: Dell, 1978), pp. 37, 62.

37. Julia Kristeva, "A quoi servent les intellectuels?," ed. Jean-Paul Enthoven, *Le Nouvel Observateur*, June 20, 1977.

38. Mary Gordon, "On Mothership and Authorhood," *New York Times Book Review* Feb. 10, 1985, sec. 1.

39. Ibid.

40. Mary Gordon, "Agnes," in *Temporary Shelter: Short Stories* (New York: Random House, 1987), p. 75.

41. Tillie Olsen, "I Stand Here Ironing," in *Between Mothers and Daughters: Stories Across a Generation*, ed. Susan Koppelman (New York: Feminist Press, 1985), p. 179.

42. Dante Alighieri, *The Divine Comedy: Inferno*, trans. Allen Mandelbaum (New York: Bantam Classics, 1981), pp. 12–13.

43. Julia Kristeva, "From One Identity to An Other," in *Desire and Language: A Semiotic Approach to Literature and Art*, ed. Leon S. Roudiez, trans. Thomas Gora, Alice Jardine, and Leon S. Roudiez (Oxford: Basil Blackwell, 1980), p. 132.

44. Fiora Vincenti, *Invito alla lettura di Primo Levi* (Milan: Mursia, 1973), pp. 67–68.

45. Juan Carlos Suñen, "Quimica de la conciencia," review of *El Sistema periodico* and *Si esto es un hombre*, by Primo Levi, *El Pais*, Mar. 28, 1988.

46. Primo Levi, *Se questo è un uomo* (Turin: Einaudi, 1963), p. 7.

47. Jacques Derrida, *The Ear of the Other: Otobiography, Transference, Translation/Roundtable on Autobiography*, ed. Christie V.

McDonald, trans. Peggy Kamuf (New York: Schocken Books, 1985), p. 88.

48. Levi, *Se questo*, p. 7.

49. Vincenti, *Invito*, p. 71.

50. Primo Levi, "A Man Saved by His Skills," ed. Philip Roth, *New York Times Book Review* Oct. 12, 1986.

51. William Abrahams, introduction to *Prize Stories, 1981*, ed. William Abrahams (New York: Doubleday, 1981), p. 10.

52. Ibid.

53. Christa Wolf, *Patterns of Childhood*, trans. Ursule Molinaro and Hedwig Rappalt (New York: Farrar, Straus and Giroux, 1984), p. 157.

54. Irving Howe, "The Utter Sadness of the Survivor," *New York Times Book Review* Jan. 10, 1988.

55. Giacomo Leopardi, *Il testamento letterario: pensieri dello "Zibaldone,"* comp. Vincenzo Cardarelli (Turin: Fògola, 1985), p. 83.

56. Bettina Aptheker, *Tapestries of Life: Women's Work, Women's Consciousness, and the Meaning of Daily Experience* (Amherst: University of Massachusetts Press, 1989), p. 54.

57. W. K. Wimsatt, *The Verbal Icon: Studies in the Meaning of Poetry* (Lexington: University of Kentucky Press, 1954); Monroe C. Beardsley, *Aesthetics* (New York: Harcourt, Brace, 1958).

58. Jean-François Lyotard, *The Postmodern Condition: A Report on Knowledge*, trans. Geoff Bennington and Brian Massumi, Theory and History of Literature, vol. 10 (Minneapolis: University of Minnesota Press, 1984).

59. Horace, *Horace for English Readers: Being a Translation of the Poems of Quintus Horatius Flaccus into English Prose*, trans. E. C. Wickham (London: Oxford University Press), p. 343.

60. Ibid., p. 341.

61. Sir Philip Sidney, "The Defense of Poesie," in *Literary Criticism: Plato to Dryden*, ed. Allan H. Gilbert (Detroit: Wayne State University, 1962), p. 425.

62. John Dryden, "An Essay of Dramatic Poesy," in *Selected Works*, ed. William Frost, 2d ed. (New York: Holt, Rinehart and Winston, 1971), p. 454.

63. Leo Tolstoy, "What Is Art?," in *Tolstoy on Art*, ed. Alymer Maude (Boston: Small, Maynard, 1924), p. 286.

64. Blanchot, *L'Espace*, p. 54.

65. William Wordsworth, "Preface of 1800," in *Lyrical Ballads*, by William Wordsworth and Samuel Coleridge, ed. W. J. B. Owen, 2d ed. (London: Oxford University Press, 1985), pp. 173, 160.

66. Blanchot, *L'Espace*, p. 101.

67. Stéphane Mallarmé, *Mallarmé: Selected Prose Poems, Essays, and Letters*, trans. Bradford Cook (Baltimore: Johns Hopkins University Press, 1956), p. 21.

5. Listening

1. Eudora Welty, *One Writer's Beginnings* (New York: Warner Books, 1983), p. 95; N. Scott Momaday, *Names: A Memoir*, vol. 16, Sun Tracks: An American Indian Literary Series (Tucson: University of Arizona Press, 1976), pp. 8, 22, 97.

2. Welty, *One Writer's Beginnings*, p. 14.

3. Ovid, *Metamorphoses*, Fable 7, Book 3, pp. 402–512, trans. Henry T. Riley (London: G. Bell and Sons, 1919), pp. 103–107.

4. Jacques Derrida, *The Ear of the Other: Otobiography, Transference, Translation/Roundtable on Autobiography*, ed. Christie V. McDonald, trans. Peggy Kamuf (New York: Schocken Books, 1985), p. 88.

5. Walter Benjamin, "The Storyteller," in *Illuminations: Essays and Reflections*, ed. Hannah Arendt (New York: Schocken Books, 1968), p. 91.

6. Giacomo Leopardi, *Il testamento letterario: pensieri dello "Zibaldone,"* comp. Vincenzo Cardarelli (Turin: Fògola, 1985), p. 100.

7. Madison Jones, "The Fugitives," in *Stories of the Modern South*, ed. Ben Forkner and Patrick Samway (New York: Penguin Books, 1986), p. 229.

8. Hunter Kay, "The Fifth Generation," in Forkner and Samway, *Stories*, p. 253.

9. Elizabeth Spencer, "The Finder," in Forkner and Samway, *Stories*, p. 413.

10. Enrique Hank Lopez, *Conversations with Katherine Anne Porter: Refugee from Indian Creek* (Boston: Little, Brown, 1981), pp. 220, 5.

11. Jane Krause DeMouy, *Katherine Anne Porter's Women: The Eye of Her Fiction* (Austin: University of Texas Press, 1983), pp. 118–119.

12. Lopez, *Conversations*, p. 215.

13. DeMuoy, *Porter's Women*, p. 145.

14. Bettina Aptheker, *Tapestries of Life: Women's Work, Women's Consciousness, and the Meaning of Daily Experience* (Amherst: University of Massachusetts Press, 1989), p. 40.

15. Stéphane Mallarmé, *Mallarmé: Selected Prose Poems, Essays, and Letters*, trans. Bradford Cook (Baltimore: Johns Hopkins University Press, 1956), p. 82.

16. Jane B. Wilson, *The Story Experience* (Metuchen, N.J.: Scarecrow Press, 1979), p. x.

17. Walter Benjamin, "On Some Motifs in Baudelaire," in *Illuminations: Essays and Reflections*, ed. Hannah Arendt (New York: Schocken Books, 1968), p. 159.

18. Katherine Anne Porter, "Old Mortality," in *Collected Stories* (London: Virago Press, 1985), pp. 194, 196.

19. Wolfgang Iser, *The Act of Reading: A Theory of Aesthetic Response* (Baltimore: Johns Hopkins University Press, 1978).

20. Porter, "Old Mortality," p. 233.

21. Ibid., p. 241.

22. Robert Penn Warren, "Irony with a Center," in *Katherine Anne Porter: A Collection of Critical Essays*, ed. Robert Penn Warren (Englewood Cliffs, N.J.: Prentice-Hall, 1979), p. 106; Porter, "Old Mortality," p. 241.

23. Lopez, "Conversations," p. 308; Porter, "Old Mortality," p. 208.

24. Welty, *One Writer's Beginnings*, p. 95.

25. Eudora Welty, *Selected Stories of Eudora Welty* (New York: New Modern Library, 1954).

26. Nancy Hale, interview, *Writers and Writing*, ed. Robert Van Gelder (New York: Charles Scribner's Sons, 1946), p. 332.

27. Margaret Walker, *How I Wrote "Jubilee"* (Chicago: Third World Press, 1972), p. 11.

28. Janet Sternburg, introduction to *The Writer on Her Work: Contemporary Women Writers Reflect on Their Art and Situation*, ed. Janet Sternburg (New York: W. W. Norton, 1980), p. xx.

29. Walker, *How I Wrote "Jubilee,"* pp. 18–19.

30. Henry James, *The Art of the Novel: Critical Prefaces*, ed. R. P. Blackmur (New York: Charles Scribner's Sons, 1934), p. 308.

31. Louise Sweeney, "Gail Godwin: Collecting People's Stories Like Seashells at the Beach," *Christian Science Monitor*, July 21, 1983, sec. B.

32. E. M. Forster, *Aspects of the Novel* (New York: Harcourt, Brace, 1927), p. 131.

33. Judith Stitzel, "Hearing Voices: Oral History as an Aid to Reading," in *Women's Personal Narratives: Essays in Criticism and Pedagogy*, ed. Leonore Hoffmann and Margo Culley (New York: Modern Language Association, 1985), p. 139.

34. Isak Dinesen, *Mottos from My Life* (Copenhagen: Presentation Books, 1962), p. 20.

6. A Sense of Place

1. D. H. Lawrence, "The Spirit of Place," in *Studies in Classic American Literature* (New York: Viking, 1969).

2. Christa Wolf, *Patterns of Childhood*, trans. Ursule Molinaro and Hedwig Rappalt (New York: Farrar, Straus and Giroux, 1984), p. 42.

3. Anne-Louise-Germaine Necker De Staël, *De l'Allemagne*, 2 vols. (Paris: Garnier-Flammarion, 1967).

4. Henry James, *The Art of the Novel: Critical Prefaces* (New York: Charles Scribner's Sons, 1934), pp. 26–27.

5. Ibid., p. 27.

6. Ibid.

7. Erskine Caldwell, "A Talk with Erskine Caldwell," in *Writers on Writing*, ed. Robert Van Gelder (New York: Charles Scribner's Sons, 1946), p. 36.

8. Eudora Welty, *One Writer's Beginnings* (New York: Warner Books, 1983), p. 106.

9. Dee Brown, *Bury My Heart at Wounded Knee: An Indian History of the American West* (New York: Bantam Books, 1972).

10. Wallace Stegner, "The Gift of Wilderness," in *One Way to Spell Man: Essays with a Western Bias* (New York: Doubleday, 1982), p. 164.

11. Robert Penn Warren, *All the King's Men* (New York: Harcourt Brace Jovanovich, 1974), p. 311.

12. Robert Penn Warren, *New and Selected Poems: 1923–1985* (New York: Random House, 1985).

13. Carolyn Forché, "An Interview with David Montenegro," *American Poetry Review* 17, no. 6 (November/December 1988): 37.

14. John Naisbett and Patricia Aburdene, *Megatrends 2000: Ten New Directions for the 1990s* (New York: Morrow, 1990).

15. Rita Mae Brown, *Starting from Scratch: A Different Kind of Writer's Manual* (New York: Bantam Books, 1988); Michel Foucault, "What Is an Author?," in *Language, Counter-Memory, Practice: Selected Essays and Interviews*, ed. Donald F. Bouchard, trans. Donald F. Bouchard and Sherry Simon (Ithaca, N.Y.: Cornell University Press, 1977), pp. 113–138.

16. Anthony Stockanes, "Ladies Who Knit for a Living," in *Ladies Who Knit for a Living* (Urbana: University of Illinois Press, 1981), p. 1.

17. Janet Kauffmann, "The Alvordton Spa and Sweat Shop," in *Places in the World a Woman Could Walk* (New York: Penguin Books, 1983), pp. 121–132.

18. William Wordsworth, "Advertisement," in *Lyrical Ballads, 1798,* by William Wordsworth and Samuel Coleridge, ed. W. J. B. Owen, 2d ed. (New York: Oxford University Press, 1985), p. 3.

19. See Ernest Hemingway, *Dateline: Toronto, the Complete Toronto Star Dispatches, 1920–1924,* ed. William White (New York: Charles Scribner's Sons, 1985).

20. Willa Cather, *The World and the Parish: Willa Cather's Articles and Reviews, 1893–1902,* ed. William M. Curtin (Lincoln: University of Nebraska Press, 1970).

21. Margaret Walker, *How I Wrote "Jubilee"* (Chicago: Third World Press, 1972), p. 13.

22. Edith Wharton, *A Backward Glance* (New York: Charles Scribner's Sons, 1964), pp. 293–294.

23. Victor Hugo, "Preface," in *Cromwell* (Paris: Garnier-Flammarion, 1968).

24. James, *The Art of the Novel*, p. 176.

25. William Hazlitt, "On Wit and Humor," in *Lectures on the English Comic Writers (1819)* (London: J. M. Dent, 1900).

26. Aristotle, *The Ethics of Aristotle*, trans. J. A. K. Thomson (London: Penguin Books, 1956), p. 70.

27. Jean-Jacques Rousseau, *Reveries of the Solitary Walker* (New York: Penguin Books, 1979), p. 27.

28. See Edgar Allan Poe, "Review of *Twice-Told Tales*," in *Essays and Reviews* (New York: Library of America, 1984); Flannery O'Connor, *The Presence of Grace and Other Book Reviews*, comp. Leo J. Zuber, ed. Carter W. Martin (Athens: University of Georgia Press, 1983); Louise Bogan, *A Poet's Alphabet: Reflections on the Literary Art and Vocation*, ed. Robert Phelps and Ruth Limmer (New York: McGraw-Hill, 1970).

29. Edith Wharton, *The Writing of Fiction* (New York: Charles Scribner's Sons, 1925), p. 223.

30. Alphonse Jacobs, ed., *Gustave Flaubert–George Sand: Correspondance* (Paris: Flammarion, 1981), p. 76.

31. Maurice Blanchot, "Reading," in *The Gaze of Orpheus and Other Literary Essays*, ed. P. Adams Sitney, trans. Lydia Davis (Barrytown, N.Y.: Station Hill Press, 1981), p. 98.

7. *Diction*

1. William Wordsworth, "Advertisement," in *Lyrical Ballads 1798*, by William Wordsworth and Samuel Coleridge, ed. W. J. B. Owen, 2d ed. (New York: Oxford University Press, 1985), p. 3.

2. Aristotle, *On Poetry and Style (The Poetics)*, trans. G. M. A. Grube (New York: Bobbs-Merrill, 1958), p. 47.

3. Horace, *Horace for English Readers: Being a Translation of the Poems of Quintus Horatius Flaccus into English Prose*, trans. E. C. Wickham (London: Oxford University Press, 1930), p. 352.

4. Acts 17: 28.

5. See chapter 17 of Samuel Coleridge's *Biographia Literaria*, 2 vols. (London: Oxford University Press, 1965); Wordsworth, "Preface to 1800," in Wordsworth and Coleridge, *Lyrical Ballads*, p. 161.

6. Wordsworth, "Simon Lee," in Wordsworth and Coleridge, *Lyrical Ballads*, pp. 57–60.

7. Wordsworth, "We Are Seven," in Wordsworth and Coleridge, *Lyrical Ballads*, pp. 63–65.

8. Pierre Corneille, "Les trois discours sur le poème dramatique," *Oeuvres Complètes*, vol. 3, ed. Georges Couton (Paris: Gallimard–Bibliothèque de la Pléiade, 1987), pp. 117–190.

9. Walt Whitman, "Preface," in *Leaves of Grass: Authoritative Texts, Prefaces/Whitman on His Art, Criticism*, ed. Sculley Bradley and Harold W. Blodgett (New York: W. W. Norton, 1973), p. 712.

10. Whitman, "Song of Myself," in Bradley and Blodgett, *Leaves of Grass*, pp. 28–29.

11. Robert Frost, *Selected Prose*, ed. Hyde Cox and Edward Connery Lathem (New York: Holt, Rinehart and Winston, 1956), p. 13; Robert Frost, "To John Bartlett," July 4, 1913, letter 53, "To William Stanley Braithwaite," Mar. 22, 1915, letter 105, in *Selected Letters of Robert Frost*, ed. Lawrence Thompson (New York: Holt, Rinehart and Winston, 1964), pp. 79–80, 158–159.

12. Robert Frost, "The Death of the Hired Man," in *The Poetry of Robert Frost* (New York: Holt, Rinehart and Winston, 1969), pp. 34–40.

13. Leo Tolstoy, "What Is Art?," in *Tolstoy on Art*, ed. Aylmer Maude (Boston: Small, Maynard, 1924), p. 208.

14. Robertson Davies, "The Pleasures of an Ornate Style," *Mirabella* 10 (March 1990): 64.

15. Luigi Capuana, *Gli ismi contemporanei: Verismo, simbolismo, idealismo, cosmopolitismo ed altri saggi di critica letteraria ed artistica*, ed. Giorgio Luti (Milan: Fratelli Fabbri Editori, 1973), p. 14.

16. Harold Bloom, *The Anxiety of Influence: A Theory of Poetry* (New York: Oxford University Press, 1973).

17. Umberto Eco, *La definizione dell'arte: Saggi di estetica e di poetica* (Turin: U. Mursia, 1968), p. 19.

18. Ezra Pound, *ABC of Reading* (New York: New Directions, 1960), p. 74.

19. Cesare Pavese, *La letteratura americana e altri saggi* (Turin: Einaudi, 1953), p. 293.

20. Pound, *ABC*, p. 90.

21. Ibid., pp. 71, 56.

22. Ibid., p. 192.

23. Annie Dillard, "Write Till You Drop," *New York Times Book Review* May 28, 1989. The essay was subsequently included in *The Writing Life* (New York: Harper & Row, 1989).

24. Horace, *Horace for English Readers*, p. 360.

25. Virginia Woolf, *A Room of One's Own* (New York: Harcourt Brace Jovanovich, 1957), p. 111.

26. Jean-Paul Sartre, "The Situation of the American Writer in 1947," in *What Is Literature?*, trans. Bernard Trechtman (New York: Philosophical Library, 1949), pp. 161–162.

27. Jean-Jacques Rousseau, *On the Origin of Language*, trans. John H. Moran and Alexander Gode (Chicago: University of Chicago Press, 1986), p. 32.

28. Jacques Derrida, *Of Grammatology*, trans. Gayatri Chakravorty Spivak (Baltimore: Johns Hopkins University Press, 1976), p. 190.

29. George Orwell, "Politics and the English Language," in *Shooting an Elephant and Other Essays* (New York: Harcourt, Brace, 1950), pp. 77–92.

30. Jacques Derrida, *Marges de la philosophie* (Paris: Editions de Minuit, 1972).

31. Wallace Stegner, "Good-bye to All T——t!," in *One Way to Spell Man: Essays with a Western Bias* (New York: Doubleday, 1982), pp. 69–70.

32. Alice Walker, *In Search of Our Mothers' Gardens* (New York: Harcourt Brace Jovanovich, 1983), pp. 20, 28.

33. Ibid., pp. 57–58.

34. André Bleikasten, "Pour/Contre une lecture idéologique des romans de Faulkner," *Sud* no. 48/49 (1983): 256.

35. Victor Hugo, "Preface," in *Cromwell* (Paris: Garnier-Flammarion, 1968), pp. 99–100.

36. Ibid., p. 69.

37. Ibid., p. 75.

38. Madame Leprince de Beaumont, "La Belle et la Bête," *Choix de Contes de Fée* (Paris: Nelson, Editeurs, 1913), pp. 353–374. For an excellent recent translation, as a children's picture book, see de Beaumont, *Beauty and the Beast*, trans. Richard Howard, illus. Hilary Knight, afterword by Jean Cocteau (New York: Simon & Schuster, 1990).

39. Hugo, "Preface," p. 100.

8. The Moment of the Subject

1. Joan Didion, "Why I Write," in *The Writer on Her Work: Contemporary Women Writers Reflect on Their Art and Situation*, ed. Janet Sternburg (New York: W. W. Norton, 1980), p. 17.

2. I am much indebted here to Jane Flax, who in her highly readable article, "Postmodernism and Gender Relations in Feminist Theory" (*Signs: Journal of Women in Culture and Society* 12, no. 4 [1987]: 621–643) very neatly sidesteps the ever present need for a summation of the relationship between "postmodern philosophy" and deconstruction by giving a mini-bibliography of "sources for practitioners of postmodernism." They include Friedrich Nietzsche, *On the Genealogy of Morals* (New York: Vintage, 1969), and *Beyond Good and Evil* (New York: Vintage, 1966); Jacques Derrida, *L'Ecriture et la différence* (Paris: Editions du Seuil, 1967); Michel Foucault, *Language, Counter-Memory, Practice* (Ithaca, N.Y.: Cornell University Press, 1977); Jacques Lacan, *Speech and Language in Psychoanalysis* (Baltimore: Johns Hopkins University Press, 1968), and *The Four Fundamental Concepts of Psychoanalysis* (New York: W. W. Norton, 1973); Richard Rorty, *Philosophy and the Mirror of Nature* (Princeton: Princeton University Press, 1979); Paul Feyerabend, *Against Method* (New York: Schocken Books, 1975); Ludwig Wittgenstein, *On Certainty* (New York: Harper & Row, 1972), and *Philosophical Investigations* (New York: Macmillan, 1970); Julia Kristeva, "Women's Time," *Signs: Journal of Women in Culture and Society* 7, no. 1 (Autumn 1981):

13–15; and Jean-François Lyotard, *The Postmodern Condition* (Minneapolis: University of Minnesota Press, 1984).

3. Charles Newman, *The Post-Modern Aura: The Act of Fiction in an Age of Inflation* (Evanston, Ill.: Northwestern University Press, 1985), p. 119.

4. Edward Said, "Opponents, Audiences, Constituencies," in *The Anti-Aesthetic: Essays on Postmodern Culture*, ed. Hal Foster (Port Townsend, Wash.: Bay Press, 1983), p. 141.

5. Jacques Derrida, "Qual quelle: Les sources de Valéry," in *Marges de la philosophie* (Paris: Editions de Minuit, 1972), pp. 327–363; Jacques Derrida, *Of Grammatology*, trans. Gayatri Chakravorty Spivak (Baltimore: Johns Hopkins University Press, 1976).

6. Elizabeth Abel, ed., *Writing and Sexual Difference* (Chicago: University of Chicago Press, 1982); Elaine Showalter, ed., *The New Feminist Criticism: Essays on Women, Literature, and Theory* (New York: Pantheon, 1985); Sandra M. Gilbert and Susan Gubar, *The Madwoman in the Attic: The Woman Writer and the Nineteenth-Century Literary Imagination* (New Haven: Yale University Press, 1984).

7. Harold Bloom, *Ruin the Sacred Truths: Poetry and Belief from the Bible to the Present* (Cambridge: Harvard University Press, 1989), p. 3.

8. Maurice Blanchot, "The Absence of the Book," in *The Gaze of Orpheus and Other Literary Essays*, ed. P. Adams Sitney, trans. Lydia Davis (Barrytown, N.Y.: Station Hill Press, 1981), p. 145.

9. Maurice Blanchot, *L'Espace littéraire* (Paris: Gallimard, 1955), pp. 53, 15.

10. Michel Foucault, "What Is an Author?," in *Language, Counter-Memory, Practice*, pp. 113–138.

11. Jean-Paul Sartre, *L'Etre et le néant* (Paris: Gallimard, 1943), p. 15.

12. Tillie Olsen, *Silences* (New York: Laurel/Seymour Lawrence, 1983), pp. 52–53.

13. Foucault, "What Is an Author?," pp. 123–124.

14. Virginia Woolf, *A Room of One's Own* (New York: Harcourt Brace Jovanovich, 1957), pp. 49–50.

15. Ibid., pp. 50–51.

16. Walter Benjamin, "On Some Motifs in Baudelaire," in *Illuminations: Essays and Reflections*, ed. Hannah Arendt (New York: Schocken Books, 1968), p. 159.

17. William Wordsworth, "Preface," in *Lyrical Ballads 1798*, by William Wordsworth and Samuel Coleridge, ed. W. J. B. Owen (New York: Oxford University Press, 1985), p. 173.

18. René Girard, *Deceit, Desire, and the Novel: Self and Other in Literary Structure*, trans. Yvonne Freccero (Baltimore: Johns Hopkins University Press, 1961), p. 310.

19. Julia Kristeva, "Motherhood According to Bellini," in *Desire and Language: A Semiotic Approach to Literature and Art*, trans. Ursule Molinaro and Hedwig Rappalt (New York: Farrar, Straus and Giroux, 1984), pp. 237–270.

20. Simone de Beauvoir, *Les Faits et les mythes*, vol. 1, *Le Deuxième Sexe*, 38th ed. (Paris: Gallimard, 1949), pp. 364–365.

21. Julia Kristeva, "Julia Kristeva: A quoi servent les intellectuels?," ed. Jean-Paul Enthoven, *Le Nouvel Observateur*, June 20, 1977, p. 108.

22. Mary Gordon, "The Parable of the Cave: In Praise of Water Colors," in *The Writer on Her Work: Contemporary Women Writers Reflect on Their Art and Situation*, ed. Janet Sternburg (New York: W. W. Norton, 1980), p. 29.

23. Rachel Billington, *Occasion of Sin* (New York: Summit Books, 1982).

24. Virginia Woolf, "Professions for Women," in *The Death of the Moth and Other Essays* (New York: Harcourt Brace Jovanovich, 1970), pp. 235–242.

25. Alice Walker, "One Child of One's Own," in Sternburg, *The Writer*, p. 126.

26. Julia Kristeva, *Revolution in Poetic Language*, trans. Margaret Waller (New York: Columbia University Press, 1984).